A FRENCHMAN

A FRENCHMAN IN KHAKI

By

PAUL MAZE

D.C.M., M.M. *with bar*, C. de G.

With a Preface by

The Rt. Hon. WINSTON CHURCHILL

P.C., C.H., M.P.

Printed and bound by Antony Rowe Ltd, Eastbourne

In Memory of
Major F. Swetenham, Royal Scots Greys,
killed in action at Cerizy,
August 28th, 1914.

CONTENTS

PART I

August 1914
The Advance to Mons—The Retreat from Mons
page 1

PART II

1915
Neuve Chapelle to Loos—Battle of Neuve Chapelle—
7th Division—Aubers Ridge
1916
The Somme—Pozières
page 97

PART III

1917
Winter on the Somme—Summer at Ypres—Passchen-
daele, and the return to the Somme
page 197

PART IV

1918
The Great Retreat of the Fifth Army—The Fourth Army
Breaks the German Front—The End.
page 263

ILLUSTRATIONS

MAPS

INTRODUCTION

THE author of this vivid book has good right to tell his tale. M. Paul Maze had a close and prolonged view of the fighting front. He saw it with French eyes from the English Staff. He was a *sous-officier* who was the friend of generals. He was a liaison officer without a commission. He was a conscript whose physique and health denied him at the outset his right to serve, but who nevertheless was always to the end among the shells and bullets.

One would naturally ask how it was that this young French gentleman, whose status was thoroughly nondescript, was able not only to make a footing for himself with an English cavalry regiment in the first confusion of the invasion of France, but how he acquired and preserved the confidence and regard of two of the best known army commanders in the British Expeditionary Force. Under Gough and upon his supersession, under Rawlinson, Sergeant Maze became in the words of Sir William Robertson "an institution." He was unique and indefinable; like Lord Godolphin he was "never in the way and never out of the way."

Of course he is an artist of distinction whose quick comprehension, keen eye and nimble pencil could record impressions with revealing fidelity. As a British private, who watched him one day sketching in a heavily bombarded trench said, "Your pictures are done in shorthand."

But we cannot think that this admirable gift, even when sustained by a charming personality and a perfect knowledge of French and English, would have sufficed to carry M. Maze for four years through the iron-clad regulations of the armies in the field, and from the jealous strictness with which the slightest privilege or irregularity was suppressed. Our author had an additional passport, the validity of which though constantly examined, tested and "visa'd" was never disputed by the authorities. His courage and self-devotion were tireless. Year after year, battle after battle, wherever the volcano erupted most fiercely, amid the smoke and poison fumes and frightful detonations, thither our author made his way, and thence his "seeing eye" and recording notebook brought back calm, trustworthy, lucid and increasingly experienced information. Acting largely on his own initiative, enjoying a most unusual freedom of movement, he set forth, he saw and he reported. The troops in the line and their officers knew that he told the truth about their ordeals and the two distinguished generals felt that they were getting something direct which they could measure and weigh.

One may imagine the tact which was required in this anomalous figure, neither French nor English, neither officer nor soldier, nor indeed civilian, who collected the conversation of colonels and captains in the most deadly danger, formed his own view upon the local situation, and then was allowed that night to walk straight into the Army Commander's private quarters and tell him all that he had seen and heard. In pursuance of this delicate and self-created task M. Maze received four wounds, and was successively awarded most of those decorations which the soldiers prize because they come only from the fire.

Not the least of our author's risks, especially in the early days before he became "l'institution Maze," was to be taken for a spy. The poignant, thrilling story of his adventures in the retreat from Mons, when by the orders of a British divisional general he was actually being led out to summary execution by the firing party, and was saved only by the chance passage through the village of the Royal Scots Greys, one of whose officers recognised him as their vanished interpreter, is here told with a self-restraint and modesty which adds emphasis to every page. No doubt it was this grim deliverance which gave our author the footing at headquarters which he knew so well how to preserve and consolidate.

For the rest we have the battle-scenes of Armageddon recorded by one who not only loved the fighting troops and shared their perils, but perceived the beauties of light and shade, of form and colour, of which even the horrors of war cannot rob the progress of the sun. This volume should be acceptable alike to the artists and the soldiers of the two great nations whose cause of freedom its author so ardently and enduringly espoused.

WINSTON S. CHURCHILL.

Chartwell: August 22, 1934.

PART 1

August 1914

The Advance to Mons—
The Retreat from Mons

B

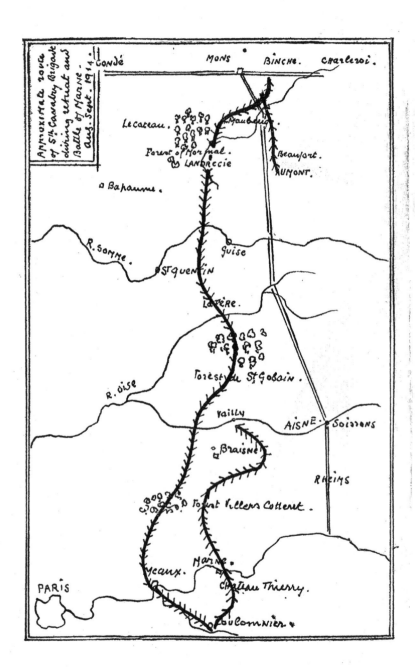

Approximate route of 5th Cavalry Brigade during retreat and Battle of Marne. Aug. Sept. 1914.

Condé   MONS   BINCHE.   CHARLEROI.

Le Cateau.   Maubeuge.

Forest of Mormal.   Beaufort.
Landrecie   AUMONT.

Bapaume.

R. Somme.   Guise

St Quentin

La Fere.

Forest de St Gobain.

R. Oise

Vailly   AISNE   SOISSONS

Braisne.

RHEIMS

Forest Villers Cotteret.

Marne.

PARIS   Meaux.   Chateau Thierry.

Coulomnier

CHAPTER I

On the morning of August 18th, 1914, I was standing on the pier of Havre that reaches out into the estuary of the Seine, gazing at the file of transports bringing the British Expeditionary Force to France.

It was a perfect day; the sea, without a ripple, glittered like a mirror, reflecting the sails of scattered fishing-smacks floating motionless in the calm. The smoke from the escorting destroyers curled over the convoy and rose into a cloudless sky, where it hung like an arch. The eyes of a dense crowd were set on the leading ship, which was growing every moment in size, followed by others cutting through her wake. Suddenly she loomed before us, her decks pink with gazing faces. Gliding into the narrows, the clang from the engine-room bells clearly resounding, she parted the green water into two silver waves and gracefully sheered into the harbour, the red ensign flapping limply at her stern.

Too restless to wait to see the rest steam by, I ran towards the docks to see the first landing, leaving the crowd dumb with the significance of the moment. I had to walk a long way round to get to the docks where some ships were already berthed, while others were squeezing their massive forms through lock gates, belching black smoke out of their red funnels.

On approaching, I saw cranes swinging guns, carts, and horses from the holds on to the quays in a merry-go-round motion; alongside every ship a steady line of soldiers loaded with kit moved down the gangways.

The rapidity with which men and material of war were being disgorged was amazing. Men swarmed all over this immense wharf; guns, limbers, sappers,

3

pontoons were lined up everywhere. Immediately units
began to form and take shape. Men hurried to shouts of
command, and out of this huge confusion of khaki, files
sprang up like yellow walls, moving to the right or left to
find contact with each other and fall into proper battalion
formation. I gazed in admiration at the speed and
discipline of it all.

With drum and fife playing, battalions started towards
the town, curving across the sun-baked wharf like centi-
pedes; baggage transport followed behind with the rolling
kitchens already at full steam. Artillery and ammunition
columns were also under way—the space they left being
immediately taken up by others landing.

In the midst of a large body of cavalry, a regiment with
grey horses had particularly attracted me. I stood watching
them, my mind a blank, as though fate had linked me with
them. As they moved off I asked one of the men where
they were making for, meaning to find them again, as
already my mind was made up to get off with them to the
war. Although it seemed a mere dream at the time, the
fact remains that within twenty-four hours I was leaving
for the front with that regiment, having over-ridden every
rule and obstacle that stood against my wish.

The arrival of British troops had filled the town with an
admiring crowd; hotels were invaded by staff officers who,
wearing red bands round their caps, were taken for
Generals; even young A.D.C.s were mistaken for Com-
manders-in-Chief. Cars with fluttering flags on the bonnets
rushed about in all directions, and innumerable motor-
cyclists wearing blue and white armbands tore through the
traffic. The troops marched through the streets, inspiring
the inhabitants of Havre with admiration.

     ·   ·   ·   ·   ·   ·

All this activity created for me an atmosphere very
different from that I had left in the country-side of Italy
barely a week before. An accidental glimpse at a local
newspaper had then revealed to me the seriousness of the

European situation. From that moment I was unable to settle down again and enjoy the peace of my surroundings— even a starlit night on Lake Trasimeno felt full of fore-boding; the frogs croaking on its silver banks jarred on my nerves—I had to leave. . . .

I remember my last glimpse of Florence from the train as it skirted the town at an increasing speed, all the roofs glowing from the light of a gorgeous sunset; my arrival in Paris early in the morning, the station shaking with the rattle and hiss of trains, the movement and talk of soldiers; the whistling and bustle as I wended my way out through countless pyramids of luggage. American travellers searched desperately for porters who had already all gone to join the colours—they could not understand why nobody in the midst of this turmoil would attend to their "grips" so that they could hurry for the next train to a port and sail back to the States out of this European mess.

An old horse-cab drove me to my hotel which, oddly enough, happened to be situated opposite the German Embassy. Paris seemed very stern as I looked through the window and heard the shouts of men selling special news-paper editions—everyone stopping to discuss the scanty news, and wondering and commenting on what England would do. . . .

As I came out of a restaurant that night, several shots rang out, and a throng of people emerged from a café shouting: "They've killed Jaurès!" The street was in-stantly filled with a mass of excited onlookers. Jaurès, who was France's greatest socialist figure, had only that after-noon rallied all the socialists to the cause of war—his name had been on every lip—what a fatality that he should then fall dead from a bullet fired by a lunatic! A white ambulance marked with a big red cross dramatically arrived on the scene; the corpse was brought out followed by a surging crowd; at a gallop, escorted by Republican Guards with pigtails and long black coats, the procession cut its way through the people whom the police by that time could hardly restrain. I never felt the tension created by human passion as I did at that moment; Paris seemed electrified. . . .

I had only reached my hotel with great difficulty, for the street was closed at both ends by a cordon of police holding back crowds who had come to see the departure of the German Ambassador and his staff. Embassy cars were being loaded with documents. From my hotel window I saw the whole of the staff get into their cars and the Ambassador and his wife step into theirs—not a murmur rose from the crowd as the cortège quickly drove away to the station. The concierge wiped his brow with relief and closed the big gates, on the pillars of which the stone eagles were to remain throughout the war, proclaiming Germany's might.

As I came out of my hotel the next morning shouts of "à Berlin" were heard everywhere. A regiment of Cuirassiers marched across the Place de la Concorde very smart in their cuirasses, the officers wearing white gloves— the tramp of the horses mingled with the shouts of the crowd throwing flowers to the men. The whole day long infantry battalions passed through Paris on their way to the stations; when the artillery passed, the guns were festooned with flowers and women jumped on the limbers to kiss the men.

All this excitement, however, failed to conceal entirely the anxiety weighing on the atmosphere. I walked about buying every paper announcing news—the first engagement with enemy patrols had taken place. . . .

Not liable to be called up with the colours, as I had not been passed fit for my military service at the age of twenty-one, I felt out of it all; a conflict was rising within me—I had to do something. I went to a recruiting depot to volunteer; there I met with my first disappointment. To my consternation a poster at the Invalides notified that no volunteers would be taken until August 18th, as the military authorities would first call out all the reserves. As my face dropped on reading this, the sergeant on guard said to me: "Why worry? You'll get all you want before the end. Have a good time while you can."

At that moment there passed over Paris, shining like a lemon in the blue sky, a large airship; everybody waved and shouted "à Berlin!" Troops were still moving along towards the stations. Carried away with the general enthusiasm, I fell into their step, racking my brains for a plan that would take me to the front before the war was over.

I moved about the Paris streets for several days dazed by the reigning tension. England meanwhile had declared war on Germany, following the invasion of Belgium.

However, a telegram from my brother filled me with new hope. He urged me to come to Havre, where the British Army was expected to land, and to which he himself was being attached as an interpreter. This wire, written *en clair*, for inexplicable reasons passed the censor!

Soon after dawn next morning an American friend was driving me in his car to Deauville, where his family had been spending the summer. We had the roads to ourselves as cars had been requisitioned by the military authorities, and the traffic on the roads, apart from troops, had practically ceased. For breakfast we halted at Evreux, a small town, and sitting at the terrace of a café we saw recruits march out from the barracks to the drilling-ground, most of them still wearing civilian clothes. It was cold, misty and cheerless. "Un, deux; un, deux"; shouting himself hoarse, an N.C.O. marched on the heels of an elongated, spectacled man in the rear ranks, whose bent back and pointed beard indicated a professor. Sipping a greenish drink at a table next to ours sat an old ranker who, glancing towards the disappearing men, uttered in a gruff voice: "That's all good material. With their bayonets they will soon be in Berlin."

Deauville was pathetic. A few bathers were enjoying their last dip in a blue sea broken by silver breakers that rolled softly on the yellow beach. Under coloured parasols elderly women were sewing, listening to their husbands who read aloud the latest news, while children in multi-coloured bathing-suits made sand-pies with perfect detachment. In the town everything was shutting up as at the end of a season. To get across to Havre we embarked on an old steamer with a ridiculous funnel. The estuary of the Seine was a glory of sunshine, and Deauville, full of holiday memories, soon receded in the heat haze. . . .

CHAPTER II

ONCE in Havre, watching English troops disembarking, I became part of the general activity, and no longer felt at a loss about what I should do. Here was order and direction, and my mind was made up.

Before repairing to the hill where the English cavalry was encamped, I went to see the British Consul, who was a friend of mine; he gave me a letter of introduction to the military authorities. With the thrill imparted by the feeling that one's instinct is guiding one in the right way, I reached the camp where the rows of horse-lines, shining saddlery, piled-up arms, and white tents standing against a background of rich foliage, at once went to my head. The town lay below, flat and blue like a lake, with coiling smoke rising from its chimneys; rays of sunlight bursting out between clouds silvered the roadstead animated by destroyers busily moving around a British convoy awaiting the tide to enter the harbour. From the stations trains kept moving out on to the glittering tracks, and puffed their way to the frontier—the whistles from engines and the clang and crash of trucks constantly re-echoed across the town.

Having discovered my grey horses, I was led by a sentry to a tent where Colonel Bulkeley-Johnson, commanding the Royal Scots Greys, stood talking to an officer. Tall and handsome, he had a very distinguished personality. In a kind voice he asked me what I wanted. I handed him my letter of introduction, and told him that I wanted to join his regiment. He smiled and asked me a few questions. Making the most of a few days' training I had had with the B.C. Horse in Canada, which I had then looked upon as a mere joke, I said that I knew German

9

and the country where they would probably be fighting. He seemed at least interested, for he replied that he had been allotted interpreters whose knowledge of English was not very good and who were not used to their ways. "Certainly a man like you would be useful to us," he said, "but you see, I cannot take the responsibility of taking you without first seeing my Brigadier. If he gives his consent, well and good." While this conversation went on, men moved about the camp, feeding their horses, who were stamping on the ground and swishing their tails; their gleaming coats told of their good condition and of the care given to them. I was told to return the next day.

The next morning, slightly anxious lest the regiment might have gone, I drove up to the camp. To my dismay the Colonel had not seen his Brigadier, and he said that in the circumstances he couldn't possibly take me. I had gathered that the regiment was leaving that very day for the north, and felt that I was playing my last card. Major Collins, the second in command, had come out of his tent to talk to me, and after a while I heard the Colonel say to him: "It's all very well, but we have no kit to give him." A sergeant-major who all the time had been standing by, listening, assured the Colonel that he could procure everything except a cap. On seeing Major Collins produce one of his, I realised that their minds were made up. "We shall take you with us," said the Colonel. "Go and get your brush and comb and return in the afternoon. We leave this evening."

Already partly dressed in khaki that I had found in the town, I rode a new bicycle to the camp, accompanied by friends who came to see me off. In the party was a charming young English actress, well known at the time in England; she immediately conquered all the young officers who surrounded her. Given in charge of a stout Scottish sergeant-major, I was at once initiated into military routine. My bicycle was exchanged for a horse; everyone offered advice—I was assured that after the first scrap I would collect all the kit I was short of. They were all

Scots, many with a strong Edinburgh accent, a very good lot of men, full of life and humour. Neighbouring regiments were already saddling up, and one by one they left the camp for the town. Our turn came, and we formed up, facing the camp now completely empty. The horses were slipping on the pavé road, so we dismounted going down the hill into the town. As I led my horse along the street of my native town I could hardly believe I was my real self—everything had developed so quickly. When we reached the boulevard that runs alongside the sea, the sun was setting beyond the cliffs. Early memories were forcing themselves on my mind as if to make an indelible impression—I had so often seen the sun dip in a blaze exactly behind that house on my return from school. . . .

We began to entrain our horses as soon as we got to the station. It took some time to get us all packed in. The men were travelling in cattle-trucks filled with straw. I found a place amongst the Headquarters mess servants who had charge of the food stores. They never stopped eating the whole journey long. After much whistling, bumping and noise, we cut through a cloud of wet steam and followed other troop-trains. Tired out, we soon settled into a sound sleep.

We seemed to run all night; stiff and drowsy we looked through the carriage windows as dawn was just breaking—the train had stopped; a woman was reaching out handfuls of oranges which she was selling. "Where are we?" we asked. "At Havre," she replied, and the station loomed before us through the mist. During our sleep the train had merely manœuvred to make room for other trains.

After a long wait our rocky train started off again with great determination, its engine shooting puffs of whirling smoke tinted by the colour of the rising sun. We ran through stations and towns with that disdainful air of things in motion. Stations were crowded with waving throngs—at every level-crossing the chins of the gazing populace rested on the iron gates where children had stuck

their faces through the bars, showing rows of fair heads.
At Rouen the train was stormed by the townspeople,
who loaded us with cigarettes and food; we gave them our
badges in exchange, and when a girl stepped forward with
a large bouquet of flowers, I took her in my arms and
kissed her amidst general approving laughter. Cheered by
the crowd, we steamed away through a filthy tunnel. Shot
out into the brightness of the sunlight, we looked on to the
wonderful panorama of the town underneath—a sea of
glinting roofs, out of which rose the glowing stonework
of Gothic churches with the lofty spire of the cathedral
stabbing the sky. In the distance the sides of bright yellow
rocky hills sloped gently towards the wide river, where
steamers unloaded in an atmosphere of blustering smoke
and waltzing cranes. Barges were being towed up the Seine
by gay-coloured tugs passing under the webwork of a
metallic bridge that held the banks in gigantic claws.
Another smelly tunnel tore us away from that lovely scene,
and presently we sped through the very heart of Normandy.
     The day was warm and lovely; the train squeaked along
the rusty rails on a track overgrown by green grass and
buttercups. Dangling our legs over the side, we watched
the white balls of smoke from our engine curl and drift
over the gentle landscape. Constantly we heard the whistling and rolling sound of other trains on distant tracks.
Fat cows, tethered in line, ruminated in rich clover-fields,
and gazed at us in their vague way as we went by. Golden
crops of corn, bright yellow mustard-fields, orchards
covered with ripening fruit interminably slid by with the
country-side. It was all very gay; the men were in high
spirits; the open doors of carriages were ripped off by
tunnel walls; but, by the mercy of God, there were no
accidents. Some men were left behind; they caught us up
later. We passed a few stationary trains crammed with
soldiers. We all cheered out of pure happiness, exhilarated
by the beauty of the country we were traversing. We had
forgotten the war.

          .   .   .   .

The sun had already set some time when we arrived at a big railway junction called Aulnoye. Trains went no further. But for us, the platforms were deserted. Rails and telegraph-wires still shone from the yellow light left on the skyline. Signal-boxes were abandoned and the round discs of the signals along the lines appeared ominously still.

Men and horses were eager to get out of the train. One by one horses were led out and slipped on the stone platform with a loud clatter. Captain Toby Long was supervising, handling the men with humour, as was his wont.

The train that had brought us, quietly began to slip away as the squadrons were forming up on the road. The red signal on the last coach seemed to watch us like an eye as the train wound itself away into a tiny square and eventually faded out of sight; after a few puffs of smoke had shot above a distant wood like the parting wave of a handkerchief, we were left to the impressive stillness of our surroundings.

After a hot day, night was falling over the earth, and the noises of a busy life had died down. We broke at once into a trot, making for the town of Beaufort further north. The air was fresh and scented with a strong smell of hay. It was late when we arrived. . . .

I slept with the men under the sky amongst the horse lines in a clover-field. The horses kept scraping the ground with their hoofs, and the mechanical action of their teeth munching hay constantly woke me up. The warmth of their breath was pleasant. It was cold. The country was wrapped in mist, lying low like a cloud. Above, the sky was clear—when the moon rose, the atmosphere became palish green; the men were snoring loudly. . . .

Wet with dew, I was up at dawn. The sun soon rose, quickly gaining power, and shone on the soaked plains. Fires were crackling—an odour of frying bacon drifted in the air. We warmed ourselves. Only a night spent in the open can make an early meal taste as delicious as that one did.

We groomed our horses and proceeded to dye them with a mixture of Condy's fluid that turned them a dirty brown; it seemed a pity to spoil the appearance of our fine steeds, but being grey they offered too conspicuous a target. Later, the regiment received the order to advance towards Belgium.

We mounted and started off under a blazing sun; our road lay for miles through crops, bending under a breeze. Large straw hats of men and handkerchiefs over women's heads could be seen scattered about the coloured fields, where the shadows of drifting white clouds were softly passing. Swallows, perched on telegraph-wires, were like the music notes of a summer's tune. I felt happy—I wanted to sing—I loved the regiment. . . .

As we advanced, now and then we heard the distant report of explosions. We could not make out what they were until we reached the fortified area of Maubeuge, where presently a row of houses blew up sky-high—the garrison was clearing the field of fire for the artillery. Some French troops could be seen here and there digging trenches, laying out barbed wire and erecting observation stations in the forks of trees. They waved as we passed, exclaiming: "Ah! voilà les Anglais!"

We rode over the suspension bridge and through the archway of Maubeuge, built by Vauban; the steel plates thundered under our horses' hoofs, and the frogs basking in the sun flopped into the stagnant water of the moat.

The streets of the town were deserted—all the inhabitants had been cleared away from the fortified areas. Sentries challenged us outside the town; not having the counter-word we had to wait until an officer came.

We were again in the glittering light of open country— the dust whirling from under the horses settled on the foliage bordering the road. Riding lightly in the saddle, we kept up a steady cadence.

Out of the hazy distance rose the broken outlines of manufacturing towns—we were nearing the Belgian frontier. High chimney-stacks shone like minarets among the dark slag-heaps of coal-mines rising like pyramids. We crossed the frontier at Jeumont, an industrial town where life had come to a complete standstill. Raising a cloud of black dust, we kept to the shady side of the street along the drab factory walls. Families of pale-faced miners, with dark rings round their eyes, gazed at us, surprised by the break the war had brought in their monotonous lives. The sky, usually blurred by smoke, was suddenly clear above their heads.

Late in the afternoon we came on a French liaison officer who was waiting for us at a cross-roads. We were ordered to hurry on to Binches, where the brigade was to concentrate. The enemy had been reported at Nivelles. The news travelled at once through the ranks, creating a slight stir. It was extremely hot. We rode at a steady trot, stopping several times in villages, where the inhabitants were waiting with cigars and cigarettes for us, and buckets of water for our horses. All this attention brought out the remark that "it was too bloody good to last.". . .

By a large convent we had to draw up on the pavement to make room for the infantry to pass. A regiment of Black Watch, kilts swinging, marched by in great style. Girls and nuns leaning over the balustrade of the terrace were excited and kept up an incessant chatter. Two of them were talking German. I pricked up my ears and gathered they were Austrians. "What a shame to see all these youths probably going to meet death." I had never thought of this before. As the regiment broke away, one of the sisters pressed into my hand a small silver medal. "It's the Virgin Mary, she will preserve you. Keep it," she said. . . .

We overtook more infantry marching to their positions of assembly and then, striking across open country, found ourselves in the calm and isolation peculiar to great spaces, at the end of a hot day. The sun having come down, its rays were levelled on prominent places, projecting them forward; fields were still bright, except in the valleys. . . .

We drew rein in the quiet of a cup-shaped dip, fringed by tall poplars. The girths of the horses were loosened and they were given a feed, the men settling alongside in picturesque attitudes, weary from their march in the heat. Flat on my back I lay, watching the sky grow paler and the sunlight gradually switch off from the tips of the trees. Everything felt calm—nature and humanity had relaxed. A scent rose from the crops—birds were twittering, crows were calling to each other fluttering in the trees, which were turning now in the coolness a dark olive-green. I dozed off, remaining conscious of the beauty of the moment; I felt the rising dampness; every sound was very clear; the metallic note of a trotting horse on a far-away road rang clear as its shoes struck the ground; some cows were lowing in the distance. . . .

It was an effort to remount after our rest. As we moved up the slope the valley we were leaving was white with mist. Striking the top we faced the sky westwards, still a glory of yellow, where strips of clouds fringed with gold hugged the horizon; the light suddenly catching all our sunburnt faces, brought them out like oranges. It was getting late; a solitary star appeared—the earth was gradually turning into a vast shadow, ending in a sharply defined line against the sky, where the trees bordering a distant road stood out like a row of balls. We were now moving silhouettes merging with our surroundings in the falling darkness—only the road still faintly gleamed from the lingering colours of the sunset.

Presently we saw the flickering lights of French patrols moving about on their round. Nobody talked; the muffled sound of the horses' hoofs sinking into the powdered dust and the jingling of swords and kit against the saddle kept up an absorbing rhythm. We rode through a thick wood, encased in the darkness of the rich foliage where stars glittered through gaps above our heads. Once in the open again the fresh air fanned our faces and the sky opened out in all its intensity. Never was there such a lovely night —I wondered if the Germans, who were also on the road, thought the same. . . .

Late at night we finally reached Binches. The squadrons

took up their billets in the town, and the regimental head-quarters settled in a fine old monastery called "La Belle Espérance," situated in a park to the south of the town.

Our supplies having gone astray, I searched the roads for our transports, where troops, coming up, were making a fearful dust. Sore and worn out, I got a bath in a huge brass tub the monks used for cooking fruit. They were most helpful, but anxious; they kept asking questions we could not answer. . . .

We slept our last night of peace in comfort, while our outposts watched the darkness waiting for dawn.

C

CHAPTER III

THE ADVANCE INTO BELGIUM

AUGUST 22ND.—We were up very early—the men were grooming their horses in the park, soaked from a heavy dew. I was awaiting my breakfast which the monks were preparing, when a plane droned above, and like a huge bird, its wings skimming the trees, passed over the house. I saw plainly the observer looking down from the cockpit of his "Aviatik" marked with black crosses on the wings.

The servants having packed up the mess kit, the Headquarters made off, leaving me and another man behind to take on any message that might come from the Brigade. We basked in the sun, enjoying the stillness of that lovely park. The morning wore on, then a cyclist rode up ordering us to rejoin the regiment at once. We took a steep shady road towards Binches, and came upon the headquarters squadron at a main cross-roads where a signpost indicated Charleroi to the right and Mons to the left. Beyond the northern bank of the road, the ground sloped gently down to a wide valley, where fields extended into a hazy distance. Scattered belts of trees and villages broke up the flatness. In the near distance the little town of Péronne lay below us, its roofs shining in the sun. Along the banks of a dried-up stream wending its way to Binches we had two squadrons in position and scouts were out patrolling. We kept contact with these units by visual signalling. With the 12th Lancers and the 20th Hussars about on our left, we formed the extreme right wing of the British Army. J Battery, Royal Horse Artillery, covered our 5th Brigade under the command of Sir Philip Chetwode.

The French Army was supposed to be somewhere near

on our right, but we were not in touch—we had not yet seen a French soldier that day. It might have been a scene on manœuvres as we stood that morning on the high ground observing the distance, surrounded by a crowd of villagers who contemplated us with the utmost curiosity. Handing each other tortoise-shell opera-glasses they looked northwards, gesticulating as though a miracle was expected. Amongst them, wearing a cassock stained by many meals, was a priest, whose self-confident superiority on military matters was obediently accepted with bated breath by his parishioners. He asked us such indiscreet questions that the Colonel who had heard him talk a language that he could not understand ordered me to keep an eye on him; he was really speaking Walloon—a dialect of the north.

The day was so lovely that it was difficult to realise we were at war; the sun filtering through the foliage of trees flecked our horses standing on the road with high lights; the shade was cool—it was an ideal summer sensation—nothing, so far, suggested the impending drama, although in the far distance to our right a rumble of guns, like thunder, was at times audible.

Suddenly the Colonel, who had been looking through his telescope, handed it to me, saying: "Look, I see uniforms crawling about there," pointing to the distance. "Tell me what you think they are." I focused the telescope on to a railway embankment some 2,000 yards away, and saw in a circle of vivid light a number of little grey figures scrambling down on to the flat. Moving along the railway line more and more were appearing and beyond, from behind a slight rise in the ground, others were coming up.

The sight of the enemy had an immediate repercussion on the crowd. Women started to wail, and rushed for home, followed by the men, while children, torn by curiosity, lagged behind turning back to see. At once the atmosphere changed—in a few seconds all these civilians were fleeing along the roads while the invasion, creeping up like a tide, steadily gained ground. In their Sunday clothes, carrying in their hands their feathered hats which they had not stopped to put on, they wheeled perambulators, wheelbarrows, bicycles and anything on wheels and fled with their babies and terrified men. The few favoured owners of motor-cars led the retreat, leaving a cloud of dust; those with horses and carts had piled into them all that they could hurriedly save of their home belongings. The enemy had now become visible to the naked eye. We could see perfectly distinctly with field-glasses, their formations advancing across fields, their numbers increasing every moment. I began to wonder what the regiment would do; the Colonel stood still, perfectly calm. . . .

Two French cavalrymen at that moment were seen galloping in the valley, zigzagging like hunted animals. We lost sight of them for a moment, and then they appeared again riding up the slope of our hill; they stopped before our squadron, their horses lathered in sweat, trembling with excitement and exhaustion. They had been cut off from their brigade after being on outpost, and with difficulty had succeeded in working their way through the enemy. They said that German troops were detraining in large numbers all along the railway-line, and they had seen their artillery on the road.

While we were talking with them there rode in one of our own scouts, who informed us that the patrol he had come from had exchanged shots with Uhlans, but had failed to hit them. Quietly he was ordered back to tell his colleagues that another time they were to keep their heads and shoot straight.

Suddenly we saw a line of gun-flashes and the atmosphere quivered with a quick succession of loud reports— with a crash shells were now bursting over the village down below and swished past our heads to explode in the trees behind us; our horses pranced and reared. The men, startled, laughed nervously.

Our outlying squadrons, which had been ordered to fall back, came then for the first time under shell-fire, and the regiment suffered its first casualty, having an officer

wounded. A horse-drawn ambulance silently drove up on
rubber wheels—we saw the first blood-stained field-dressing; it marked a moment. War had indeed started. . . .
The Colonel all this while was absorbed in the dictation
of messages to his adjutant; signing to me to come forward,
he said: "I want you to ride to the Brigade with this
message," and showing me the place on the map, he added:
"You must deliver it only into the Brigadier's hands."

Thinking that a bicycle would be quicker than a horse,
I borrowed a signaller's push-bike and started off at once
for the cross-roads two miles away as rapid volleys of
musketry were fired from below.

It was hot as I pedalled up the steep hill past the
monastery where we had spent the night. The enemy had
lengthened his fire and his shrapnels were bursting wildly
in the air. As I passed under a vaulted archway over the
road, men who were posted on top with a machine-gun casually asked me: "What the hell was happening?" I told them
to keep a good look-out, as the enemy was not far off. I
reached the flat and presently came up to a château. Sleeping cuirassiers and their unsaddled horses were spread over
a large lawn. At once I told the sentry where the enemy
was, and shouting: "Debout! ennemi," he roused the men,
who sprang to their feet. This sudden uproar brought the
Colonel out on to the balcony, wearing a white night-cap.
I rode up to tell him what was happening, and after shouting some orders, he thanked me.

I continued on my way, and eventually saw the Brigade's
red pennant hanging from a lance at the door of a small
café. Jumping off my bicycle I walked towards an officer
seated before a kitchen table, who was receiving dispatches
from orderlies who, after handing in their message, waited
in a queue for the receipt. Very curtly he told me to take
my turn; on my insistence that I should see the General
personally, he threatened me with arrest. Happily, Major
Seligman, who commanded J Battery, had witnessed the
incident; he led me at once into a small room, where Sir
Philip Chetwode stood before a map, smoking a Turkish

cigarette in a long amber holder. After reading my
message he promptly wrote something on a dispatch-block,
enclosed it in an envelope and said: "Rejoin your Colonel
at once with this; the regiment is falling back on to this
place," which he showed me on the map.

I gulped down a glass of cold coffee handed me by Major
Seligman, climbed on to my bike and again found myself
pedalling as hard as I could along the sun-beaten road.
Soon, through a cloud of dust rising in the distance, I saw
coming towards me the red trousers of French cavalry,
which passed me with a terrific clatter and dust—they were
the two regiments I had awakened. The Colonel, recognising me, waved, and said: "Merci, mon garçon." They were
an impressive sight, but how hot they must have been wearing those breast-plates, though they were covered by khaki
cloth to prevent them glittering.

The dust of the road caked on my lips. I turned to the
right at a cross-roads, went through a small hamlet, and
then hesitated at the next fork-roads. Which way was I
to take? Following my instinct, I bore left, giving a wide
berth, I thought, to the enemy creeping up from the north.
I was half-conscious of a figure moving behind a tree half-
way up the steep road I was leaving on my right. I did not
pay any particular heed, being only fully aware of it after
I had turned off. I caught up with a lancer cantering back
to his troops, who said that he had just spotted two German
cyclists on the road. I grabbed the side of his saddle, and
as he cantered I free-wheeled along, resting, until he broke
off into a different direction from mine. Alone for some
time on the road and not hearing a sound (the enemy shelling had ceased), I began to feel uneasy. At the bottom of
a steep hill one of the two cuirassiers we had seen earlier in
the morning appeared. He didn't seem keen to run after
his regiment after hearing that German cyclists were about.
He said he would remain with me, and as he was tired of
his horse, would I let him ride my bicycle? I climbed with
difficulty on to his overloaded saddle and we set off
together, he in front—a funny sight with his heavy helmet,

cuirass and bulging haversacks. We had gone only a short distance when two sharp shots suddenly rang out and, like the flutter of a large beetle, something whizzed past my ear, the dust flicking up on the left side of the road in front. Without a word we were rounding the next corner, my French companion showing the large seat of his red trousers, as he bent over the handle-bars like a professional cyclist. Galloping on behind, my beastly horse was pulling and jerking his head back all the time; I never had such an uncomfortable ride. I couldn't stop the brute even when I came on one of our squadrons deployed among corn-stooks in a field; like John Gilpin, I rushed wildly past them and just managed to hear Captain Long shouting to me that the Colonel was in a sunken road 100 yards beyond. I galloped on to him and gave him my message, at which he said, "Well done!" With a smile he asked me what I had done with my bicycle; the cuirassier turning up at that moment, his face shining like a rising sun, there was no need to explain.

The regiment, partly dismounted, waited for the enemy the whole day long. We were all on tenterhooks. We heard some firing on our distant left and then, far away on the right, the constant rumble of cannonade that came from the French—for some unaccountable reason we never saw a German again that day. Were they working around our right? If so, what would happen when darkness fell? At dusk we fell back a little. Infantry had come up and were digging a trench as we went through them. We found places for our horses in a small village reeking of manure and settled for the night as best we could. I curled up in a wheelbarrow, smiling at the anomaly of making my bed at the end of my first day of war in an implement so symbolic of peace. I was aroused sharply from my sleep by the return of one of our runners who, unknown to me, had been sent, soon after me, with a duplicate dispatch to the brigade. Cursing in broad Scotch, he said he had "never found the bloody place," and had been shot at.

CHAPTER IV

THE RETREAT

(1)

AUGUST 23RD.—The regiment was astir before daylight and immediately moved forward and awaited orders. A fierce engagement had started early on our distant left, and never stopped raging throughout the day. We saw infantry march forward and some retire, but could understand nothing of what was going on. We could get no news. We remained roasting in the sun, expecting to be called forward at any moment. As the day passed the first casualties of the battle began to go through in ambulances—the reports we got were more gloomy than convincing. A fierce battle, anyhow, was being fought at Mons. As night fell, a division came up to allow the retirement of one that had fought all day long—we ourselves withdrew through them, being ordered to Givry for the night, the sound of cannon having then died down.

I found myself with the whole of the transport of the 5th Brigade jammed together inside an enclosed field with only a narrow gate for entrance; every wagon on its way through had barged into the gate-post, and when the last one squeezed itself into place there was hardly room for the horses to move when unharnessed. It was a pitch-black night and chilly. In the remotest darkness over on the German side haystacks which had blazed all day were now smouldering; flames would rise from them now and again and gradually die down, plunging us in the dark until an enemy searchlight began to sweep the sky. French gendarmes passed on the road, clad in heavy coats and leading their tired horses. They told me that the French 5th Army had fought a fierce battle at Charleroi and was now retreating. They wondered why we were remaining. Having had no reports from the battle at Mons, I began to consider our own situation. A peasant's cart squeaked along the road; from inside the lit-up hood rose the pathetic wail of a newly-born child; the shadow of the mother was projected against the canvas. Then started a solemn procession of convoys of wounded, followed by the infantry retiring.

Keeping my reflections to myself, I went over to the men who had lit a bonfire to cook their dinner. I tried to impress upon them that we were in full view of the enemy, and the folly of the risk they were running, but they merely roared with good humour, standing silhouetted against the glare of the blaze. The cook, an immense fellow with curly hair, was dishing out bacon or brandishing a great club-like stick as a poker. The fire lit up every corner of the bivouac, where rows of horses were placidly feeding.

.   .   .   .   .   .

AUGUST 24TH.—It was still dark when the transport got orders to pack up and retire south at once. There was an immediate sign of hurry about our camp, as horses and men moved about, tripping and banging over the wagon poles. Gradually they extricated themselves from their tangle, and as the last one got clear of what remained of the gate, the first burst from an enemy shell heralded the daylight.

The convoy consisted of the transport wagons of the three regiments of the brigade, some of the headquarters staffs and led horses, among which were a nice lot of polo ponies, which were to fall next day into the hands of the enemy. As escort we had a few mounted men and cyclists. Major Seymour, who had landed in France with a broken ankle, added a picturesque note to the column by driving an old-fashioned cabriolet he had bought from a peasant, with horse and harness complete.

Three German Dragoons, taken prisoners the day be-

fore, had been handed over to us and were riding as
passengers on the top of a loaded cart, exciting everybody's
curiosity and attention. We spread over about half a mile
of the road. The whole echelon was under the command
of Major Collins. The Colonel had ordered me to stand
by him, as I would be of help; he expected confusion on
the roads, owing to the general retirement.

The sun was climbing quickly when we started—the
light was white, promising torrid heat. Transport wheels
ground along the road and guns boomed loudly on both
sides; uneasiness dominated the atmosphere. From the
road I looked into a valley where deployed infantry was
advancing across fields, while squadrons of cavalry galloped
round the base of a spur to occupy a position. Having the
road to ourselves for the time being we retreated steadily
across the country. Soon the heat became trying—there
was not a cloud in the sky. We avoided Maubeuge, after
crossing the French frontier, and went through elements
of a French division deployed for action. Men were
hidden behind crenellated walls, showing only the muzzles
of their rifles—we saw a great deal of their field artillery,
everybody standing ready for action. They did not seem
to understand why we were retiring, and the information
I gathered from them tended to show that they knew absolutely nothing of what was happening.

We continued our journey at the same pace, all the
horses pulling well. The sound of guns was increasing all
the time—the deep reports that must have come from the
heavy guns of the Maubeuge fortifications soon added to
the general uproar. We were alone most of that morning.
Looking up we saw a bright yellow airship overtaking us,
droning through the limpid blue, a tricoloured streamer
whirling in its wake. The frontier and Maubeuge had
steadily receded—the country all the time was opening out
before us as though we were riding towards infinity. The
gun reports had dwindled down into a faint rumble—we
were glad to get away from them.

Fields were marked everywhere with heavy-wheel traffic

and trampled down by infantry, indicating the passage of a considerable number of troops. Civilians had all gone on—no one was to be seen in the villages we went through. Towards the afternoon the red and blue of French uniforms were seen streaking the plains on our left, moving parallel with our road. Later we fell in among them. They belonged to the 5th French Army, had fought at Charleroi, and were the tail-end of a division that had gone on ahead. Although hot and dusty the men appeared to be in good spirits; we progressed easily with them until well on in the afternoon, when we were held up in a village for a considerable time. Apparently we had caught up another body of the French retirement. The road ahead of us was a blue tape of uniforms.

The ground rose as we went on, giving us an extensive view of the country, with marching troops everywhere. Soon we were tightly pressed by French infantry marching alongside; rifles, haversacks, sparkling mess tins were moving up and down around us like a choppy sea. Everywhere they overran the fields, a blue mass shuffled forward through the dust on what seemed millions of feet. Feet, feet, moving everywhere. I was never so conscious of the use of feet as when I saw this army on the march. Often we had to stop to let units cut across our road; we were in the thick of the general French retirement. The sun beat down on these sweating hordes, where each individual, his tunic wide open at the neck, reacted in his own way to the heat, the weight of his pack and his ill-fitting clothes. But the lean and the fat, the tall and the short, all kept up. Although many feet were dragging along the ground they certainly didn't look like beaten troops. Many were pensive and perhaps anxious, but there were also the men, always to be found in armies, whose unquenchable high spirits bucked up the others. They joked and greeted us as we passed, some having festooned their rifles with flowers. The figures of the officers on horseback rose above the sea of heads as though they were floating along on the

stream. Regimental flags were furled up in black oilcloth.
At every village we met with increased congestion. Constantly we had to stop. To add to the confusion refugees
and their carts were now mixed up with the troops—herds
of cattle were being urged forward, but they kept to their
own pace, turning their anxious eyes, as though sensing
the drama of it all. Dogs barked; peasants whipped forward their horses as batteries of French seventy-fives
glided endlessly by between oat-sheaves and corn-stooks.
We were in a cloud of dust, through which at times we saw
the sky, intensely blue. Soldiers, civilians, beasts, all
sweating, were heading south, following the general movement of retirement, which was to go on for eight days. . . .

At length the civilians encumbered the roads with their
vehicles to such an extent that they were compelled to
halt to allow the army to get on. They watched us go by
with the patient look of resignation of people who have
already suffered enough not to care any more.

All the time the sound of guns pursued us—we didn't
go fast enough to get clear of it. As night closed in on us
we entered a large village, having successfully extricated
ourselves from the current of the French retirement and
branched off to the right.

We filled the entire square of the village with our
wagons, and unharnessed the horses, tying them up around
a bandstand. I slept propped up against a pile of music
stands, vaguely conscious of an incessant tramping of feet
that gradually died away like the flow of a tap.

CHAPTER V

(II)

AUGUST 25TH.—With the first glimmer of light, men were up and about, feeding their horses. An ominous calm hung over the village. But for the stragglers lagging behind their division, which had gone on, no troops were now passing. A few motor-cyclists rode in looking for Headquarters, whose whereabouts we didn't know. I managed to find some petrol for one who had run short—we drained the last drops from empty petrol tins in a garage, the door of which we found unlocked, indicating the owner's hurry to get away.

As the transport got under way, Major Collins, who since the previous morning had not been in touch with the regiment, told me to remain behind and ascertain what troops were still to the north of us. I was to catch them up again at a village where they would halt, some miles further south. The works of the village church clock ground lazily, striking an early hour as I passed on my way to the outskirts of the village. It was the only sound I heard after the rattle of the convoys had died down.

On reaching a broad field I made for a haystack standing on a slight rise, which gave a view looking forward and behind on two immense semi-circles of country. As I took up my position the sun was barely showing over the horizon, climbing in a patch of glaring light that strained my eyes and made me feel all the more the nervous weariness of the early morning.

Moisture from the night still gripped the land; everything was uniformally grey and indistinct. But the sun, climbing fast, showed up villages, woods and prominent

29

features, which stood silhouetted a milky-blue in a rim
of silver light.

I still felt the chilly air of the morning—my horse snatch-
ing at the straw of the sodden stack kept pressing me
against it, making my side all wet. A smell of cows rose
from the land, the dew glittered like jewels. . . . The
country seemed completely abandoned, nothing in it was
stirring. It was the hour when the smoke would rise into
the still air from farm chimneys, when the early meal of
the peasants is prepared, when the cows begin their lowing
and turn towards those who come out with the milk-pails.
All that life seemed to have ceased. Implements were now
lying about, hurriedly dropped by the men called away to
the colours, and then by the older men who to the last
had stuck to the soil. . . .

The landscape was now full of colour; trees bordering
the roads made distinct squares and triangles across it;
corn-fields were streaked by the regular shadows of stooks,
lined up like regiments. My horse had become restless,
champing at his bit and stamping the ground. I moved to
another haystack, as much to overcome a feeling of uneasiness that I felt creeping within me as to quieten him down.
This huge space in all its solitude was weighing on me.
Suddenly, between the regular intervals of trees on a distant road, the red of French trousers appeared, moving
rapidly southwards on bicycles; a short while after, one
of our motor-cyclists rode up from the village, and I cantered towards him. He had been searching in vain for a
battalion to deliver his dispatch to. I advised him to read
it, as it might supply him with the necessary indication.
Happily it did, and he rode off at full speed, leaving me
in the dreaded quietness, although the booming of guns
was now audible far away on my right and left. It seemed
extraordinary that there should be so few troops just here.
My attention was drawn towards an aeroplane that
swooped down round a belt of trees and glided to earth
like a partridge—for some unknown reason it immediately
rose again, gaining height at great speed; it showed the

allied colours on the wings.

I had made up my mind to rejoin my transport when a detachment of men sprang from some hidden ground below me, riding across the fields. I moved forward so that they should see me and they drew towards me, their officer in front, cantering on a polo pony as he would have done on a polo ground. They had just left a patrol of their own regiment, which a short time before had been exchanging shots with Uhlans. They were falling back on their regiment, and I was advised to get quickly back to my transport. As they turned off to the left and I began to retrace my steps towards the village, I was suddenly seized by a feeling of panic, which for a few seconds I could not control. I reined in my horse who, at the slightest pressure, broke into a canter and remained for a while until things assumed their normal proportions again in my mind.

After going through the village I crossed over a railway track; the stones flying against the metal from under my horse's hoofs made musical notes that broke the unnerving silence. I scurried up a slope of cut corn, and at the top drew rein to look back. The roofs and pale stones of the village were glowing in the heat, the golden tail of the weathercock on the church steeple caught the sun; beyond, the plains rolled away towards the distance, full of shimmering uncertainty.

Facing a new vista of shining fields, I cantered down the reverse slope, trying to get my direction from the lines of telegraph wires cutting across country. Coveys of partridges rose on my way. Larks were singing, hovering high in the sky. What a day! . . . On the right I could see for miles; a wood limited my view on the left. A troop of lancers remained outlined for a time on a far-away ridge, and then dipped out of sight over the other side. I saw later the silhouettes of tiny figures bent forward, echeloned on what must have been a road—probably stragglers or civilians—I was too far away to tell.

On entering another village I found four men resting in the shade of the street, one or two of them with puttees

undone or boots off. They lay exhausted next to their unstrapped kit. I loaded my saddle with their haversacks,
urging them to get up and come on. They had reached
the stage where, although the mind is still willing, bodily
strength fails to respond. But they got going again, en-
couraged by the eldest, who kept repeating, "Stick it, the
Queens." Suddenly dropping their packs and leaving the
men to march on, I trotted on, having seen their chance
of a lift with a halted transport ahead of us. I cantered
up and found the wagons with poles down in charge of
a young officer. He objected to my suggestion about taking
the men, and when I told him that he had better be pushing on with his convoy, he replied that he was awaiting
orders, and I had better mind my own business. However,
I hastened back to my stragglers who, with a final spurt,
managed to climb on a cart as the transport was moving
on; without referring to it the officer had changed his
mind. . . .

Keeping off the road on the soft field I soon left them
behind, having for direction a forest spreading to the south
in front of me. I had a map, the cover of a New Year's
calendar giving the topography of the department, and
although not very detailed it was better than nothing.

I had to trot many miles to reach the village where the
transport had halted. I kept an eye on the kilometre stones
on the road, and realised how long I had lingered on behind. To my dismay they had left the place, but, thanks
to the information given me by some French cavalry
soldiers who had seen a transport, I was able to catch them
up further on the road. It was then about 10 o'clock in
the morning; the day had hardly begun and yet I felt I
had lived a lifetime! I gave Major Collins all the information I could, and didn't hide from him the urgency of
moving on. The transport rattled on without a stop; the
country was still open all round us and there was no sign
of troops anywhere. Guns were firing level to our right,
miles away. . . .

Towards the end of the afternoon we saw ahead of us

French troops retiring to the Marne. August, 1914

the sky blurred by dust, indicating movement on the roads; as we went on the noise of transport became audible, together with the now familiar shuffling sound of march- ing feet. Coming down a steep hill leading into a townlet we saw French troops pouring into it. Again we had fallen in with the French retirement. We managed to enter the place after waiting outside to let some artillery go through. The khaki of our column struck a discordant note as it mixed with the red and blue of uniforms of French soldiers which swarmed in the town. They were smothered in dust; many were exhausted, lying with boots off among piled-up arms and haversacks, contemplating their sore feet with an expression of despair. The alert ones were fighting their way to fountains and into houses to refill their water-bottles. The heat of the sun striking the exposed side of the street reverberated as from an oven, while the shady side cast a chilly cool. As we crossed the dazzling square in front of the Mairie a great many staff officers stood gathered near motor-cars, one of which flew a blue and red pennant fringed with gold.

A Colonel of Hussars in a brilliant uniform whom I had seen observing us as we came on, walked up to Major Collins, to tell him we were in the area allotted to the French retirement, and advised us to get away from it as soon as we could, for the congestion was very great farther south. There was a disturbing feeling of bustle and tension about the place. A tall French General, in a fever of agitation, was giving orders to officers arriving and de- parting—he said something about using their artillery and seventy-fives and then, looking at our transport in the middle of the reigning confusion, briskly stepped towards us, a map in one hand, a crust of bread in the other, and said: "Can't you see that you are congesting the whole of my retirement? You must get out of our way." His manner was anything but pleasant. I translated what he said in milder tones. Pointing to his map and addressing me, he added, "Tell your officer to get on to this road as soon as he possibly can." With that he precipitately

D

entered his car, which cut its way through the troops and
disappeared. The Colonel most charmingly excused the
curtness of his General, and explained what he could of
the situation. "We are all retiring south to chosen positions: we shall attack when a propitious moment arrives—
la situation est sérieuse, mais pas grave." The atmosphere
seemed charged to bursting-point.

Following our orders, the transport moved away as best
it could, being held up every few yards by large agglomera-
tions of troops and endless columns which were cutting
across our road. When we struck the road indicated, it was
easy to realise that it led due west and as the enemy was
falling on us from the north, it was evident that the sooner
we veered south the better for the safety of our convoy.
Away from French troops we seemed to fall into an
unoccupied gap, which gave us a feeling of uneasiness. We
headed in the direction of a large forest, which we could
either skirt by keeping to our road, or enter, by deviating
to the south. We drove through; the silence of the forest
made distant sounds more perceptible—somewhere on our
right heavy skirmishing was going on.

At a junction of cross-roads and lanes which cut diagon-
ally through a wood, I suggested taking a track which
would make our direction still more southerly. The C.O.
hesitated a good deal—those intermediate arterial roads
were not marked on the map, it might be risky. The
transport was waiting, the horses' heads facing either way
while he trotted down the line to confer with an officer at
the end of the column. Drivers and horses were impatient;
I had only to make a sign and the columns were in the
lane. I didn't know where to look as Major Collins rode
up again, but by then the horses were pulling hard and
whatever he wanted to do we could not turn back now.
When the path began to narrow down and the branches
on both sides of the road in places swept our horses, I
became concerned. The wood seemed completely deserted;
there was no sound apart from the dangling chains and
the steady strain of our horses. This sudden isolation re-

laxed my tension and for a while I gave myself up to
its peace. Eventually we branched on to a broader alley
nearly parallel, and the change from a rough on to a
smooth surface suddenly induced our horses to trot, as
if they understood the danger threatening.

Leaving the forest with its lovely shade, we emerged on
to a glaring main road where, after a time, we were relieved to see the dust rise from a British ammunition
column trotting in front of us. A signpost indicated the
way to Landrecies. While we were halted for a short
rest an obsolete-looking motor-car crawled up with the
strangest man at the steering-wheel, wearing a bowler hat
and spectacles on the tip of his nose. He blew a tiny sharp
horn. Among the family was a child buried under a pile
of luggage, holding in its hand a cage with a bird. "Look
at the circus turn-out," exclaimed one of the men, as the
machine shook past, propelled by irregular bursts from
its engine.

We had completely lost sense of time—a day seemed
endless. The light lingered on a long time after the sun
had set, and in the coolness we progressed with relief. We
passed the bivouac of a French brigade of territorials, all
busy cooking dinner. A Colonel and his staff, whom I
thought I knew, drove up to us; indeed, it was the Colonel
who commanded the 129th Regiment of Infantry at Havre,
and years ago I had followed the regiment on manœuvres,
often playing truant from school, unable to resist the
temptation. I stopped to tell him the situation as I knew
it. I was amazed when he replied that he had no orders at
all, and that certainly he could not retire without any.
Instead, he commanded the cooking-pan to be kicked over
and drew up his men. I met him in Paris after the war, a
drawn, thin figure. Well he remembered meeting me then.
"Ah!" he said, "we were only a brigade of old men; after
a short fight we were overwhelmed from all sides and had
to surrender."

In a village further on, the Mayor met us, wearing a red,
white and blue sash round his large stomach. He was very

excited, as troops had stolen fruit from the gardens, saying that, "In the name of the Republic" he would forbid it. He seemed completely off his head—he alone remained. I wondered then what the Germans would do with him and his apples.

We were all worn out when, after midnight, the transport unharnessed in a village. I had found rooms for the C.O. and myself, and it was understood that should the transport move in the night I was to be called. Without undressing, I flung myself on a bed—my last sense of consciousness in that stuffy room which had never known an open window, was facing an enlarged photograph of a French soldier hung over the mantelpiece in a shiny gold frame. His mother who had shown me into the room had pointed it out to me, saying with the tears on her cheeks, "Perhaps he is already dead!" . . .

CHAPTER VI

RETREAT

(III)

AUGUST 26TH.—I woke up suddenly—it was daylight. I didn't know where I was—I only felt the weight of my boots. I looked at my watch—I had slept five hours. Not a sound came from the village. I peeped through the window—the street was deserted.

I slipped down the stairs into the kitchen shouting for madame. Her bread and coffee lay on the table. I got no response. Full of apprehension I ran up the stairs, and as I seized my cap and revolver belt, I heard the clatter of horses' hoofs—the square tops of Uhlan helmets were passing right under my window! I paused, breathless; then a motor-car rushed through the streets, carrying a party of Germans, revolvers in hand. I had to push the window open gently to see if anyone else was coming. The two riders I had seen turn off to the right were now out of sight.

I had to act quickly. Fortunately the village was small. Each farm opened on to a yard. I had to avoid the roads. The kitchen door was locked—it gave on to a small garden. I jumped out of the window and climbed a wall covered with pears, crossed over a lane into a farmyard, slipped through some stables into an open space and made for another farm where a few hens, pecking at a manure heap, ran off with much fluttering. At the next farm, looking through a window I saw some people in a room. I rushed in—they were terrified, reviving themselves with brandy. "Quickly," I said, "which is my best way out of the village? Have you seen many German troops?—how long have the English been gone?" They all talked at once. One little

37

fellow, a hunchback, caught hold of my arm and said, "Suivez-moi," and I followed him. After much dodging about we came to a wall—I peeped over and saw an expanse of country that looked like the whole of France spread in the sunlight. The trees of two main roads divided the landscape. One led to St. Quentin. I shook the hand of my guide, who said, "Bonne chance, sauvez-vous vite." Hiding the best way I could, I crept towards the road, shuffling noisily through a wet cabbage patch that soaked me to the skin. After a short run I flung myself headlong into the ditch bordering the road. Carefully I looked around—not a soul could be seen anywhere. I put my ear to the ground, but detected no sound. I got up and ran, dodging from tree to tree, which happily were thick and not far apart, stopping only to recover my breath. I watched every haystack, keeping all the time my eye on a village to my right.

I had just paused a moment and was on the verge of rushing forward again when there, standing against a bright wall, were three Uhlans, their shadows distinctly reflected on the wall. My eyes glued to them, I dared not move. A cold shiver ran down my spine as one of them rode his horse across the open towards a group of small haystacks about 200 yards from where I was. Stopping suddenly, he stood up in his stirrups and looked through his field-glasses. He took his time, concentrating on certain places. I could see his dark horse lash the air with his tail. Nothing, evidently, had arrested his attention in my direction, but when he waved to the others and they promptly joined him at a quick trot I thought I was finished. They stood a while conversing, then looked round, and to my relief turned their horses and started at an easy trot, moving back towards the village, their lances with folded pennants rocketing above their heads.

As I had my eyes fixed on them I heard coming up a kind of flapping sound. It was a dog running straight at me. I gave a sudden jerk as he neared; it frightened him off, and with a suppressed yelp he swerved and ran on, his tail between his legs, trailing a lead. Meanwhile, the Uhlans had neared the village and were vanishing behind farms. There was nothing for me to do but run. I looked in every direction first, and crawled to the other side of the road, seeing as I did so the dog, away in front, still running for all it was worth.

What saved me was the depth of the ditch and the bank on both sides of the road; by bending down, I could run along nearly sure that I could not be seen from the fields. What distance I covered I don't know, when two sharp shots rang out ahead on my right, echoing from wood to wood. I felt the atmosphere relapse into a drawn silence as I lay with my face to the ground, expecting to hear more firing. Nothing more happened. I got up again, looking intently to the right. I was inwardly so anxious and excited that I could hardly see; the light was also too bright. I was now nearing the line of trees along a road crossing mine and as the ground rose slightly towards it on my left I couldn't actually see all of it, so I crawled back to the other side. No sooner had I done so than a few more shots were fired, and distinctly I located the report coming from a bushy belt of trees, where for a second I imagined seeing the khaki of our uniforms. The light was so dazzling I dared not yet believe my eyes. But at that moment, unmistakably, two of our cavalry strode across the road away in front. Hopes raised, I waited; there among the leaves I could see red faces. I was now sure. Having advanced a little more, I cleared the bank, waving, and bolting across the distance that separated us, I shot in amongst them as between two goal-posts. They were our cavalry, dismounted—their horses were just at hand a few paces off. For a moment I could hardly talk. The officer told me that I was lucky, for German patrols were about and they had been firing at anyone who showed himself. "You are lucky they didn't see you. Your regiment must be about somewhere, they passed early in the morning. You had better walk to brigade headquarters at . . . . . . two miles away: they may be able to direct you."

Having joined a Highland Light Infantryman who had strayed from his battalion, and who was walking the same way, I heard the details of a severe scrap in which he had been engaged. His haversack was full of raw apples, which he kept munching and spitting out. Red-haired, tall, as brown as a berry, with a terrific Border accent, he looked the picture of health, in spite of his weary march. The village we walked into was occupied by our infantry, and in the middle of the market square there stood a throng of officers obviously engaged in stern conversation. Among them was a stoutish man with a grey moustache, General Sir Charles Monro, who commanded the 2nd Division. As I was still new to the Army, the sight of red tabs had not the sobering effect on me, that it had on a regular private. I rashly imagined that the staff would welcome any information that I might be able to give. I boldly approached the group of officers, saluted and inquired the whereabouts of the Scots Greys or of their transport with which I had lost touch. I was about to say where I had come from and what I had seen, when the General cut me short, looked at me from head to toe and replied that the Greys had passed through the village earlier that day, but that he had no idea where their transport had gone. Suddenly his face twitched and he abruptly asked my name; I saw suspicion in his stare. "Where have you come from?" I mentioned the village. "The place has been occupied by the enemy since early this morning," he replied. I felt a stir amongst those listening—one officer walked quickly away.

"What village did you say you were in?"
I could not remember the name. . . .

"What is the name of your colonel?"
My memory failed me entirely. . . .

"What squadron are you in?"
My mind was a blank. . . .

I had the sensation of the ground receding under my feet as I was seized and my belt and revolver taken from me. I was immediately searched, right down to my puttees. Handcuffed, my legs trembling under me, I was led off to join a party of German soldiers and Belgian civilians who were standing by the headquarters baggage, tied to one another. We were marched off at once, escorted by men with fixed bayonets. . . . I could hardly realise anything. The General and his staff soon after passed us in his car without even looking at us. It was no use my appealing. I heard a man say, "Here's another blasted spy." It made me realise the situation I was in.

It was useless to try to get a hearing from my escort. I could not talk to the German prisoners, who all the time were mumbling to me, "Bist du Deutsch?" I dared not answer. I heard them discuss me—they couldn't make out what I was. The three Belgians looked such ruffians I thought it wise not to address them at all. We were made to step out, to keep well behind the rear of the transport.

There was a general sign of hurry about everything—riders were driving their heels into their horses, the infantry alongside us were marching fast. The dew had laid the dust, but the sun was very hot, although it was still early morning. Staring at the wagon before me I followed the sound of its squealing as one does a tune. I walked on dazedly, as though in a dream, not realising yet the full extent of what hung over me. A loud rumble of guns on our right grew nearer and nearer.

In a village where we rested later in the day, the exhausted refugees livened up as they saw the "espions." They spat at us and threw stones. One French territorial, for some unknown reason alone in that village, came up to us seething with rage, waving his bayonet. Our guard became furious and handled him very roughly. He was foaming at the mouth.

We resumed our weary march, picking up as we went on a considerable number of stragglers belonging to all sorts of regiments. From their appearance it was evident that they had had a bad time—but they looked determined and walked on, keeping in rank. Motor-cyclists and staff cars would rush past, raising a cloud of dust. Artillery would cut across fields, leaving the road free for the infantry—everybody was bent on pushing on. Every echo I heard of the situation sharpened my apprehension.

We overtook a halted wagon line, and as ill luck would have it, three German prisoners we had had with the transport the day before recognised me and waved. As they had been with us for a whole day I had chatted to them a good deal to try to get some information out of them, so of course they knew me quite well. How could I explain to the guards who had seen them greet me the circumstances of our acquaintance! The incident was at once reported to the military police, and nothing I could say made things any better. I was in a divided frame of mind, for, although I stood accused and knew I was hated and despised by anyone who caught sight of me, I could not help liking and admiring these soldiers.

When night came I was led to a small shrine on the side of the road. Tired out, I lay down, a meek statue of the Virgin Mary above my head. I remembered what the nun had said on my way north as she had pressed the medal into my hand. Indeed, I needed now all the help in the world, even hers. . . .

The night was very cold. Troops went by incessantly. Above the shuffling of feet I heard my sentry solemnly remark, "Why don't they shoot the bastard and be done with him, instead of keeping us shivering out here all night." Somewhere in the darkness a fierce engagement was taking place, not many miles away. . . .

CHAPTER VII

(IV)

AUGUST 27TH.—I was led out of my shrine into a thick fog at an early hour. Artillery, transport and infantry seemed to be all mixed up, and as units extricated themselves from the reigning confusion and got on to the road, an officer shouted out where they were, giving them directions. The three German prisoners were brought up; I joined them at once and we followed in the wake of a large column of infantry. We were given biscuits and a tin of bully beef. Something serious had happened during the night—I didn't know what it was, but I sensed it by the way the horses pulled and the chains strained, by the voices of the drivers, the pace of the marching men; all indicated the gravity of the situation. The enemy was obviously pressing on. In all this I wondered what would happen to me.

After we had been on the march for some hours, the day cleared brilliantly. Suddenly, as I marched alongside some kilted men, my eyes fell on a French soldier who happened to be a friend of mine. I hailed him and we walked along together. He had fought at Charleroi, and lost touch with his regiment. As he knew no English it was difficult for him to explain that I was an old friend, but he managed to tell an officer who understood French. Unfortunately, this didn't help me, as the troops became separated from each other and I even lost touch with my friend. We walked on all that day—my feet were sore. I had thought much; so many problems and possibilities had flooded my weary mind that I could think no more. All I felt were my feet. A fierce battle was being fought over on our left—I detected the rumble of the French seventy-

43

fives. Late at night I was taken into a bedroom of a large modern house standing in the street of a fairly big place plunged in utter darkness. There were two beds in the room—we were three—I took one. For the first time since leaving Mons my guards took off their boots. I couldn't remember when I had last done so. It didn't seem a relief at first, rather the opposite.

One of the guards was a Cockney whom I felt was sympathetic. The other man, a Scot, never answered when I spoke. Only once did he speak, to say, "Dinna worry, if ye're a spy, ye'll be shot allrecht; if ye're no', ye willna be." It was logical enough. My Cockney was much more loquacious. Left once alone with me, he had even told me that he knew they were all wrong—that I was not a spy.

I had been resting a little while when the Provost-Marshal walked in with my haversack. He produced several things belonging to me and asked if the razor inside was mine. Yes, it was; a German razor bought in Hamburg years ago, and I added that if he had had any experience of German or Swedish razors he would use one himself. He went out smiling. After his visit I couldn't sleep—I listened to the guns booming to the east and west of us, the sounds increasing intermittently in an alarming way. The air was heavy with a tension which overpowered all my feelings. I watched the dawn filter into the room. It was barely light when the stairs suddenly trembled with loud footsteps and the banging of rifle bayonets. The door was flung open. The Provost-Marshal stood framed in the doorway and the raucous voice of a sergeant-major behind him ordered the prisoner to be marched out. Quickly my guard and I slipped on our boots, the Cockney looked up enquiringly. "Never you mind, me lad, get ready quick. Atten-shun, march down," and without a word I followed, ready for the worst. There was a tremendous bustle in the street, created by baggage wagons and the infantry hurrying through the village. We waited for a chance of getting across. I heard the clatter of horses and mens' voices shouting, "Make room for the cavalry!" My eyes then fell on Major Collins leading an approaching squadron of Scots Greys. I shouted, "Major Collins!" He turned at the sound of his name, but didn't see me, for he went on. Desperately I shouted again, but my vain appeals were drowned in the tumult of the rushing traffic, while I became hidden from the rest of the troops by the passing wagons. "There you are, none of the Greys have recognised him," said one of my escort, but as they were preparing to bundle me through the clearing made by the disappearing horses, Major Swetenham appeared leading the next squadron. I didn't have to shout to him. He had seen and recognised me. His arm was raised and the squadron had halted. He asked in a puzzled way what I was doing here under arrest. In a few words I told him. "Sergeant, where is the Provost-Marshal?" He had gone on. "Lead me to him," said the Major, and we all hurried across the road, where the escort and I were told to wait. In a few moments both the Major and the Provost-Marshal were walking towards me with a smile on their faces. "Come along quickly," said the Major, "they were going to shoot you," and stopping one of J Battery's limbers, he told me to jump on it as he had no horse to spare. I felt everything suddenly widen around me.

The battery immediately bolted along the main road towards La Fère, shaking me out of all bearings, but a feeling of relief had surged through the whole of my being. After going on for some time within sight of a small village called Cerizy, on the St. Quentin–La Fère road, we came on to part of the Greys halted in the middle of a cup-shaped plain. J Battery drew up and I immediately went towards Colonel Bulkeley-Johnson, whom I saw sitting on a heap of stones on the side of the road, talking to Major Swetenham. He looked pleased on seeing me approach, for he had concluded, after missing me for the last two days, that I had been taken prisoner. He expressed in his charming way much sympathy for what I had gone through. He said, "You must remember that the 2nd Infantry Division have had a very bad time and they have been very nervy about spies. One can hardly trust one's brother these days, such odd things have happened." He told me to remain with J Battery in the meantime, as I would be in good hands with Major Seligman, who commanded the battery.

The 20th Hussars and the 12th Lancers were near-by. The whole of the 5th Brigade was concentrated. Patrols were out, while a whole squadron of Greys commanded the approach of the entire valley in which we were sheltered. The brigade was thus well safeguarded against any surprise.

Everybody was resting, lying in the hot sun, when at about 11 o'clock the report came in from one of the outlying patrols that it had withdrawn from its position, having been engaged by enemy scouts. Two German squadrons had been seen advancing a little way behind them. There was an immediate stir, Major Swetenham galloping off with his trumpeter and our squadrons mounted and dispersed with a section of guns. I remained with the limbers, expecting every moment something to happen. After what seemed an age, for we were left on our own, the rest of the battery was ordered up, and I jumped on to a limber following. By a high bank, where the led horses of one of our troops had been left, we stopped. At that moment rapid musketry fire opened from the top of the bank and just as I reached the men who were firing from behind a hedge at an advance guard, bullets whistled through the leaves, coming from half-way up the distant spur, where a large body of enemy cavalry had dismounted, and over which J Battery's shells were properly bursting. The next second the enemy's horses, which were being quickly led to shelter, were stampeding, scampering up the hill, caught in the rapid fire of another of our squadrons with machine-guns. What followed was timed to perfection like an event at a tattoo, when suddenly, from a corner of the ring, deployed cavalry appears and a charge finishes the tableau. J Battery lifting its fire, the 12th Lancers, which had worked round the right of our troops unobserved, sprung on the scene at full gallop, dashing for the flank of the disorganised Germans. The charge went through them like a flash, the men pulled up their horses, re-formed, and once again rode through the enemy. By the time the Greys had come on ready to charge, the work was done; only a confusion of dead and wounded was left on the ground.

I ran down into the valley as one does towards the scene of an accident. Remounted squadrons with drawn swords were also hurrying to the scene. As a few Germans were hiding in the corn-stooks lances and swords were thrust through the hay and I heard fearful yells. The horses were very excited, as were the men, who were showing to each other the blood dripping off their sword-blades. Others were busy picking up souvenirs.

Meanwhile, I had propped up a wounded German Dragoon, who was vomiting quantities of undigested un-ripe gooseberries. He had a nasty sword-thrust through his chest. In broken English he told me that he had only left the Ritz in London twenty days before, where he had been a waiter, but what I was interested to find out was whether they were the vanguard of a large force of cavalry. He said that several divisions were in the vicinity. I wrote this down on a piece of paper and had it immediately sent to the Colonel. By then the regiments had re-formed and were drawing away from the scene, and as I could see my-self being left behind again, I hurried towards where I had left the limbers. I was just in time, for they were off, and I was cursed by the sergeant for leaving them, as he said that an officer had instructed him to keep an eye on me. At that moment our guns unexpectedly fired again. It was Captain Dendie who, just as his section was limber-ing up, saw another advance party of enemy Dragoons on the reverse slope. Taking advantage of a target with open sight, he ordered his guns to re-open fire. This oppor-tune intervention gave the brigade time to withdraw at leisure. As from my limber I looked around I saw Major Swetenham's trumpeter coming towards us leading a horse

with an empty saddle. I guessed at once what had happened—Major Swetenham had been killed. I felt his death
deeply. He, with another officer who had been shot
through the hand, and six wounded men were our only
casualties in that engagement.

Making three long columns, the three regiments were
now trotting across stubble fields in the wake of the
brigade staff, who were cantering ahead with escort, a red
pennant fluttering from a lance. The shining bamboos
of lances and the bright coats of the horses encircled the
battery, whose wheels noiselessly crushed the straw. A
dog that had suddenly appeared from nowhere, moved
in rhythm with the cavalcade, delighted with his new
attachment. A feeling of satisfaction ran through the
ranks and the horses stepped out proudly. There was every
reason for this elation—the enemy cavalry had been dealt
a blow which would make them realise that they still had
to reckon with the British cavalry. They would in future
not advance as they had done that morning without taking
the rudimentary precautions. It seemed incredible that
a large force of cavalry with their reputation should have
moved over open country without throwing out strong
patrols to reconnoitre the ground.

The country we were traversing consisted of vast
stretches of fields rolling away on all sides. The golden
stacks surrounding scattered farms were like the turrets
of isolated fortresses guarding that lovely country that was
being hastily abandoned to the enemy. No living thing
could be seen moving in this immensity except a few cows
running wild for want of milking and far patrols left behind, dwindling, as we advanced, into little dots in the
distance. The land of France never appeared more noble
or beautiful than it did then, glittering in the sunlight,
facing another invasion. An Englishman could not be
expected to feel the same heart-rending as a Frenchman.
It was not his country. This retirement was to him merely
a military affair—part of the routine of war.

Sitting as a passenger on my limber, I began to relax

after all my emotions. It seemed an age since dawn. We had left the fields for the road. J Battery's fine horses, in perfect condition, trotted smartly along. Limbers were jerked off the ground, facing at times every direction except forward; with difficulty I held on.

The lovely day wore on. We felt care-free, halting in places for long periods, knowing that our pursuers would leave us alone that day. Indeed, even their patrols failed to follow us, and our infantry, whose retirement we were covering, was thus getting well away.

It was late and very dark when the battery drew up in a village in which there was not a sound. Everybody appeared to have left. We flashed our torches on to a big pile of rations, topped by sides of raw beef, erected like a monument in the middle of the square. This food was a godsend to the troops. It was dumped everywhere along our line of retreat, and as the troops marched past they picked up what they wanted; we never once ran short of food. As we had to leave a great deal of it behind, the enemy must have concluded that we were running away in a panic.

I tried to get into the Mairie to find some accommodation for the troops. As I pushed the door open a man appeared on the balcony in his night-shirt, a flickering candle in his hand. He was the mayor, terrified, for he thought we were the Germans. In one of the rooms an old woman sat by a stove in the dark. She had seen the Germans before, she said, in the '70 war and, nodding her head, declared with assurance that she was not afraid. We unpacked baskets of mess silver which the battery carried unnecessarily, and which I think she probably took for loot. Presently I went into a yard, where from a wall came a smell of rabbits. I heard something making little jumps. I pushed my hand through wire netting and got a firm hold of two slippery ears and produced to the mess a magnificent rabbit for our dinner. The smell of onions frying in butter made an immediate impression on our tired minds and bodies.

E

I cooked the dinner myself, and those now alive who were present will remember what a jolly meal we had. Major Seligman's good humour and the aroma from his cigar dispelled any feeling of anxiety that night.

CHAPTER VIII

RETREAT

(v)

AUGUST 29TH.—We had our longest sleep since Havre that night. Up to 10 o'clock in the morning no orders had come in. The men were enjoying their first proper wash and were talking of an indefinite spell of rest. Instead of drawing away, the Brigade had gone forward again to try to get some observation of the enemy's movements and cover the retirement of our infantry. The enemy had obviously relaxed their strain upon us. It was a godsend for the tired infantry of the 2nd Division, which was now leisurely drifting south.

We returned quietly to billets that night, everybody a little browner from the sun. We had heard vague reports about a stand made by the British at Le Cateau, and also knew that the French 5th Army that day had turned on Von Bülow's army and given it a nasty smack at Guise, so things were not so bad after all.

Personally, I was hopeful. One must have faith in something. My faith lay in Joffre. I had only seen him once, and all the French Army had faith in him. What I had seen of the British Army gave me also every reason for confidence, although their whole army was, of course, a small item in this huge affair. Anyhow, something kept telling me to wait and see, and at every opportunity I tried to instil my optimism in others.

AUGUST 30TH.—The high ground between the Oise and the source of the Somme was now behind us. We seemed the whole time to be in a gap between the French and the British Armies, for throughout all that day's retire-

ment we hardly saw any troops. The three regiments of
the Brigade and J Battery kept together on the road going
through lovely country more closed in, passing charming
old towns, all completely deserted. In one place the nuns
in charge of a lunatic asylum, under the impression that
they could get a train at the station, had taken to the road
with the inmates who kept breaking away like children.
Finding no train, they were now trailing back. We had no
time to help—we left them.

We ate all the time on our march. We would pop into
gardens and gather any fruit that was there, and whenever
we caught sight of chickens we looked for eggs, though
often we saw the marks of those who had had the same idea
before us. I myself practically lived on lettuces and bread
and cheese. Being in the open air the whole day, we were
bursting with health. To keep fit I walked whenever the
battery stopped trotting.

We did a good fifteen miles, and entered the shelter of
the St. Gobain Forest, a haven of peace. We rode for
miles over a carpet of moss cooled by the shade of high
trees that met over our heads like arches of cathedrals—
the drive was like an endless aisle. Frightened deer, seeing
us, would stride across side-rides and shuffle through the
branches which the sunset lit up like smouldering twigs.
We were not hurried; the beauty of nature at that moment
was sublime. There was no end to this forest in which we
never saw a soul. The freshness of the evening was rising,
birds were singing from every tree; rabbits, who owed
their peace to the war, seemed quite bold as they hopped
back into the bushes as we passed. The sun had sunk, trees
had turned dark and the road was a creamy white as we
emerged into the open again. It was just light enough to
find out billets in the village at which we drew up for
the night. Of the enemy there was neither sound nor sign.

August 31st.—Again we were not hurried that morning.
In a routine manner we took to the hot road. It was
another perfect day with rolling pink clouds in a blue sky.

We were having a wonderful spell of weather. We had lost touch with our infantry until noon when, at the beginning of a long climb, we fell in amongst them. The heat was rising from the hard road, unmerciful to sore feet. Sweat was pouring down the men's red faces—their necks were tanned by the sun. We climbed and climbed, feeling the heat slackening the men's stride while the horses pulled harder on the strained chains. Once over the brow of the hill everything relaxed—the ground suddenly giving under tired feet, we seemed to be sliding down the winding road. With renewed life the columns tramped down like an endless centipede, their feet making a noise not unlike pouring rain. Below us lay the country, a vast panorama cut by roads, where marching troops were raising a veil of dust like caravans in the desert. Our ammunition column followed the winding descent. The unceasing movement of haversacks sent me off to sleep, my head dropping to one side, then to the other. At a turning we had the sensation of planing over a town, slightly blurred by the heat haze below us.

As we passed through the town we saw French soldiers hurriedly burning documents in the middle of the barrack square—a wonderful old building looking forlorn without its regiment. We watered our horses and had a rest in the shade of the town.

Under way again with monotonous regularity we cut through the lengthening shadows of poplar trees bordering the road until we came within sight of a large river, where men were splashing and swimming. The sun caught the banks and lit up their faces, their shirts and naked limbs. It all looked very gay, in spite of the fact that sappers were laying the charges to blow up the bridge. The infantry had now gone on, the cavalry remaining behind to guard the crossing. The shadows had crept into the fields and were now vanishing with the light. My ammunition column was trotting away. In the stillness of the falling night sounds rose very clearly. We felt refreshed. We heard distinctly the explosion from the bridge. We felt quite secure as we stopped, unharnessed the horses and prepared to settle down for the night, but during dinner rumours of the enemy spread which made us wonder whether after all we should get a night's rest.

We had hardly got between fresh sheets when our doubts were dispelled by the appearance of an orderly from the brigade with an order to pack up at once and resume the retirement. Orders were shouted out through the window; everyone rushed to his job—in a few minutes the battery was leaving the village at a quick trot in the mysterious darkness.

We thundered through country and empty villages. Not a light was showing anywhere. Wherever possible we kept off the roads to rest our horses from the hard surface; the wheels running on the damp fields made a soothing sound. Anxiety kept us awake. There was no sign of any regiment of the brigade following the battery, and we wondered what was happening. After a considerable time the echo of marching feet rose from other roads, together with the dull roll of hurried transport. We fell in with hordes coming from every direction, all converging towards the small town we were making for. Units were squeezing themselves into the town which subsequently disgorged them on to the main road outside in a chaotic crush. Moving along the street this flow of shadows emphasised the stillness and emptiness of the town.

J Battery forced its way into the drift—infantry was marching sullenly on. We were crammed as if in a tunnel. Wheels were grinding, axles squeaking—all sounds united in a cacophony, above which the metallic notes of cavalry horses' hoofs rose in a harmonious *leit-motiv*.

We moved on and then began to be held up. No sooner did we stop than we immediately fell asleep, vaguely conscious of other troops moving past us, which intensified our sense of immobility. When it came to our limbers to advance it was torture to be stirred by the sudden jerk of the horses' pull. We were constantly being overtaken, and then, in turn, overtaking others. The halted infantry

dozed, crouched over their rifles, weighed down by their
packs. The general apprehension seemed anæsthetised by
our weariness.

When a late moon appeared, ascending slowly into a
perfect round above the dark line defining the far distance,
the trees silhouetted against it appeared to slide backwards
as we moved forward. The figures of lancers off the road
were gliding noiselessly by like ships in the night, leaving
us behind—shadow lantern forms under the veil of night.
Rifle-fire broke out now and again not far away.

SEPTEMBER 1ST.—The chilly air gave us the first intimation
of dawn. The darkness above our heads rolled away like
a curtain, and what seemed to have been walls surrounding us steadily crumbled down. All the fantastic shapes of
things that had followed us through the night were vanishing, real things were now appearing. We felt a sensation
of freedom and relief as the day grew, slowly unfolding unexpected new scenery.

Light brought us the revelation of ourselves; we were
soaked with dew. With a sudden blaze the sun came out,
casting a violent, tiring white light. Spread like a dark
deep carpet the verdure of the forest of Villers-Cotterets
lay in front of us. When we reached the outskirts, we saw
the Guards entrenching, preparing for immediate action.
The tail of the 2nd Division was hurried through, and we
had to wait to let the infantry pass. Apparently the enemy
had drawn very near. At that moment everything presaged
imminent danger.

We had hardly entered the forest when the outskirts
flared up with rifle- and gun-fire. The trees shook from
the reports. We galloped on, and although we felt anxious
none of us realised then the danger from which we had
successfully drawn away in the night.

Out of the forest we dropped into country bearing a
new character—up-and-down hilly country having open
views on glades and valleys with winding streams banked
with tall poplars. Thick verdure fringed the distant hills,

where villages clung to their slopes showing the architec-
ture of each picturesque church catching the full sunlight;
every village in the valley with cultivated gardens aligned
in patterns of colour made a classic picture. We rode over
the Marne; in the water the gay reflections from the
summer-houses mingled with those of the trees. Along the
banks were lovely gardens frequented by Parisian families
on Sundays. One could imagine the scene as they lunched
out of doors while the brilliant mahogany canoes and boats
darted past in the water, coloured by white flannels, bare
limbs, bright frocks and sunshades. A restaurant advertis-
ing its "trout" perfected the air of suburban holiday happiness. All was desolate. A previous Sunday's bill of fare
still hung, half torn, at the entrance. The terraces running
down to the water's edge with tables and chairs upside
down presented the rakish apppearance of things that had
once been gay. Rows of fishing-boats painted a light green
were chained up on the bank. The fishers had all gone;
but the river was flowing gaily on, its weeds still hiding
the trout, writhing in the light or shade of the current. I
heard the plop of a rise, but already the shadow of the
impending invasion had paralysed the place.

We billeted that night near the Forest of Retz. The
atmosphere had grown tenser, for the enemy had brought
renewed pressure to bear everywhere, and although we
made a firm stand when the opportunity occurred, we had
only to look at the signposts indicating the nearness to
Paris to realise how grim things were.

CHAPTER IX

RETREAT

(VI)

SEPTEMBER 2ND.—Early that day the 5th Brigade were on the move, covering the retirement of the infantry over the Marne. The ammunition column followed the Brigade transport which had been sent on ahead. Throughout the day the sound of fusillade rose in the distance with the spasmodic loud reports of explosions as bridges were blown up behind us.

We reached the hilly ground above Meaux in the afternoon and descended towards a large valley, where the town lay trapped in a white heat, from which rose the faint lines of its majestic cathedral. J Battery joined us shortly after we had unharnessed.

We were surrounded by small suburban gardens such as are to be seen from the train as one nears Paris. I wandered away from the battery, and on looking over the hedge of one of those gardens my eyes fell on a young girl weeping. She was a charming-looking girl, dressed with the care and simplicity of young Parisiennes. She told me that she had come that morning to fetch away her grandmother, but she was unable to get the luggage away as no conveyance was now available. Having made sure that the battery would not move off—it often did so at short notice, and I dreaded being left—I secured a wheelbarrow and made two journeys to the station with her luggage. The last trams still running to Paris were packed with fleeing civilians—trains were being hurried away continuously. When I returned we sat on a large pumpkin chatting. I held her well-shaped hand, conscious of sensations that seemed to belong to another world. The English khaki and the red and blue of French troops were streaming down from the hills as water does after a storm. The volume of congestion on the roads in the valley was swelling like rivers in spate.

As we parted with tender embraces I saw the sun set like a red ball on the fringe of the hill skirting the town. The dust and mist oppressed the atmosphere. The Greys had dismounted alongside J Battery. I saw the Colonel. It was the first opportunity I had had of talking to him for three days. I told him that the idea of being a mere passenger with J Battery rather worried me. Although the officers and men had been very good to me, it was no use denying the fact that some were not altogether convinced that I was not a spy. I had sometimes noticed that whenever I approached a group of men talking they would at once stop their conversation; wherever I went I had the sensation of being watched. This may or may not have been fancy; nevertheless, I felt it. . . .

I suggested going to Paris and getting properly enlisted with the French Army, with a view to becoming an interpreter. The Colonel thought it a good idea, and wrote me a letter, in which he made the request that I should be attached to his regiment. Sad as I was to leave, it was the best alternative.

I jumped on to the last train that steamed out of Meaux. Flashes from firing guns were revealing the brow of the distant hills in the dark. A shell whizzed over our train—the whistle from our engine gave an alarming yell, terrifying the people in my compartment. It seemed then that only a miracle could save France. . . .

The journey to Paris lasted barely an hour, and emphasised the nearness of the enemy to the capital. We tumbled out of our carriage half dazed with sleep. A great many of the passengers had nowhere to go.

When I passed the Place de l'Opéra I rubbed my eyes, amazed at being in Paris. I went to a café, where my dishevelled appearance attracted attention. I had not shaved for a week. People asked questions about the battle—I answered in optimistic terms. An English officer in red tabs enquired what I was doing in Paris and to what unit I belonged. I thought I had aroused his suspicions. I realised that I was wearing an artillery officer's greatcoat, which had been lent to me for the cold nights. I went to the Ritz that night: I had a luxurious bedroom. They refused all payment. I shall never forget the sensation of my first bath and a good bed with clean sheets.

One can only enlist at the recruiting depot of one's native town. As no ordinary trains were running to Havre, I managed to wangle my way into a compartment of a boat-train taking the passengers to an Atlantic liner sailing from Havre. Once seated, I was not bothered about tickets, but I only felt completely reassured when the train moved off. I sat next to a pretty American girl. The train took ages to get to Havre, so we had time to make friends. We arrived in the town plunged in the silence of night, and I followed my friend on to the liner, having nowhere to go at that hour. We settled on the upper deck lying on deck-chairs covered with rugs. The sky was silvery; a breeze blowing in from the open sea caressed our faces as we chatted, watching the reflections of the port-hole lights zigzagging on the dark water below. Soon after dawn visitors were hurried ashore, and slowly the huge steamer moved away into the pearly atmosphere of the outer harbour. I waved to my charming companion until her features were lost amidst the pink faces leaning over the deck railings. I got some breakfast and made for the barracks.

I had made up my mind that on no account would I remain stuck at the depot. I was shown into a room reeking of tobacco and old files. Obscured by a screen of cigarette smoke, an officer in white with gold stripes on his sleeves sat at a table. Without raising his head he asked what I wanted. When he realised that I had come from the front, the expression on his face changed, and in an anxious way he asked me for news. They knew nothing, he said. I told him all I knew. War had evidently disturbed a peaceful existence and the routine of bureaucracy. As he tried to read the letter I had handed to him it was obvious that he could not understand English. I watched his collar pressing into a roll of fat at the back of his neck as it turned from red to purple; I feared a stroke. I then explained that I merely wanted to be incorporated in the French Army and sent back to the Colonel of the British regiment, whose request was in this letter. He didn't know what to do; never before had he been faced with such a situation—"But I will do what you want, since you wish to get back to the front." He wrote and puffed and filled sheets of paper. At last I was handed my military papers and given an order to go to a depot in Paris, the headquarters for troops attached to the British Army. He gave me a pass to leave Havre, but no trains were running. I was so anxious to get away that I walked straight into a motor shop and bought a motor-bike. I had never ridden one before. It took me no time to feel confidence in my Triumph engine—I flew through the country.

I had a lovely ride as far as the barricades of Paris. There my troubles started. The territorial guards would not let me through, in spite of my pass. They didn't seem to know whom they were to allow in, and stopped everybody indiscriminately. I took my chance when the excitement had reached its height with the arrival of some suspected persons—I slipped through and soon found myself rounding the Etoile and speeding down the empty Champs-Elysées. I rode into the barrack-square, my Triumph engine purring like a cat—the sentries at the gates wondering who the devil I was.

After seeing the head of the mission, I discarded my British uniform and was dressed from top to toe in new clothes. I emerged as a French cavalry soldier, covered with kit that included a cavalry carbine and enough ammunition to keep me going for a war on my own! As I was to rejoin the front the next day, I was given leave, and I spent the evening walking the boulevards, where special editions were being shouted out with news of our victory on the Marne. The Germans were in flight! It was difficult to believe.

The next morning I was *en route* making for General Sir John French's headquarters.

SEPTEMBER 13TH.—The quays of Paris were deserted. The zoo was crammed with cattle to feed Paris, which had prepared for a siege. Again at the outer gates, in spite of my pass showing clearly where I was bound for, excited territorials made difficulties about letting me through. I was glad to be free of them; they had an uncomfortable way of thrusting their bayonets too near one's face.

The road ran absolutely straight, the trees and milestones sliding easily by. I saw no movement on the road until a convoy of private cars passed carrying some wounded. I followed along a canal where a fleet of barges were held up with nobody on them except dogs jumping from barge to barge barking anxiously.

As I went through a village, a line of bayonets summarily stopped me. I was marched into a barn and held under arrest. Apparently I had not stopped immediately on being challenged, and they had orders to arrest a soldier on a motor-bicycle. . . . I waited until an officer came; he was a very nice fellow, who looked at my papers and then turned to his men, saying: "It's terrible to be in command of imbeciles." Their faces dropped with disappointment.

I arrived at the headquarters in the evening, finding an atmosphere of intense elation. The next morning I saw General Huguet, the chief of the French Mission. He congratulated me on my initiative in bringing a motor-bike. He said he would not send me back to the Scots Greys, as I would be more useful at the headquarters of a cavalry division. As all my particulars were being taken down in the office the clerks came across my brother's name, who was attached, as an interpreter, to a battalion of Cameronians; he was reported missing. I remember how it impressed me at the time that the fate of one individual could already be recorded in an organisation strained by a battle that meant nothing less than the salvation of the Allies.

My orders were to report to General Sir Hubert Gough's

headquarters, somewhere on the Aisne. He had just taken
over the command of the newly formed 2nd Cavalry Division. The atmosphere was fresh after heavy downpours of
rain as I gladly set out on my journey. Meaux, which I
went through again, was weighed down as though a hurricane had swept over it. The old bridge had been blown
up and the river was flowing fast past its crumpled remains.
I followed some French soldiers over a pontoon made by
our engineers; it was not easy to get over with my machine,
as the current strained the unsteady footbridge.

I climbed the height out of the town with the throttle
of my machine fully open, watching the cathedral grow
more and more conspicuous as I rose above the lovely
valley in which it stood.

The country-side soon revealed signs of the recent fighting. Telegraph-poles were down, riddled with bullet-holes,
the wires lying across the road in diabolical coils. A broken
rifle or a bayonet stuck in the earth marked a soldier's
grave—red képis were scattered about amidst spent and un-
spent ammunition; shells had made deep gashes everywhere. Dead horses were lying about with most of their
entrails protruding, infesting the air with a smell of putrefaction. Away in the fields solemn groups, identifying the
dead, were moving amongst inert red and blue uniforms
clinging to the ground.

The drone of my engine broke the silence of death.
The muzzles of shattered guns could be seen still looking
defiant and menacing. I got off my machine and walked
across fields to look at the wreckage left by the armies that
had battled and gone on. Limbers were twisted by shell-
fire into the weirdest shapes. Dead men appeared asleep
by their guns; some lay in strange contortions, their faces
calcinated by fire. Judging by the number of Frenchmen
prostrate on the ground still holding their rifles with fixed
bayonets, I could imagine the severity of the fighting as they
had swept forward. What struck me then was that death
seemed to have united enemies in a common peace, and the
sight of all those waxen faces did not horrify me at all.

I walked back to my bike, shining so brightly in the midst of this devastation. Crows, disturbed in their gruesome pursuit, looked very dark against the grey sky, hovering over me with outspread wings. I rode on, facing an endless stretch of lonely road. A plane swooped down from the sky, and seeing black marks on its wings, I got off my bike, to fire two clips from my carbine. Whether I hit it or not, I had the satisfaction of seeing it take to higher regions. I had also tried my rifle, which bruised my shoulder. I went on, depressed by the acute hopelessness of my surroundings.

Far away in front on the road, an indistinct group of people was moving along. I had to ride up close to them to make out what they were. Two French Cuirassiers, tucked under the same coat, were riding on one horse—I couldn't see their faces. Asleep on another horse rode a French Dragoon, his head bandaged with a dressing which the blood had stained until it looked like a red turban. His body jerked backwards and forwards with the movement of his emaciated horse stumbling along. A lance was hanging down from the saddle scraping the ground. A few steps behind followed a dejected German. He alone raised a tired arm as I spoke—they were beat to the world.

After riding up a long steep hill, I passed through the town of Château Thierry, shattered and silenced. A company of French sailors were going out of the town, pulling some tiny guns along with ropes. They looked out of place on land. Plaster and dust covered the street; every roof showed gashes. Window-shutters swung sadly on their broken hinges; every wall was riddled with bullet-holes. Bedding and furniture had been thrown out and many Germans lay about, shot apparently as they had come out of the houses.

The sun had broken through a small wood as I had entered, shining on some dead French soldiers stretched across the sodden path. I noticed one wearing patent-leather boots, the pathetic relics of happier occasions. A lonely horse with elaborate German saddlery was grazing

with its fore-leg caught in its reins. I freed it and went
on till I came to the bifurcation of many roads giving
observation along the rides that cut through the forest.
Against the dark green foliage two riders were revealed
moving in my direction. Rather startled I waited, my
carbine cocked, as I saw they were German soldiers
mounted on black horses. They raised their hands on
seeing me. They were lost and had been searching for
someone to whom to surrender. I took both their revolvers and a pair of field-glasses and made them march in
front of me until we came to the main road, where we
waited for someone to turn up. I eventually handed them
over to a French column of artillery, and they promptly
asked for food; they were so fat that a little fasting could
have done them no harm.

The noise of gun-firing could now be plainly heard,
particularly coming from the direction of Rheims on my
right. It was at least a sign of life. As I neared the Aisne
the roads became more animated with the traffic of French
ammunition columns going back to refilling points—the
horses were crawling along, very thin and some with
terrible sores on their backs. The men were worn out,
asleep inside their long caped blue coats. A few Paris
motor-buses went by, crammed with infantry. So far there
was no sign of British troops.

I stopped by a fine old château that had suffered much
from artillery-fire, flying a Red Cross flag on its roof. The
park was swarming with German prisoners in different uniforms—Guards, bearded Bavarians, Death's Head Hussars,
Dragoons, Uhlans. The latter were smoking long porcelain
pipes.

French surgeons, wearing blood-stained aprons, were
smoking cigarettes, contemplating with an air of satisfaction the catch of prisoners below them. German Red
Cross men were carrying to waiting carts the wounded
who lay on stretchers on every step of a broad marble
staircase. There were no ambulances—the medical
arrangements seemed very inadequate. A convoy of

private motor-cars with English wounded passed on the road, making for Rothschild's château at Chantilly that had been turned into a hospital.

At last I was to see the British Army again.

I fell into a turmoil of life and agitation when I entered the town of Braisne on the Aisne. The noise of marching troops and the incessant rattle of convoys of wounded mingled with the furious sound of guns. I was informed that the British 1st Corps had pushed the Germans beyond the Aisne and the 2nd British Cavalry Division was somewhere near Vailly, where a battle was going on. Cartloads of wounded lying on straw streamed past me on my way there. Immediately beyond the village of Chassemy the shattered remains of one of our batteries stood in front of a wood under full observation of the enemy, holding the heights of the north bank of the river. Every gun and limber had been pulverised by their fire, and judging by the number of men lying about, few of our gunners had escaped. German artillery were still spattering the road with shrapnel at the time.

I had to wait in a ditch for a lull. I could see the flash of every shot and the dust drift over the fortifications of Fort Condé, that very visibly fringed the heights rising sheer from the river. The holes, the dead horses and smashed-up carts lying on the road, testified to the accuracy of the German shelling. I had to dodge these obstacles as I quickly rode seeking the shelter of a wood within sight. There I saw a General's red pennant, and then I found the British Cavalry.

Standing talking amidst a group of officers was General Gough. I presented my orders; he at once broke into French, saying: "Splendid, I am going to make use of you right away." He knew of my adventure with the Greys. "Would you like to go and see them? They are holding the bridge-heads at Vailly; you will report to me how things are there." Smartly booted, the General struck me as a typical cavalry officer, gay, keen and alert. I liked him at once.

F

Vailly bridge was no health resort. The Greys held
the south bank of the river facing a bridge over which, on
retiring that night, they had suffered heavy casualties. I
sought my way about, the tac-tac of machine-guns echoing
along the river-bank. The heavy enemy shells were bursting, scattering a black smoke and showering chunks of
mud all over the place. The prospect of dislodging them
from their new position seemed remote, as they overlooked
us from everywhere.

Having worked my way along the outskirts of a small
wood, I found myself speeding up the drive of a lovely
estate with a Louis XIII château facing an immense lawn
encircled by the verdure of an extensive park. The bricks
of the building reflected their pink tones into the water
of a moat, where frightened swans, flapping their wings,
were aquaplaning in their attempt to rise from the water
at each sharp report of our field-guns hidden in the bank;
otherwise the place seemed empty.

Two German Red Cross men were stretched across the
white marble steps in a large pool of blood. The door of
the château was ajar, and my curiosity led me into a room
where everything had been turned upside down. Pictures
had been torn, frames smashed, every drawer burst open
and emptied. Everywhere were the remains of food and
empty bottles. A strong smell of sour wine came from
below the stairs, which presently I descended. A sense of
insecurity gripped me on reaching a dark passage at the
bottom as I began to splash about in cold fluid, stepping
over broken bottles, feeling with my hand the damp wall
leading to the cellar as though I were in a sewer. Two
diagonal rays of light filtering down from some ventilators
above met in a luminous circle on the dark pool of wine.
I flashed my torch across the cellar, where lying on
mattresses on dripping barrels were some inert human
beings—German wounded. The liquid lapped the walls
with a steely sound as I moved. I shook one man, but he
never stirred; another, who gave a moaning growl. I
couldn't tell which was asleep, drunk or dead. Tiptoeing

upstairs with relief I reached the hall facing the park glittering in the sunlight, and rushed out into the fresh air.

Among the German dead lying about the ground were some of our cavalry; an officer was lying crushed under his horse. I noticed that his saddle-bags had been opened and searched. I could not resist taking a tin of tobacco, although I felt something was watching me, and the roar of the guns sounded like a reproach.

I found the Cavalry Divisional staff where I had left them. I dozed for the remainder of the day with the rest of the officers, with the roar of battle tinging our sense of safety with uncertainty.

At dusk we rode on to Braisne, putting up for the night in a lovely château. Although both Germans and French had been in it in turn, it had retained its air of great comfort and the cultured atmosphere created by the owners still prevailed in the rooms. Autumn had turned the nights very cool. I made my home in a little hut, a part of the greenhouse, smelling of dry earth and plants, and I lit a fire. The gardener's blue apron hung on a nail in the wall just as he had left it. His gardening tools stood in a neat line with rows of flower-pots placed according to size. A quantity of fruit lay on planks for ripening. The place was a model of method and tidiness. Having acquired two rugs from a bedroom, I slept the night in the greatest comfort. In the morning the sun warmed the walls that were covered with wild pink roses. The noise of traffic rose from the town with the distant reports of cannon.

As the headquarters were moving off, I saw General Gough, who asked me how I was. He kept in close touch with everyone around him, and always looked very cheerful.

The Division was in reserve, and remained so during the next few days. There was no more question of pursuing the enemy who, in his turn, was attacking us. The infantry was having a very trying time—the weather had broken and the shallow trenches into which they had dug themselves gave little shelter either from rain or shell-fire. Casualties were increasing, arriving in the town in large numbers.

Days were growing shorter—autumn had set in. We rode back to Braisne every evening, surrounded by gun-flashes darting out of the darkness. The return of the inhabitants to the town had increased the bustle and movement—shops were reopening. One heard tales of the German occupation. Women came forward with all kinds of stories . . . how they or their daughters had been violated by German soldiers. One, whose looks and age might have sheltered her from such outrages, ended her statement by saying: "Mais, je dois le dire, pas brutalement."

The organisation of the evacuation of the wounded was gradually being taken in hand. Every available place in the town was receiving cartloads of what looked like khaki and mud. A new English Division was arriving—men fresh from England. Battalions were singing.

One evening I went into the old church, turned into a hospital. I slipped in with the draught as I opened the door, which banged after me with a muffled sound, immediately shutting me off from the outer world. The wounded covered the slabs of the transept and the nave, forming a cross of human suffering. Lit by the shimmering lights of a few tiny lamps, caps of French nuns, not unlike the wings of albatross, were moving silently about. The place was cold and damp, with a weird mixed smell of disinfectant and incense.

When I got outside again, the moon was shining brightly on every roof of the town. In the lit-up room of a house shadows were bending over some undefined shape forming a group, as in a picture of the "Adoration of the Magi." A strong smell of ether drifted in the air, blood-stained pads thrown out of the window were falling with a ticking sound into the shining eddies of a stream. Operations were being performed. I walked away following the bloody bandages, which were carried along on the current that sang its little tune. . . .

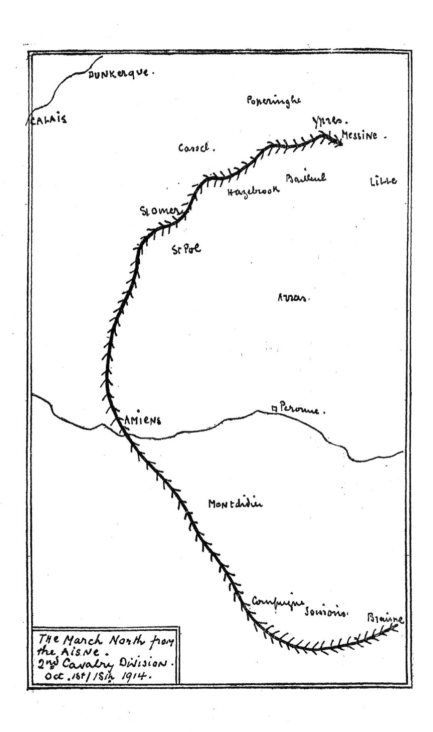

DUNKERQUE.

CALAIS

Poperinghe

Ypres.
Messine.

Cassel.

Lille

Hazebrook

Bailleul

St Omer

St Pol

Arras.

Peronne.

AMIENS

Montdidier

Compiegne
Soissons
Braisne

The March North from
the Aisne.
2nd Cavalry Division.
Oct. 1st/18th 1914.

CHAPTER X

A CHANGE was soon to come for the British Army. We were to be called upon to check the enemy's movement on the French left wing in his attempt to reach the coast, which developed into a race in which both sides were constantly extending their wing in order to overlap the other. General Joffre met Field-Marshal French in the town hall of Braisne. Both came with an elaborate staff, crowding the main square with staff cars flying all manner of pennants, the Commander-in-Chief's Union Jack striking its distinctive note with General Joffre's blue, white and red braided with gold. I saw Joffre, tall and stout with a white moustache, coming out of the town hall looking incredibly calm—unostentatious among a galaxy of brilliant uniforms. He walked towards his car, his eyes fixed on the distance, mysteriously pensive and distinguished, in spite of his heavy gait and badly fitting leggings. . . .

The whole of the British Army was to be relieved by the French. The infantry was to go by train, the cavalry by road. We all welcomed the change.

The cavalry started trekking north towards Belgium on October 1st, 1914. Horses were going begging, so I had acquired one. I put my motor-bike on a headquarters lorry and rode all the way.

In those early October days the cavalry looked picturesque moving like coloured ribbons in the hilly country and wooded land turned by early frost into a gamut of lovely browns. I often kept back to watch them at a distance and impress the picture it all made on my mind.

We were always within sound of guns, and kept in touch with the developments on our right. Sometimes I trotted alongside General Gough, who was keen to talk French, which he did extremely well. His conversation was always full of interest, he asked questions about everything he saw. He understood and loved the French. At night it was my business to find him his billet. I saw that he had the best that could be got, and then looked after myself. There was, of course, plenty of competition and success depended on one's wits.

Looking for a billet for myself one evening, I rode up the avenue of a small château which promised hospitality and comfort. The noise of my approach had brought out the gardener, who, hat in hand, held my horse as I dismounted. As I climbed the balcony steps a fat cook was grinning at me through the bars of the kitchen window, from which came a delicious smell of food. A very pretty maid had answered the bell—it promised well. The rotund lady of the house appeared, a picture of health; a big bunch of keys jingled at her waist. She asked me for news in a tone of authority. Like D'Artagnan, I put on a martial attitude, assuring her that she had nothing to fear, as I had arrived! It was obvious that she had already recovered from the fright of invasion and that her spirit of hospitality was limited to the minimum of her obligations. The head of a very skinny individual wearing a black silk smoking-cap emerged tentatively through a door and greeted me kindly. From the look his wife cast upon him I gathered who he was and who was boss. The maid was rung for; after being shown into a bedroom in the servants' quarters I was taken to the kitchen, where I was given the warmest welcome by the staff. A good soup was steaming in the plates as I sat down to dinner next to Lucie, the pretty maid, who, unfortunately, had constantly to leave me to attend to the dining-room. Later the mistress of the house reappeared, condescendingly suggesting that I should go up and have coffee in the "salon" with them— the last thing I wanted to do. I blushed with shyness, offered excuses and managed to look so uncomfortable that she did not insist.

British Cavalry trekking North from the Aisne. October, 1914

I helped to wash the dishes and clear the kitchen, and longing for rest went up to my bed. Through the skylight of my window stars appeared in a clear moonlight night—everything was still and perfect. Presently I detected the sound of furtive steps, and then somebody gently rattled on my door. It was Lucie enquiring if I had all I wished. . . .

I was off very early in the morning. The gardener brought round my horse and I mounted from the steps to the main entrance like a knight going off to the wars. The fog was very thick. I could only guess how the park lay, melted as it was into the grey vapours of the atmosphere. Garlands of cobwebs, woven during the night, sparkled like jewels on the hedges bordering the red paths that were dotted with fallen leaves. Huge trees might have been fountains in a world of fantasy, their dripping leaves perfecting the magical illusion.

The Division went on ahead early, leaving hardly any trace of its passage. I followed slowly in its wake, knowing that I would catch it up again somewhere during the day. Sometimes we moved only at night so as not to be seen by the enemy.

I loved being on solitary roads, left to my own reflections while the early morning mist gradually vanished and the first burst of sunshine flooded the country. A battle going on in the distance would strengthen my feeling of being in a pocket of peace outside the circle of the rising cyclone. Although I stopped where I liked for food, I could not linger too long, for the Division would be getting over the ground. We had passed Montdidier and Moreuil, reaching Amiens at night, all animated and lit up. The sight of crowded streets and bright shops was intoxicating. Amiens is celebrated for cakes and sweets, and we bought them and ate them greedily like children.

OCTOBER 11TH.—The roads were congested with Paris omnibuses rushing up French infantry to stem a violent German attack. The Division stood by to render assistance, but our services were not called upon, and we proceeded to Doullens, the country suddenly taking on a different aspect with its low red-roofed villages scattered about the flat land connected by roads lined with wind-tortured trees. The sky seemed larger and clearer as in Holland. One felt the proximity of the sea. Having received the news that the French had been pushed out of the Forêt des Nieppes, the Division was hurried on. The sun had slipped down below the horizon simultaneously with the rise of the moon, so that it hardly got dark. The air had become chilly, but trotting kept us warm. The fields exhaled a smell of peat and the mellow lights of isolated farms glowed while smoke from chimneys curled in a silvery atmosphere.

We halted late at night. Supplies were waiting for us, and the first mail arrived as a complete surprise.

OCTOBER 12TH.—The morning was very foggy, with the visibility restricted to a very few yards. I was sent forward to gather information, and passed through the village of Caestre. I was hardly able to define the other side of the road where the vague figure of one of our lancers stood immobile against a hedge braided with dew-drops. He informed me that Uhlans had been reported in the vicinity, and that some men of his regiment were ahead along the road. The visibility seemed to grow less as the fog rolled by like an endless cloud in the slight breeze.

I left my motor-bike and started carefully on foot. I had not gone many paces when a horse whinnied near-by. Thinking that it must be our cavalry, I strode towards it, when two German horsemen loomed before me and then turned and went off in a shower of sparks and clatter of hoof-beats. I leapt back into the fog as quickly as they had appeared—I was practically within touching distance, and they must have been as frightened as I was.

I retraced my steps, not knowing what I would bump against next, when the ominous silence was suddenly broken by a puffing engine pulling a squeaking train that

stopped somewhere below me, emitting hissing steam.
Carriages recoiled violently, doors were opened and
banged, shouts from Frenchmen rose above the infernal
din of tin-cans and banging of rifles. What could it all be?
I slipped down a deep bank and then down a railway cutting and landed on to a platform amidst a rabble of French
territorials detraining. The fog had now slightly lifted.
Pushing my way through I found their old colonel, who
could hardly be heard above the tumult, in spite of his
shouting. He looked as though he had been suddenly
landed from a balloon. When I informed him that an
English Division of Cavalry was in the vicinity he exclaimed: "Que bonheur! I haven't even got a bicycle to
scout for me. I have been sent into the blue—my orders
are to detrain here. Me voilà. I have no idea where anything is." I had to tell him that a patrol of Germans was
within a hundred yards of the station, and at once he
attempted to get a semblance of order among his men,
who, judging by their accent, came from the South of
France. They never ceased talking. "Des Uhlans!" they
exclaimed—nothing could have surprised them more.

I had to go at once and report to General Gough the
sudden apparition of this French infantry.

By then the sun, like a red ball, had appeared through
the dispersing mist. Very soon, as though a curtain had
lifted, rising out of flat green plains, a hill dotted with
windmills and neat red-roofed houses, sprang into view.
Our cavalry filtering through the German outposts were
at once fired at. The crack of rifle-shots came from every
hedge close at hand. Immediately our guns came into
action, smothering the whole hill, wreathing in smoke the
monastery of Monts des Cats perched on top, and obliterat-
ing the peace of that charming Dutch-looking landscape.

General Gough was quick in getting off his brigades to
the attack of the hill-side. He tried to get the support of
the French territorials, but it was time for "la soupe," and
besides, "we are only poor territorials, and not attacking
troops," said their colonel. They eventually made a show

and deployed behind the advance, gathering with glee all the prisoners on their way to the rear. Each company claimed their share and insisted on keeping them. Poor devils, they little knew how much their services would be needed later on, and how well they would all behave in far more trying circumstances.

Giving the enemy no respite, we cleared him out of the heights of Mont Rouge and Mont Noir, driving him into the plains beyond Bailleul, our brigades pursuing hard on his heels. Many houses were found gutted; a number of dead French Hussars were lying about the roads.

I followed the pursuit on my motor-bike and entered Bailleul by mistake before the Germans had completely left. I sailed into the Grande Place, the inhabitants rushing at me pointing in the direction the Uhlans had just gone. "They are not far," they said. "Look, here is the dung of their horses still smoking: you can get at them." I had no intention of catching them by the tail, and waited until some more of our people arrived.

The Divisional Headquarters rode back to Caestre for the night, where I was asked to see about a coffin for Prince Max of Hesse, who had died of wounds received that morning. I saw the Mayor and the undertaker of the town about it, who were both very much exercised as to who was going to pay for the coffin. The conversation was carried on before the body of this fine, fair-looking, dignified youth who lay in his Hussar uniform in a corner of the room.

Every morning a thick mist hugged the earth and delayed our pursuit. To our surprise one day we saw an English civilian wearing grey flannels drive up in a white racing car, on the bonnet of which he had fixed a repeating rifle. He drove his car backwards and explained that in an emergency he could get away without turning, as the Germans would immediately have shot him if they had got hold of him. Casually he said that he had been shooting at a German gentleman, "a walking one." He had come down on his own from Antwerp and had attached himself to General Rawlinson's 7th Division. Two Belgian civilians in armoured cars had done the same.

The enemy had now been driven beyond the towns of Wytschaete and Messines, withdrawing before us, offering very little opposition. It almost seemed as if we were being lured into a trap. The country we were now in was flat, covered mostly with turnip and sugar-beet fields stretching like the sea towards a streak of blue, suggesting a distant coast. A few roads with straggly trees wended their way towards the drab districts of Lille and Armentières hidden behind the rusty-coloured trees of Plogsteert Wood. Except for farm-houses scattered about, the country offered no natural cover whatsoever.

One morning after rain, the country looked all washed up and shone as though it had been polished. The air was fresh. I had joined a patrol—we stood behind a haystack watching the little village of Gapaard—the wind brushed the wet straw against my face as, leaning against the stack, I looked through field-glasses, while the men held their horses, tightly bunched, out of view. Suddenly I caught sight of a mounted man advancing across the fields who, coming from that direction, could only be a German, although at first his uniform was indistinct. Gradually he grew very visibly within the radius of my glasses in the clear way binoculars have of reducing distance and projecting objects forward in a vibrating light. I could see every movement he made as his beast strode slowly forward and he looked round with an unconcerned air, nearing his impending fate. The steely click of cartridges slipping into rifle-magazines checked the feeling of mercy which had been rising within me. As he came up we were wheeling slightly round the haystack out of his sight. A farm-house hid him from our view for a moment, and then he reappeared casually as though attracted by a magnet, making straight for us.

A silence followed the cracks from our shots as a flock of plovers swooped down from the sky. The man, doubling up like a knife, had rolled off his saddle. We had to look carefully round to see if we were being observed. Some of our own scouts were seen moving out of their hiding-places like animals often do after the sound of rifle-shots—then nothing stirred again.

While, with difficulty, I unbuttoned the dead man's tunic to get at some papers bulging inside his breast pocket, those with me were collecting souvenirs. A red stain had spread on his white shirt. Watched by his wounded horse we rushed back to our own horses. Later I read some of his mother's letters giving news of his father and several brothers all on different fronts—they were very pathetic. War seemed to me a very horrible thing that morning, and I remained pensive all that day. . . .

On our way back another patrol handed over to us a German in civilian clothes who had deserted in the night, having discarded his uniform for clothes he had found in a farm. We took him to headquarters in Messines, where he remained under arrest for examination. He didn't seem to realise the gravity of his case; as he had been caught in plain clothes, orders had come from Cavalry Corps that he was to be shot. It fell to my lot to tell him.

As I walked to where he was detained, I prepared in my mind what I would say. It seemed inconceivable. On my entrance he sprang to attention. I looked at him—his face betrayed so little anxiety or knowledge of what was in my mind that I hardly knew how to give him the news. I ordered the men who were guarding him to leave the room and, left alone, I uttered the words sealing his fate. Standing dazed before me, he said: "I am not a spy, I am a deserter." All I could answer was that I felt very sorry for him. Something was urging me to do everything I could to save the poor fellow—was it that he was unconsciously recalling the same position I had once been in myself? I asked him if he would care to write to his relations, promising him that I would see that the letters reached them. I left him then and rushed back to General Gough, imploring him to spare him; he said that he could not go against orders. I was on my way back to get this miserable fellow's letter when I met the firing-party coming up the road making for the spot chosen for the execution. Bravely he gave me a letter to his mother and one to his girl. He was quite collected. The escort was ready to take him when, with his two letters in my hand, I rushed back to General Gough in a final effort to save him. The General was already in his motor which was moving off. It was a question of seconds—"Look, sir," I said, putting my head through the window. "Let's not shoot this fellow. A German more or less is not going to affect the ultimate result of the war." "Well, do what you like with him," he retorted. I ran back as though I had wings—the gruesome party was on its way. Back again inside the house everybody seemed delighted. The military police, who were guarding him, looked at each other and said: "Well, we had better give him back the souvenirs he gave us," and they handed him his watch and chain and shook him by the hand.

CHAPTER XI

DURING the next few days, although little resistance was encountered on our front, our advance came to a standstill. The General made use of me by sending me out to gather all the information I could from patrols. My motor-bike enabled me to keep in touch with our squadrons, who were scattered in the country, taking cover behind farms or where they could.

Our attempt to get into Warneton one night broke the usual silence that had prevailed on previous nights, when hardly a rifle-shot had been fired. As we thought this little town was not strongly held, we tried to occupy it by creeping into it in the dark. But our patrols found barricades across the main streets, so the wheels of a gun were muffled with sacking, and men with their boots off pushed it into position so as to fire point-blank up the street at the barricades. The sullen boom of this gun, followed by the crash of glass and the sudden flood of light from enemy Verey lights, made a weird impression in the dead silence of the night. A heavy rifle retaliation obliged our gunners and men to decamp quickly, and the land once again relapsed into silence.

Thereafter the enemy's resistance stiffened whenever we attempted to advance. It was his turn to be bold, and in places he tried to dislodge us from our positions. Their guns had come up and were booming again, and the first shells crashed into Messines, where General Gough had his headquarters. It was a clean little town with a grey stone Mairie facing a wide pavé square with a few poplar trees. The charming old houses with polished brass handles on the doors were very Dutch in character. Towering behind stood a great old stone church. The children were again attending school. Our arrival had brought the villagers a false sense of security. My billet was in the Mayor's house, which had a charming garden with a small greenhouse, where heavy bunches of grapes hung in line. I looked at them the first day, helped myself freely on the second, and after that I took a regular cure of grapes. Only the Mayor knew—he didn't like it, but what did it matter? Within a week even the house was no longer standing. I nearly paid heavily for my fondness for grapes, for when Messines was being heavily shelled, I hurriedly gathered my kit to clear out of the place, and as I went for my last bunch a shell landed plumb in the garden.

The shelling on Messines had increased daily, and was very severe. The headquarters had retired back to Kemmel and all the inhabitants had left. Often as I was on the road I saw terrified peasants coming from distant farms wheeling their belongings away. They settled in the village of Wytschaete and in the neighbourhood which, already filled with our troops, became very much overcrowded.

As an Intelligence officer had come from G.H.Q. to re-connoitre our line, Colonel Greenly, the G.S.O.I to the Division, told me to accompany him and show him round. He rode a heavy motor-cycle, and at our first contact I took a very strong dislike to his ways; with several revolvers round his waist he had a cowboy air. We set off together, the roads very slippery after the rain, paved as they were with large cobblestones. I had the advantage of riding a very light machine, and dropping my feet on the ground I could brake, and even turn the machine by merely lifting it by its handle-bars without stopping the engine. Having lost touch after a few miles with the troops in the vicinity, we plunged into an atmosphere charged with the sudden silence of a danger zone. It invited prudence, but no—my leader had gone on ahead without even bothering to listen to the information I picked up from a passing peasant. German cavalry had been seen that morning quite near-by, and shots had been exchanged. I was catching up at a reduced speed, keeping my eyes fixed on the bend of the road ahead as my officer was then turning at right angles. Immediately two sharp shots rang out. I made a *volte-face* and rode for dear life. He was wounded and taken prisoner.

Immediately after, I was greatly relieved to find a party of 3rd Hussars, whose squadron was concealed behind the buildings of a big farm near-by. One of their interpreters was a great friend of mine. He carried with him a bottle of champagne, which he meant to uncork only on the occasion of the final victory—he was an optimist. We drank it on the spot. From them I gathered that French cavalry were on their left, so I pursued my round in their direction. The road ran between two high banks, and offered little sense of security, as I could not see the fields on either side. I proceeded carefully. Leaning against an estaminet front were some bicycles. I looked through the window inside where several French soldiers were drinking coffee. They were quite startled when I entered. One of them was going back to a post along the road, and I went with him. A little further on three men were hidden in the ditch by the road, and on the top of each bank a look-out man was posted behind a tree. While we chatted, a little fellow with a Parisian accent was sharpening a pen-knife with a stone on which he continually spat. Suddenly the sentry above us reported in a hushed voice that a peasant was coming across the field. I jumped on to the bank and saw an elderly man carrying a parcel wrapped up in a white napkin. He was trying to run, and anxiously kept turning his head back as though he were being followed. To re-assure him I went to meet him, keeping along the top of the bank. I hadn't gone more than thirty yards when two Uhlans suddenly appeared from a side lane. I ran back hearing a volley of shots from my French companions, and the clatter of the German's horses turned quickly about. By the time I reached my friends the Parisian had already resumed spitting on his stone. As for the poor peasant, he was petrified with terror—the Germans had hailed him from the distance, he said. . . .

Such incidents showed me how careful I had to be,
although there was a special fascination in going about as I
did. One day on my way back to headquarters on the main
road to Wytschaete, I saw the superb and unexpected sight
of a Bengal Lancer, sitting like a statue erect in his saddle.
Showing his brilliant teeth, he smiled, and I managed to
make out that he was enquiring in a suave way if I was a
German.

.   .   .   .   .   .

The Headquarters of the 2nd Cavalry Division were now
at Kemmel in a red-brick château adjoining a pond in
which ducks chased each other swimming through reflections of the park's autumn colouring. A continuous shower
of leaves fell spirally on to the water. A whole brigade of
cavalry, bivouacked in the park, made a lovely picture.
Already, from Kemmel, the increased enemy artillery
sounded very near.

The Headquarters moved forward to a report centre
early every morning. Night reports from the front tended
to indicate that the enemy was taking the initiative everywhere, particularly on the right in front of our infantry
corps by Armentières and on the left in front of Ypres,
which was now being very heavily shelled. We retaliated
with our field-guns as far as our ammunition allowed.
Those two towns did not then seem to us as important as
they were to become within a very short time.

J Battery was in the vicinity, in position just off a
sunken road in an open field. At that time no camouflage
was necessary, as few aeroplanes were about.

.The first contingent of the Lahore Division arrived—a
fine lot of men. General Gough, thinking of defence, had
ordered the digging of trenches in front of Wytschaete on
which his cavalry could eventually fall back. As all
squadrons were in outposts, there were not many extra
men available for the work with the Divisional sappers.
General Gough asked me to round up a number of the
Wytschaete able-bodied inhabitants and put them on to a

part of the work. They all tramped down the slope in front of the village carrying their picks and shovels and I settled them down to dig. We were making a trench running more or less parallel with the road to St. Eloi. It all went well until a few shells whizzed over their heads, when they immediately dispersed, leaving me with very few. Seeing a big ditch running parallel with the road and anxious to save time, I had the idea of running our trench towards it to link on. I had only to bank up the side facing the enemy, thus saving much digging. I regret to say that when the position was occupied, shells, ranged on the houses, exploded behind the men's backs, causing many casualties.

All this was the prelude to a fierce battle which was to become known as the "First Battle of Ypres," and which was to earn for the British Army everlasting glory.

CHAPTER XII

THE BATTLE OF YPRES

THE 2nd Cavalry Division had moved its report centre to the lodge of Hollebeke Château, which though on our left was at first the point most threatened by the enemy. A lovely drive led to this lodge with a double alley of silver-stemmed poplar trees. As I drove up and down, falling leaves were twisting and circling towards the ground like yellow butterflies. The sky was a very clear blue—the sun shone softly on all this lovely colour, impressing on my mind the last glory of summer.

The situation on our front had become threatening. The enemy's big guns, having newly arrived, were now in action, and the black smoke of their shell-bursts of "Jack Johnsons" was multiplying everywhere. Our few guns, rationed short of ammunition, were retaliating as best they could—many of them having broken their buffer springs were completely out of use.

I was inside the White Château, as it was always to be called, the day we were compelled to abandon it to the enemy. I was wondering at the time what could be done to save the ultimate destruction of the lovely things in it which included a collection of miniatures, that could with ease have been carried into safety—but war seemed to justify the callous attitude adopted towards such things. . . .

While I was looking around, the whining of shells passing over the house had become continuous, and the reports of loud explosions were coming from the park. I looked out of the window and through a screen of smoke and splashing shells, I saw an ominous animation about the ground. Indians who had wandered from the line were being rounded up, regimental horse transport was hurrying through, reserve squadrons of cavalry, ordered up in

support, were cantering across the wide lawn and a General
with his brigade staff was falling back to safer quarters.
The fire of musketry was coming alarmingly nearer,
together with sudden outbursts of machine-gun-fire. We
were being heavily attacked as were the divisions on our
right and left.

General Gough had already removed his report centre
to a small estaminet early that afternoon at the cross-roads
of St. Jean and Ypres. Things were not looking too good
when I got there. I was immediately sent with a message
to a division on our left north-east of Ypres, which, from
where we were, could be seen wreathed in the black and
yellow smoke of bursting shells. As I passed through the
town I realised that its destruction had started. Many
houses were already holed and the empty streets were
littered with debris. All the inhabitants had been sent
away. The absence of our troops struck me as I went along
—they must all have been up in the line, except for some
reinforcements I passed later walking up the same road
that I was on.

The château where Headquarters were established
offered a lamentable appearance encircled already by
shell-holes, some of them large craters. The trees of the
park were shattered and across the paths dead men were
lying. In spite of the persistent shelling a few sappers were
repairing cut wires and motor-cyclists kept rushing in and
out, running the gauntlet. Inside the place vibrated from
unceasing explosions, spattering the walls outside. Staff
officers were engrossed in their work like men at an
examination. Eagerly I waited to receive the receipt for
my message as plaster fell from the ceiling and clerks typed
hard in the next room; the plaintive note of the Morse
kept calling in vain. . . .

Darkness fell on my way back and the rain set in. In
the suburbs of the town I bought two cold chickens from
a shop which was hurriedly packing up. The country had
immediately sunk into a set depression. Gun-flashes were
holing the darkness everywhere, and from the line rose an

alarming tumult of musketry and machine-guns. London
omnibuses were splashing their way through to St. Eloi
packed with the London Scottish—those sitting on top were
sheltering under shiny, dripping mackintosh sheets. The
roads had become very slippery. I was skidding all over
the place. Once I was laid out and saw my chickens
crushed under a bus wheel—the General's dinner had gone!

Again the Headquarters had moved off, leaving no one
behind to say where they were. I looked about, but saw nobody. A sudden lull in the firing at the time was producing
an eerie effect. I took the road to Oostavene, where I fell
on a dismounted troop sullenly waiting in the dismal dark.
I heard that the line had fallen back considerably in my
absence, especially on the right. Going along the
Wytschaete road, I reached the part below the town and
realised that the line of trenches I had dug was just off
on my left. A fluttering sound whizzed past me which at
first I took to be rain falling on my hot engine. I became
very agitated, barging into obstructions lying across the
road. Bullets were thumping into the fronts of a row of
houses. Suddenly a voice shouted: "What the hell do you
think you're doing, riding here with a motor-bike?" It
was an officer of the Household Brigade, who informed me
where my headquarters were.

The line had now fallen back on the Messines—
Wytschaete trenches. Having turned on to the Kemmel
road immediately beyond the high ground, I saw a mass of
men sitting on their horses immobile in their long blue
coats. They were French Cuirassiers, dripping wet.

The prospects for the night were not reassuring when
later on, without undressing, I lay down on a good bed. I
had not been asleep long when I was roused by a roar of
musketry, the intensity of which I had never heard before.
I thought the enemy had got into the village. After
fumbling for my boots, I slipped my tired feet into them,
having the presentiment that something very serious was
happening. I walked over to the office and waited—
General Gough had ridden off somewhere; Colonel

Greenly, his Chief-of-Staff, calm as usual, said to me: "Go
to Wytschaete and find out all you can—we are being
heavily attacked."

_I set off into an atmosphere of electrifying anxiety. I
followed the line of a light railway parallel with the road
from Kemmel to Wytschaete, making straight for the infernal din. A motor-cyclist passed me, skidding on the
greasy paving like myself. At a small hut, a tram halt, an
officer was forming up a group of men, gathered from the
officers' mess servants. Every spare man that could be
found was being sent up in reserve.

Meaning to walk the rest of the way, I lifted my bike
over the ditch on to a sugar-beet field just off the road.
As I pushed it through the wet leaves, my body crouched
over the saddle, my chin pressed against the handle-bars, I
faced the flashes of some guns firing near-by, and heard
myself remarking: "J Battery!" And so it was. In my excitement something within me was calmly registering. The
rattle of musketry had spread over Wytschaete, and
sounded like a wood on fire. The glare from the burning
farm was rising and falling. A few peasants on the road
were shouting in the Walloon dialect as they ran for dear
life. Shells were bursting about the road. At the bottom
of Wytschaete village, where units were being gathered
together, I fell into the centre of confusion. I ran up the
main street to the church behind a vague group of men
and jumped on to the low wall of the cemetery in the
Square out of the way of glinting bayonets that were rushing towards an uproar coming from the lower end of the
village, where the enemy had got into our trenches. It
seemed at times as though a distant band was playing. I
thought I was imagining things, but, no—a German band
was playing their men into the battle with the "Wacht am
Rhein." In the midst of this turmoil German prisoners
were shuffling their way through to safety following their
escort. Without quite knowing what I was doing, I succeeded in reaching the right of the town and descended on
to an embedded space near the Wytschaete–Messines road.

Inhabitants fleeing from the Germans. Belgium, October, 1914

The row was infernal. Flashes from unexpected places were the only indication of people's whereabouts. Forms were scrambling hastily backwards and forward. Then, suddenly, a glare of light brought out lines of men advancing in formation through the confusion. It was a battalion of Lincolns! I talked to a man whose face I couldn't see. I made out he was a Colonel of cavalry who was looking for his regiment, I believe the Carabineers. He certainly knew less than I did about what was going on. After wandering about, gathering information here and there, listening intently to the firing, I was able to form the opinion that in spite of all this commotion, the enemy had not succeeded in breaking through to any depth, for we still held part of the high ground. He had also been cleared out of the trenches below the village. I got back to headquarters and told the Chief-of-Staff that I had seen the Lincolns move up to the battle. He said: "This is splendid—we have sent them up to counter-attack with the Northumberlands on the left. We are also expecting a French brigade to arrive, it will relieve the situation."

On a sack of saddlery I lay waiting in the hall watching drowsily the comings and goings of dispatch-riders. I fell asleep, but was awakened, as by a recurrent nightmare, by the sporadic report from a gun making the queerest sound, as though something were wrong with it.

General Gough presently came in, his face flushed with the fresh air. Not knowing that I had been up to the line, he said: "Well, Maze, go on to the road to Wytschaete and send forward every man you see." Once outside, the uproar from the battle fell and seemed more patchy. Dawn was breaking as I entered the outskirts of Wytschaete. Guns had eased off, firing more spasmodically as if exhausted—then, suddenly, the battle abated. In the growing light men were gathering together, shaking themselves. Wounded were dribbling down in ones and twos— ambulances were on the road as far up as they could go. His kilt in rags, looking utterly exhausted, a sergeant of the London Scottish was forming up his men who stood

like sailors being photographed on a shore within sight
of their wreck.

German prisoners, uncertain of their fate, were being
marched down under an Indian guard, tied together with
a rope round their necks. I helped to search them for
documents; one in his eagerness handed me his spectacles,
which I stupidly kept. Shortsighted as he was, I thought
he must suffer such inconvenience that later I traced him
down and returned him his glasses, for which he was very
grateful.

Preoccupied by the events on our immediate front, we
didn't realise the seriousness of the situation in front of
Ypres, where, behind the scenes, General French was at one
time contemplating retiring to the coast, and General Foch
was imploring him to stand for the reputation of the
British Army until French help arrived.

General Gough and his Chief-of-Staff were riding back
from the line when I entered the château gates on my return. Looking happy and bright, he said: "Go and have
some rest, I don't think the Germans will come on again
for a while."

French infantry were arriving all next day, and spread
themselves over the country, bringing a welcome relief to
the still dangerous situation. They invaded the country in
no time, followed by their transport, made up of a comical
variety of vehicles which came up at a slow pace behind
in their usual matter-of-fact way.

General Conneau's fine cavalry corps also came up, his
regiments trotting by for hours, tall fine fellows in their
long blue coats riding well in their saddles. The number
of French guns coming into action multiplied daily—we
became surrounded with batteries.

The best part of our division had been taken out of the
line and kept in reserve, but every morning the headquarters went up to a report centre, turning out well and
smart in spite of conditions and moving off not unlike a
hunting field does to the covert.

We spent one day waiting in a smith's shop. General

French Regiment of "Chasseurs" in Flanders. November, 1914

Gough had his office in a small house next door. Amongst irons, tools and anvils we made ourselves quite comfortable. With a pair of large bellows we blew up the fire and kept ourselves warm. Through the window one could see across the road. The rain was pelting outside—a little way in the fields beyond, screened by a belt of trees, French gunners were firing unceasingly their seventy-fives, which echoed through the country.

Sometimes a detachment of Spahis with their red burnous would ride past on white Arabs. . . .

Then one day the place began to be heavily shelled. The staff ran for their horses and galloped away. My motor-bike would not start. I had to wait for the storm to abate, lying in the ditch. In the middle of it I saw a French soldier walk down the road, taking no notice of the shells that were pitching on to it. He was covered with caking mud. As he was passing me without saying a word I hailed him. He wouldn't answer. "Look out," I called, "where are you going?" and in a southerner's accent, steeped in depression, he turned and said, "What's that got to do with you?" After the shelling had died down I brought him into the shattered smithy and asked him what was the matter—I felt something was wrong. Then in a resigned pathetic way, he said, "It's not that I'm any more frightened than the others; the shelling I don't mind, the war I don't mind, but tell me, can the sun never shine in this God-forsaken country?". . .

We got talking—what a decent little fellow he was. He had unstrapped his haversack—but then he had given up the idea of running away. I gave him some of my spare under-clothing. As he carefully rolled it up and put it in his sack among the few things that comprised his intimate portable home, the photograph of a woman and two children slipped out of a note-book. Presently he cheered up and slowly began to re-harness himself—he picked up his rifle and started walking back towards the trenches he had left. I went with him as far as the first communication trench and we parted with a handshake. As I was watch-

ing the erratic movement of the muzzle of his rifle bobbing
out of sight, the body of a French officer on a litter made
of branches appeared over the parapet, carried shoulder-
high. Lying among the leaves he looked like a Roman
warrior with his waxen face spotted with blood. There
was something very stately and dramatic about this procession, which I followed as far as my motor-bike, which
was lying among the débris littering the road. By the
mercy of God the engine responded with a turn.

Our division was now clean out of the line, relieved by
the French, but we were kept in reserve near at hand, for
the situation was still precarious. In front of Ypres the
battle was going on as fiercely as ever—we still wondered
if the line would hold. By then the weather was absolutely
vile; the days had grown very short—every evening the regiments tracked back into their billets in the neighbourhood
of Bailleul. The roads were like sheep-tracks, nothing but
liquid mud that filtered through everything and clung to
the horses, who had now grown their long coats. It was
hard on the men who looked after them.

Bailleul was a fine town. The town hall was an old-
fashioned belfry, standing in a large pavé square, where
markets were still held. The shops were open, inns were
packed and hotels like the "Cheval Blanc" were serving
meals unceasingly. Officers and soldiers rode or drove into
the town from everywhere around to get a good meal. The
existence of town comforts, relatively near the line, where
conditions were appalling, gave one always a sense of surprise.

Reinforcements kept marching through the town. One
night the Liverpool Scottish arrived, being, with the
London Scottish, one of the first territorial battalions to
land in France. As they went by I had the surprise of
recognising amongst them many old friends who, years
before, had belonged to the Birkenhead Park Rugby
Football Club, of which I was a member. In those days
I used to hear them talk of their drill in connection with
the territorial regiment. I had also seen them parade on

a summer Sunday, marching afterwards to church in full-drill order, with bagpipes playing. Neither they nor I thought then that it was for serious business they were preparing, or that we should meet again in a French town on the way to the firing-line.

We foregathered that night at the "Cheval Blanc"—they were all eager to hear about the conditions. The night was wild, I remember, and above the rushing wind and the rain beating against the windows rose the loud rumble of cannonade. As we came out into the dark a Zeppelin, lit by the moon, quickly passed high up between two clouds, shining like a silver cigar.

Two days later I was looking for the graves of most of these friends in the little cemetery by Kemmel Church. They were caught in the thick of it the moment they went into the line, sharing the fate of all the badly-needed reinforcements that daily were being hurried into the battle. Like a crop, crosses were sprouting out of the ground.

The 2nd Cavalry Division went at last into billets for a rest, concentrating in the area round the village of Vieux Berquin. Like all the northern villages it was a dull place; a main street, the usual square and the inevitable ugly new church. Immediately from the main road you stepped into beet-fields or into a forest of hop poles. Every farm stank from the manure heap placed right in the middle of its yard, a few steps from either your mess or bedroom window —the smell could not be overcome.

I had found for myself a very comfortable billet in a curé's house. At first he wouldn't take me, but on enquiring whether I was a good Catholic and I having replied that I was a bad Protestant, perhaps he had seen the chance of making a convert. I stayed three months in his house. He had a darling old servant called Louise, who was a great character. She was about seventy years of age, tall and, like her house, spotlessly clean. Her frail, lined face was framed in a huge white bonnet that fell into a white collar, spread over her broad shoulders. A blue apron covered her large front, tidily buttoned into a bodice.

Over her stockings she wore knitted jersey spats and walked on dainty clogs. She and the cat breathed the happy atmosphere of a bright tiled little kitchen, sprinkled with sawdust. Monsieur le Curé was inclined to boss her, but she held her own. Yet she looked upon him with profound respect and, being herself unable to read or write, thought him a most learned man. Posing as an intellectual, Monsieur le Curé, amidst his books and faked mediæval carvings, sat reading in his library, where the light, filtered through the saints and virgins of his horrible modern stained-glass windows, fell on his tonsure. Obsessed with the thought of enlarging his odious church, which he took for a work of art, he asked everyone he came across for money. Louise, followed by her cat, would come in and call him at dinner-time; she was not going to have her soup get cold—she stood there until he sat down.

I contributed towards the household food with my rations, which in those days were more than plentiful. Louise always made an excellent meal. His stomach resting comfortably on the table, the curé kept loosening the large knot of his napkin, too tightly tied round his neck by Louise. Having seen him start to eat, Louise was in a state of absolute beatitude watching all his movements, and the cat waited to lick the empty plate.

The room I loved most was the kitchen—the tall figure of Louise bending over her pans, the cat warming himself by the stove—the sawdust sprinkled on the floor. A native of a wind-swept harbour on the northern coast, she would talk of her youth in the sand-dune country. Her stories were always either tragic or romantic. She had days for everything; the great day was ironing day; how she worked in that atmosphere impregnated with the pungent smell of rapidly-drying linen! I would watch her, fascinated, as she ran her iron over the steaming frills of her bonnets, which, when finished, hung over the stove like bunting glorifying her day's work. I always told her that there was nothing to fear. She would say, "On ne sait jamais." Alas! In 1918, the village with that neat little home was completely destroyed. What became of her and her curé I shall never know.

.   .   .   .   .   .

Christmas came. To perfect the illusion, snow fell and a frost set in, covering the flooded fields with a thin film of ice. Every soldier in the line received a parcel from the Queen containing a variety of toilet requisites, ingeniously chosen. It was a charming thought, greatly appreciated; not a man was forgotten.

PART II

1915

*Neuve Chapelle to Loos—Battle of Neuve Chapelle—
7th Division—Aubers Ridge*

1916

The Somme—Pozières

H

CHAPTER XIII

JANUARY, 1915

THE winter was by then well upon us, with cold and rain. We had settled into a routine; reliefs of divisions brought a certain animation; long columns of lorries went through the village with the daily supplies of food and ammunition.

Horses were in good condition again and regiments were once more smartly turned out. To keep the men fit we played football; an officer brought out a few hounds from England. One day a whole pack was produced. Hounds ran through every open door. They were chased around counters, shops and everywhere; the population rose in a chorus of protestations—they couldn't understand why English soldiers wanted to amuse themselves with dogs at such times. We had a few runs with the hounds; Colonel Goodwin, our head doctor, afterwards Governor of Queensland, broke his collar-bone jumping a hedge. Of course it was a captured German horse that did it. The General said it served him right! Eventually hunting was stopped.

After their long rest the cavalry, leaving their horses behind, were sent up to hold a part of the line. I had then little to do at headquarters. I helped in the map department and occasionally visited the line with a staff officer. I had also to settle peasants' everlasting claims for damages done to their fields or barns, and although on many occasions they had my sympathy, I thought very often they were overdoing it and told them so. Some of them still lived in their farms comparatively very near the line. They went on busily working regardless of shells, which often crashed into their gardens. Was it bravery, interest, or love of the land that made them stay? However, one day one of these farmers bitterly complained that the soldiers who were billeted on him had done a great deal of damage. An

99

Intelligence officer was sent up with an interpreter to investigate the matter. During the progress of conversation a shell crashed into the yard frightening the chickens, who went off in a flutter. "There you are," cried the farmer, "how do you expect them to lay with all that noise going on?"

One day the enemy began to throw bombs. Having none to retaliate with we had quickly to make some. I was sent up with a sapper officer to discover the official "artificer" in the town of Estaires. (The municipality employs a man every year for their firework display on July 14th.) The man had gone to the war, but we found his workshop. Using the little material at our disposal, we made the first bombs with jam tins, nails and powder. I was happily unable to be present at the first experiment, in which General Capper, who commanded the 7th Infantry Division, was wounded.

About that time the 16th Lancers had their trenches blown up by a mine and lost many officers and men. Every day the enemy sprang surprises upon us. A new form of activity was steadily developing on the whole front.

One evening I saw General Gough looking pensive, alone in a tiny garden—his brother John had died of wounds. Linked as those two brothers were, it was a bitter blow to him. John was suitably buried in the cemetery off Estaires, within the everlasting sound of marching troops coming from or going to the line.

To my surprise, I was told one day to apply for leave. It came, and I got a lift on a staff car going to Boulogne. Driving on that straight wind-swept road, we passed villages full of Indian troops looking very miserable, sitting on the edge of the pavement, gazing at the rain dripping off their mackintosh sheets. . . .

JANUARY, 1915.—It was exhilarating to be once again on board the Channel boat; a keen wind swept the smoke from the funnels into a grey sky; the sea was choppy. The boat was packed with men going on leave. Two torpedo

destroyers escorted her across the Channel, their thin bows
boring into the rough seas, which at times hid them completely. Leaning heavily over from side to side, our ship
didn't ride the waves so well and many gay faces became
solemn. It was a relief to glide into the calm of Folkestone
Harbour, where we rushed the Pullman cars. The polished
mahogany walls of the compartments, the tables with tea
already set, the little pots of jam, recalled comforts we had
forgotten. An English town looks so tidy from a train,
with its orderly rows of roofs; immediately beyond were
fields and hedges, playing fields with goal-posts. And on
each side rose the downs. England again! . . . untouched
by the war.

A week's leave is short-lived. . . . Now we are back in
Victoria Station, full of troops hurrying along the platform
—the leave train seems already full to overflowing. A Scotsman, enveloped in kit, is embracing his wife and children,
who have travelled with him through the night, so that
they may be a little longer together. A sharp whistle and
the train is off. Every carriage window frames a crowd of
anxious faces, some of them certainly looking for the last
time at one or other of those lonely figures left on the platform, staring hungrily after the moving train, which leaves
the track empty like an open grave.

Folkestone! . . . everybody walks solemnly to the boat—
the passage is going to be a rough one. Darkness is falling
fast, the rain is pelting, the wind increasing. Even in
harbour the steamer rocks, straining its squeaking hawsers,
which suddenly flop into the water; the boat heads out to
sea. We turn to see the last of England as it is swallowed
up in the darkness and the cold breeze from outside chills
our faces.

Destroyers alongside are dipping heavily in the water;
we roll like hell. Lifebelts have been slipped on by everyone—some make their way downstairs unsteadily. We dis-
embark at last, feeling wretched, and solemnly make for
waiting buses and trains. It is no use trying to sleep in
Boulogne; the hotels are crowded and, besides, they are so

dirty! . . . Nothing could be colder than the filthy leave trains, with their smashed windows.

I travelled on the top of a bus. The night was pitch dark; the bus laboured over the hill out of Boulogne and reached the plateau, where on the dead-straight road to St. Omer it sped quickly along. We swayed from side to side; instead of London traffic, wind-swept trees passed us as in a cinematograph. The rain was lashing our faces, giving everybody a false complexion of health and happiness. We had spread over our knees the clammy cold mackintosh-covers tied to the seats. For sleep and shelter we took the weirdest positions. We drove into St. Omer and dropped a few dazed men who scattered away into the sleeping town. No one uttered a word—the weight of everybody's thoughts could be felt. The bus was going on as far as Hazebrouck, so out we pushed again through wind and rain. After another long chilly spell we rattled into a big square and stopped; the radiator was boiling. Everyone got out—it was difficult to find anywhere to go at that hour; the town was fast asleep. Canteens, I believe, were open. In a room on the ground floor of a house an oil lamp standing on a table was burning low. I looked through the window; it was empty. Pages of *The Times* were strewn over the floor. On the table empty glasses had been left—the officers had gone to bed. I went in. Notwithstanding the smoke and the appalling smell of stale tobacco and whisky, I drew an arm-chair to the mantelpiece and stretched myself out, staring at the embers of what had been a good fire, my mind full of a medley of thoughts. Leave was a cruel thing!

CHAPTER XIV

NEUVE CHAPELLE

FEBRUARY 2ND.—My mind still full of my week's leave, I got back to Divisional Headquarters to find everybody engrossed in the preparations for the offensive directed on Neuve Chapelle. The infantry was to attack, break through the enemy line and the cavalry was to go through the gap. It sounded all right; most people were optimistic.

On the evening of the attack the tramping of feet and the rattle of carts had gradually died down as all units had reached their positions. Only the firing of field-guns could then be heard. We waited for dawn. The usual barrage fell and most of us stood picturing in our minds what was happening in the line. From where we were we could not see anything or gather any information—we could only hear the drumming sound of guns—all cavalry regiments were waiting, ready. Soon, singly, ambulances appeared, rushing through with the first casualties and then they streamed in, followed after a while by the first walking casualties—looking dazed at the miracle of being alive. A giant of a Highlander with a shattered arm was stepping through the traffic smoking a cigarette.

Conflicting reports were now coming through. We had scored a success somewhere, but the left seemed definitely held up. The 5th Cavalry Brigade was ordered to move up; the atmosphere at once livened up as all the horses filed away towards the line. We prepared to follow, but no orders came and the rest of the day was spent waiting in suspense. As darkness fell we were ordered back. Above the clop-clop of our horses' hoofs on the cobble-stones the constant roar of the guns rose as we tracked to our billets through a confusion of traffic.

The next day, out of pure curiosity, I went to Neuve

Chapelle to see what things were like. Though the battle
had subsided, German shells were still pitching all over
the place, making the approach to the town decidedly unpleasant. In parts we had fallen back on our previous front
line, but the trenches had been so battered that they
offered little shelter from the persistent sniping. Although
it had stopped raining and the sky was clearing, the atmosphere was depressing. From a bit of trench I managed to
look over the top of a parapet for a few seconds, and saw
rows of dead Scotsmen facing the German barbed-wire,
lying in the young grass, their kilts fluttering now and
again in the keen wind. . . .

.   .   .   .   .   .

After Neuve Chapelle there followed for us another
period of inaction. The weather had then improved; crops
were coming through the pink earth looking fresh and
vigorous. A pale sun shone on the bare trees standing like
brushes against the sky; the light was lingering in the evening, giving a presage of spring, although a cold feeling persisted in the air and something in one's heart refused to
be cheered.

In April, General Gough was given the command
of the 7th Infantry Division, and to my joy he took
me with him. The division was out of the line resting,
when one morning a very unusual cannonade rolling from
the north set us thinking. At a moment's notice we were on
the road. I rode up with the led horses, falling in on the
way with the cavalry tracking north. The most extraordinary rumours were going about—the Canadians had
been attacked; there was a vague mention of "gas."

We hurried to Caestre that evening, where we went into
billets. A great many infantry had come up in buses.
Ambulances were passing ceaselessly under our windows.
The night was very dark, but in the distance the battle
line was visibly springing up with the flares into a continuous firework. Above the general row of the artillery
the loud detonation from some of our heavies shook the

country as though to assert their power. We could hardly
sleep—troops were walking through all night. At 4 a.m.
we were roused by the women of the house, who brought
us some coffee—they had packed up and were leaving. We
made off for Vlamertinghe.

The road to Poperinghe was crammed with traffic. With
the led horses we cut across country, through hop planta-
tions, seeing on the road lines of troops moving up. There
was an incessant traffic of ambulances through Vlamertinghe, backwards and forwards.

I was sent to Brielen, where in a château the headquarters of the Canadians were established. They had been
very heavily shelled—the trees of the park had collapsed
into the moat, in which the white bodies of dead pigeons
were sadly drifting about. The Canadians had had a
terrific ordeal the night before. The Germans, advancing
behind a gas screen, had broken through a division of
Algerian troops on their left. They had retired in panic,
exposing the flank of the Canadians, who at one time were
very nearly swamped. . . . Their timely and gallant
counter-attacks had momentarily restored the situation,
but at great cost. Relief was now arriving. The 7th Division was in reserve; only its artillery was in action.

Throughout the night the intensity of the shelling increased—the noise of marching troops and traffic never
ceased; some of the regiments marched through, singing.
At any moment we expected the town to be shelled. Every
reinforcement going to Ypres had to come through Vlamertinghe, the only main artery this side of the town. The
wounded were dribbling in all the time, making for the
church, now turned into a hospital.

The shops had been quickly emptied of their stores—
every shopkeeper was leaving, getting rid of his goods at
any price—we felt the bombardment of the town was imminent. After my visit to Brielen I had come in late to
find a billet; in answer to my knock at the door of a respect-
able-looking house, a young and pretty nun, with bare feet,
had let me in. She belonged to a convent in Ypres, from

which all the sisters had fled, taking refuge for the night
in that house. She seemed very eager to talk as she led me
into a bedroom where, leaning against the door holding
a candle that lit her lovely face, she remained chatting with
me for a long time. After being cloistered in her convent,
she seemed thrilled with her renewed contact with the
outer world. Did the war not bring to all something unexpected? When bidding me good night, she turned in a
sweet way and said: "Please don't tell Mother Superior
when you see her that we have been talking together," and
she vanished along the corridor on her bare toes, her graceful shadow following her along the wall. . . .

At 4 o'clock in the morning she came to call me as she
had promised to do. Outside nothing was changed. The
stream of lorries and ambulances was still running on. I
went to the church, which by then was packed with
wounded; many were lying on the bare stone floor, as there
were not enough stretchers for all. Orderlies were giving
the wounded tea, but many of them were hardly able to
lift their pale lips to the mug—the spectre of death was
already waxing many faces. Grey German uniforms were
mixed up among the khaki, receiving the same attention;
our men were giving them cigarettes; it was difficult to
realise that a few hours before they would have been at
each other's throats. The dull light of a wet morning was
filtering through the stained-glass window. . . .

Now that the reinforcements had all gone up, the muddy
road marked by thousands of wheel tracks looked suddenly
empty—animation had ceased, but only for a time. The
rows of casualties waiting outside the church were depressing. When a casualty came in, the rug which covered him
was lifted; sometimes the mud and the pallor on his face
made it difficult to know whether he was alive or dead—he
seemed already to belong to the earth. Those who had
died on the way were immediately taken to the churchyard,
where a large common grave awaited them. A priest stood
on a heap of earth above the graves, in which rows of
corpses, sewn up in blankets, were lying like mummies at

the bottom. His white surplice flapped in the rain and the words of his prayers were swept away on the wind. Indians covered up the corpses with earth and a few privates, caps in hand, stood watching the scene. An old Belgian peasant watched too, till the noise of the guns became louder and more alarming, when his head sank into a red handkerchief and he walked away sobbing, exclaiming, "Ah, Monsieur! c'est trop triste."

. . . . . .

I went up the Yser Canal, where the Algerian troops had fallen back. They were a pathetic sight, lying in the ditch suffering from the effects of gas. It was impossible to get anything out of them. Their heads were crumpled between their legs, they looked vague, as though in a dream. Still the enemy pressure was not abating.

When I got back to Vlamertinghe a French corps had at last arrived, brought up in motor buses from the region of Arras. Fresh and well equipped, with their little bluish guns trailing behind, they were comforting to see. Sitting on the limbers with carbines across their backs, gunners gazed with curiosity at Gurkhas as they progressed alongside them through the town. I saw a rather fussed French officer in the crowd, who had just detrained with his company, which was coming to reinforce the first regiment of Algerians. As he was in a hurry to get off to Elverdinghe to get in touch with his brigade, I lent him my horse. He eventually sent the horse back by an orderly, who handed me the following note: "Thank you for your horse," it said, "I have traced my regiment. It is now 4 o'clock and we are attacking Lizernes at five. Au revoir et merci."

At five the French were attacking, after putting down a terrific barrage. I thought of that nice fellow going over with his company. . . .

As expected, the first shells crashed into Vlamertinghe; arriving in ones and twos, whistling like rockets, with that sharp, piercing noise, then coming in coveys, bursting all over the place. Everybody ran out of the town; the Greys,

tethered outside in a field, had a good many casualties before they could get away. It was much safer to leave the
wounded where they were in the church.

Night fell suddenly. From the direction of the line a
red glow had risen and spread into a large circle across
the sky. From a motor-cyclist I heard that Ypres was in
flames. I couldn't resist going to see it. I set off, cutting
my way among transports and troops, all held up by a great
congestion at the outskirts of the town. They seemed
trapped in the lurid glare which revealed them in the darkness. Shells were sweeping the road and where they had
made gaps men were busy extricating casualties from
smashed-up carts. At the canal bridge the light was playing on the rigid figures of some of the Gurkhas, whom I
had seen walk up so briskly that afternoon.

As I saw the town, a print of Napoleon watching Moscow
in flames came to my mind. It was a general conflagration
—with the Cloth Hall alone in the large square standing
in an individual blaze—the flames were lapping the roof,
already collapsing in parts with a thundering crash. Large
volumes of smoke whirled into the sky, rising through a
constant shower of sparks, which fell in cascades, illuminating the inside of the hall, as on a banquet night. The report from shells pitching into the blaze was hardly audible
in the devouring crackling noise of the flames. Ypres was
writhing in a grandiose agony. The silhouettes of some
stretcher-bearers could be seen rushing across the square.
I heard some men laughing and shouting at an old woman
who was gesticulating incoherently—one said he thought
she might be a spy—poor woman, she had gone clean off
her head. The tyres of my machine were quite hot.

On my return I found Vlamertinghe under the reaction
that places have after the passing of a tornado. The main
street was covered with débris fallen from the shelled
houses; two shattered ambulances were lying on their sides;
the church was being hurriedly emptied of its wounded,
and lorries were coming up to clear off the rest.

My nuns had remained terrified in their billet. I found

some in prayer. I had forgotten all about them, though I had promised the Mother Superior that I would get them away in a lorry; they had been waiting for hours. With difficulty I managed to commandeer an empty ammunition lorry. They were packed in like a lot of chickens. The glare lit up their white caps as they came out one by one, casting horrified looks at the state of the street.

With our counter-attacks we won back some of the lost ground. For a few days more the battle went on, then gradually things quieted down; the 7th Division tramped back to billets in Béthune.

.   .   .   .   .   .

During that spell I contracted a sore throat and felt very sorry for myself. Seeing this, General Gough ordered one of his staff cars and packed me off for a holiday, merely telling me to come back when I was fit again. Sitting on the back seat of a very comfortable limousine, I set off for Normandy, my batman beaming with joy on the front seat at the prospects of an unexpected holiday. I was driving to St. Wandrille, where my sister lived in an old abbey belonging then to Maurice Maeterlinck, the Belgian writer.

The restfulness of the place, after the turmoil I had come from, was a contrast hardly possible to describe. The flapping of pigeons' wings or the chime of the chapel bell was the only sound to be heard. A stream ran through the estate where I sat watching trout swerve about under the weeds. The park had never been touched since the monks departed years ago. Weather-beaten slabs with the faint traces of skulls and crossbones, marked the spots where some of them were buried. The wood was a tangle of trees and evergreen, through which the branches, like large serpents, had worked their way, hanging over the path.

Yet the sound and sight of war could not be kept entirely away from that haven of peace. On certain days the wind would carry the rumble of cannonade. From a look out on top of a hill the valley of the Seine could be seen receding into outspread distant forests. The sudden whistle from a siren of a ship would come unexpectedly, and like a vision the tops of the masts and funnels of a transport on its way to Rouen would appear gliding slowly above the fields. Troops would sometimes cheer as their ship passed a village on the river; sometimes they were Scotch troops and a lament from their bagpipes would drift plaintively across the plains, as a salute from the Highlands to Normandy.

Inevitably, however, I got well, and the time came when we had to leave. My batman, who had spent his holiday in the village and had made a hit with the "mademoiselles," was as sad as I to take leave of this lovely spot.

We left on a lovely spring morning for the north, parting from country untouched by war, to fall gradually into the midst of convoys, the dust and noise of villages occupied by troops at rest, which gave us that sudden horrid feeling of return. . . .

CHAPTER XV

On May 9th, 1915, an Indian and British Division delivered an attack on the Aubers Ridge. The 7th Division was in reserve, ready to exploit the breach made in the enemy line. Waiting for news, we listened the whole day to the bombardment. In the evening we heard of the failure of the 8th Division and the order came for the 7th Division to take over its front and renew the attack in the early morning.

I went to the line, accompanying a staff officer who was in charge of the relief. All trenches were being heavily shelled. We fell on one of our leading battalions endeavouring to advance as it met the disorganisation of the division that had fought. What we saw then was not reassuring for the prospects of our attack. Already there were many casualties, and we wondered how the rest would get up to the front line, what state they would be in, and whether they would reach it in time to attack at dawn. These problems were on our minds when, on our return, we entered Divisional Headquarters. We were relieved to hear from General Gough that he was cancelling the movement of his troops, for he would not expose his division to what he considered sure failure.

The next day the division was on its way further south, bent on a new attempt that was to be made on the orchard by Festubert. I was told to make sketches of the divisions' objectives. I was happy to be given something definite to do and I was much interested in the work. My way every day was along the Béthune–Laventie road that cut through Richebourg L'Avoué, a village standing nearly in the front line. This main road went through flat country, under direct observation from a row of German balloons hanging

in the air like sausages. The first real spring days had
arrived, and buttercups and green grass were growing in
the space between each pavé stone, as no one used the road.
The surrounding land had fallen into waste, shelled by
German artillery in search of our guns, which were well
hidden under camouflage.

Sometimes as I walked up everything was quiet—no
movement could be seen anywhere. Those momentary
lulls impregnated the atmosphere with a haunting hush,
broken by a sudden outburst from our batteries which, in
order not to reveal their position, fired only very spasmodically. It was really very difficult to spot the exact position
of the guns when they were firing. One saw muzzles dart
out of the earth for a fraction of a second, the grass in front
flatten out with the displacement of air, and after the
whirling dust had drifted away, everything would relapse
into a weird stillness.

Only skeletons of farms were left, but as they were
marked on the map the enemy would still obstinately shell
them. The orchards were in blossom and a few birds were
still singing.

After our ordeal of shelling in the last attack on the
Aubers Ridge, the apparent security of our new sector
seemed strange. A heavy shell would whine its way to
Béthune, passing over my head. Its report could be heard
as the shell left the enemy side and followed throughout
its journey until it found its mark with a big crash. At
times it could actually be seen for a second as it sailed
through the air.

The front line where I was to work ran parallel with
the Rue du Bois in Richebourg L'Avoué. A screen had
been erected all along the street to prevent the Germans
from observing the traffic in the day-time. It bellied and
emptied with the wind like a sail and the holes in it showed
that its protection was only psychological. One didn't
linger anywhere about there, for bullets would whistle
past, hitting with a sharp tick the tiles of the roofs, which
fell on the white pavé and broke into red pieces. Every

sound echoed alarmingly on that road—the tac-tac of a machine-gun had a searching note, as if it were picking you out.

One of the battalions in the line had its headquarters in one of the dilapidated houses. I used to go there to pick up a guide, who accompanied me on my round. I also exchanged scraps of news with the officers. After pushing aside the army blanket which served as a door, I was inside their headquarters. On a table lay a variety of literature that always included the *Vie Parisienne*. This paper was popular in every mess and cuttings from it generally adorned the walls. The inside of a battalion headquarters in the war zone always suggested to me a stage scene—the people in it appeared to play a part just as the furniture that surrounded them. The Colonel and the Adjutant were always very typical, fulfilling with traditional attitudes and expressions their definite functions. Even the guns banging outside sounded as though they came from the wings of a theatre. The spectacular entry of a sergeant-major was always dramatic, even though he only placed on the table the usual routine paper, briskly saluted and went out. The teapot, the saucers, the inevitable tin of condensed milk on the table, the green canvas garden chairs and the valises tidily rolled up in a corner, all claimed their importance in the setting.

Through ruins of farms and orchards a communication trench wended its way to the front line. In spite of the dilapidation everywhere and the many wooden crosses that were peeping over the ground, the spirit of spring was there. Even flowers were growing where the earth had not been turned up by shells.

The immediate approach to the line always gave me a peculiar sensation. In a quiet part it felt like entering a sanctuary where one was inclined to walk about on tiptoe. It seemed like any other trench at first; but then you realised that the enemy was a few yards beyond, squatting in the same way between two narrow walls of sandbags; and you would see perhaps a dead man lying on the para-

pet awaiting the night for burial; or snipers spying from
a corner the chance of a target; and the strong smell of
mildew would creep into your nostrils.

I worked in the sector held by Guards. The men were
tall and strong and always looked well turned out, even
there. You could hear the clicking of heels as an officer
spoke.

To find places from which to make my drawings was at
times difficult. I had to use a periscope and crane my neck
over the sandbags quickly and peep, but the parapet was
very high and I kept slipping off. I had to avoid attracting
the enemy's attention, for they were always on the *qui-
vive*, ready to snipe, or to phone to their guns to fire a few
rounds. The dark space one could see in places between
sandbags on the opposite side were loopholes. ·

The thick belt of barbed wire in front of the trench
looked forbidding. So far our artillery had done little to
it in the way of destruction. Our objectives beyond were
very undefined. A thick belt of trees bearing fresh leaves
limited the view. Spattered here and there the red tiles
of wrecked buildings would mark an objective. The views
had the same uniformity all along. Bodies lying about No
Man's Land broke the appearance it had of being a track.

When I left a trench and said good-bye to the men who
were going to attack, and with whom I had been perhaps
only a few minutes, it always filled me with anxiety for
them and brought home the incongruities of it all. . . .

For the attack, an advance report centre had been
arranged for General Gough and part of his staff in an old
ruined farm that had been reinforced with concrete for
the purpose. Those who could not get accommodation
had dug a home in the ground with a mackintosh sheet
for head cover that gave little assurance when, as often happened, the enemy artillery would turn its attention on the
farm.

MAY 16TH.—On our way up on the evening of the attack,
we passed troops leaving their concentration places and

making for the line in the darkness. Day and night our artillery had been shelling the German positions. As usual the cavalry had come up, bringing to a head the excitement of our preparations. Telegraphists were testing their newly-buried cable lines.

Late at night troops were still filing past our headquarters. A whole brigade had halted near-by, where lorries had brought up supplies. Extra ammunition was being dealt out to the men—iron rations were being showered from a lorry, the battalion's mail shot out of a sugar bag. Anxious faces immediately bent over the envelopes, hoping to see their names or hear them called out. A young fellow with eager eyes caught a letter thrown at him and I saw his face brighten up as he slipped away from the crowd to read it by the light of a bicycle lamp. I was standing near him when he had finished; he looked at me in a nervous way and said, "I'm all right. I can go over now."

A battalion was lying fast asleep between rows of piled arms, detached for the time being from all that was going on around them.

A few hours before the attack an A.D.C. and I were groping our way to a haystack, where we had an observation station, from which we hoped to view the battle. In the dark we kept losing our way, though we tried to stick to a path with the help of a dim torch-light. At last, after scrambling into our haystack and tucking ourselves in, we waited, shivering, until dawn.

We kept our eyes open by watching the lights from the flares quivering over the front. The Meeruts and the 2nd Division on our left had already started their attack.

At 3 o'clock our division attacked. Although the night was clear, any view we had was blurred by smoke. The German artillery began to retaliate—they were pitching their shells everywhere, some getting nearer and nearer our haystack, until one fell plumb at the base and shook the whole thing as though it had been a bale. The pungent smell of the smoke at once made us decamp. With difficulty we extricated ourselves from the hay which had shifted, scrambling across fields without any pretence of stoicism, pursued by salvoes which made "woofs" over our heads.

The first report of the attack seemed good. The division had penetrated the enemy line on quite a wide front and in parts to a considerable depth. On the other hand the 2nd Division had not been so successful. It took the whole day to sift out all the reports that came through and to get a clear idea of the situation. It was obvious that our flank was exposed by our advance and the failure on our left. There was a lull and then the battle restarted, but, instead of going forward, we were now fighting hard to retain the ground won; in places we were falling back. A number of prisoners had come through, with the usual stream of casualties.

On the following day the attack was renewed, with a view of helping on the 2nd Division. It had started to rain. One attack after another failed, and so it went on until May 19th, when the 7th Division walked out of the line. By then the artillery had resumed its routine work and any idea of further attacks had been abandoned. Again the cavalry was trotting down the road towards back areas. The A.D.C. and I went back to search for our telescope left in the haystack in our hurried retreat, but amidst the burnt hay we could not trace a single bit of it.

We went for a rest to a little village on the canal near Béthune. The weather had become glorious and warm. The sky was blue and our anti-aircraft guns dotted it with little yellow puffs when German planes flew over the town. Gordon Highlanders were bathing in the canal, their pipers marching up and down fields crimson with poppies, blowing Highland tunes. Summer had come at last. According to a new regulation order which nobody enforced, troops were supposed to wear bathing costumes. However, one day a young officer, newly arrived from England, noticed his company bathing conspicuously with nothing on. On seeing a French woman sitting on a near-by barge, he hastened up to her to apologise but, hardly raising her eyes, she said: "It's all the same to me; I'm married."

On May 26th General Joffre came and inspected the division, to compliment it on its success and to see a picked division. There was a fine march past; when he saw the Highland regiment he smiled and made an amusing remark about the convenience of kilts, which soon travelled throughout the army.

We also had a visit from Mr. Asquith. He wore black clothes and a soft hat; and watched with a look of pensive intelligence some tired soldiers passing down the road.

Lord Haldane, too, came to see us. Some of the officers objected to his visit; they couldn't understand that a man who had befriended the Germans should be allowed to come to France! Few people realised even then that we had to thank *him* for the efficiency of the Expeditionary Force in 1914.

.   .   .   .   .   .

In July, 1915, General Gough left the 7th Division to command the 1st Corps. As I followed him I began to feel that I was an integral part of his institution. General Monro, who was leaving the corps to command the 3rd Army, bade us good-bye. Passing through the ranks of the parade he recognised me and in very kind words reminded me of my narrow escape with his 2nd Division during the retreat in 1914. "Isn't that the fellow I nearly shot?" he asked. I hadn't seen him since.

The 1st Corps Headquarters were at Choques, a dull village in the midst of a coal district. The Prince of Wales was then attached to the corps. He was most energetic, riding every morning, often without stirrups, and going for long rides on a bicycle to visit the front or the various subordinate staffs of the 1st Corps. His presence among the troops was very popular; he also charmed the French people who saw him.

Our routine was relieved at this time by a tragi-comic incident. A rich brewer travelling with his wife in a motor-car met with an accident. He was killed outright, but his wife survived him two days. As he was a prominent member of Choques and staff officers were billeted in his house, we attended the funeral. People had come for miles, forming a long procession. There was a great display of candles in the church, and the sermon lasted hours. It was difficult to keep one's face straight as a fat priest leaned heavily on the rim of a marble pulpit and, with many gesticulations, shouted the defunct's good deeds and qualities. We had to march a long way to the cemetery, where again we had to listen to speeches. We were very hungry when we returned to the dead man's house. We had been invited to a luncheon, at which we sat for three solid hours eating excellent food and drinking gallons of good wine that warmed up the conversation. We managed to leave before the end. By then the *déjeuner* had turned into a rowdy banquet. The guests little knew that madame, lying on the floor above, was busy dying and that three days later they were to go through exactly the same ordeal on her behalf.

CHAPTER XVI

BATTLE OF LOOS. SEPTEMBER, 1915

THROUGHOUT the summer the 1st Corps was engaged preparing for the attack on Loos.

Early in September new divisions came into our sector, which began to swarm with troops. By then the attack was no more a secret. For days convoys of lorries had been passing unceasingly day and night through all the villages leading up to the line. . . . Guns were booming. The cavalry had arrived in the neighbourhood, increasing the congestion with all its regiments. South of us the French had prepared for an attack on a big scale. For the first time we were going to use gas.

The headquarters were moved nearer the battle front, to a drab district of coal-mines, where even summer could bring no joy, for nature had little to give to its inhabitants. We settled in a draughty château that had housed troops since the early days of the war and had suffered in consequence.

We had a Flying Corps wing near-by, where I had friends. I dined with them the night before the attack. The prospects of the morrow had filled them with an artificial exuberance. After dinner we went gaily to the hangars to see their machines standing all ready.

On the evening of September 23rd, I walked up to a slag heap in front of Vermelles village, organised to accommodate signallers during the battle. My duties were to help and gather any information I could for Corps Headquarters. Unfortunately, I did not receive my orders personally from General Gough and I remained vague as to what I was really to do. The staff had been very secretive in giving the necessary information, although I had been up to the line every day to see the preparations and knew the sector well. Being new to the corps I dared not insist.

The flashes from firing guns were lighting the pitch-dark night as I lay down on some kit to snatch some sleep in our overcrowded dug-out. Before dawn the fury of our barrage awoke me, dazed from the atmosphere in our hole. I immediately looked outside—the curtain hiding the future battlefield was slowly lifting. The slag heaps that surrounded us were beginning to show their queer shapes, as though they had been rising out of the earth. In that opaque atmosphere the coal trolleys, suspended on the overhead wires linking every pit, were silhouetted like spiders entangled in their webs.

To the second at zero hour the whole line vibrated violently with the rattle of machine-gun fire as the divisions went over. We waited, our throats constricted with excitement and anxiety. Out of the mist the towns of Auchy, Citée St. Elie and Hulloch had risen, the skeletons of scaffolding and machinery showing through the smoke. The actual front line was completely blurred. The middle distance between the front line and our slag heap was now in constant convulsion, rising in graceful columns of black earth and smoke. The gas which we had released was drifting heavily down across the left of our front, obviously in the wrong direction. We peered and peered through our glasses, trying to catch sight of anything where the smoke had drifted away. Through a gap the horizon showed up like a sinister purple streak. Suddenly someone shouted, "What's that near Fosse 8?" We all focused our glasses on to the slag heap and for a second figures appeared, as one might see bathers surge up in the troughs of rough seas.

Our telephones buzzed feverishly; messages were coming in on the wires, all more or less confused. Someone caught a visual message and spelt the words out to another, who took it down, repeating every syllable with that slow cadence that gives special significance to tidings, and leaves an indelible impression on the mind—"WE—HAVE—NO —OFFICERS—LEFT——" Then something happened—the shutter flashing the message had closed—contact was lost.

By noon the atmosphere in our shelter was more than I could bear. I rushed to Corps Headquarters, where the failure of the 2nd Division on the left had cast a gloom over the good news received from other divisions. I asked a staff officer if I might go up to the line to get more information, and he begged me to wait until further news had come through. Excited by the constant movement of dispatch riders going in and out and staff cars hurrying off, I set off aimlessly on my own towards the turmoil of movement and noise, urged by an impulse to do something, anything, rather than remain inactive. Everywhere the roads were congested with troops and traffic—ambulances with five pairs of still feet protruding from the stretchers had started streaming past with the regularity of perfect organisation.

At Vermelles congestion was holding up a brigade on its way to the line. They belonged to the 24th Division, and were sent up to strengthen the position at Fosse 8. The men looked small; they had come straight from England, wearing obviously new kit; having marched all day they were exhausted before entering the fight. One of their Colonels, an old-fashioned type of territorial, was very fussed. As they started on their way again I strode along with them.

The ground being flat they all had a clear view of the line rocking with explosions. Dead men and horses were lying on the road—green-looking casualties, mostly Scotsmen, were dribbling past their ranks—Red Cross men, shouldering their burdens, were advancing across the broken ground, moving like dinghies in a choppy sea. In contrast to the dejected mien of our men slouching up to the attack, a bunch of German prisoners were marching smartly along with their escort.

The German artillery having lengthened its fire, shells were beginning to pitch all round us. For troops just landed, their contact with war was sudden and severe. At length the old communication trenches were reached. The men, waiting their turn to wend their way up, looked around them as cattle do on entering a slaughter-house. Guides, not knowing the way, were leading columns astray —men kept telescoping on each other at every halt. Fosse 8 at that time was like a bursting volcano.

Staff officers had arrived on the scene and were endeavouring to straighten out the chaos amongst the formations. The whole front by then was resisting German counter-attacks. What would happen to that poor brigade I dared not think.

At Corps Headquarters I found General Gough's batman wandering in the château grounds trying to gather, as was his wont, any scrap of news from anyone who came in from the battle. He was a platelayer on the railway at the beginning of the war, and like the rest of his type was endowed with a great deal of common sense. He had been batman to General Gough's brother up to his death and now looked after what he referred to sometimes as "the old man," who happened to be years younger than himself. I gathered from him that Sir Douglas Haig had visited the headquarters in the afternoon and I was also informed that the gas, to use his own words, "had worked lovely." I dared not disillusion him.

In the office I looked at the map and realised how many objectives we had failed to get, but Loos was in our hands. Orders for the renewal of the attack were being issued— fresh divisions, including the Guards, were coming up . . .

General Gough looked so intensely preoccupied in the morning that I dared not approach him. I placed myself in a suitable corner in the hope that he might see me and give me something to do. After waiting for some time I went off on my own towards Loos, where the Guards were to attack Hill 70. On the road to Loos an agglomeration of troops could be seen in the distance. As shells had begun to scream over this road I kept in the open until I got over our old front line and reached an old German trench skirting a ridge, from which the view on to Loos and a wide part of the front on the left was excellent. With the

aid of my map I could make out the approximate position
of our troops, particularly where constant shell-bursts were
making a black screen of smoke and from where came the
monotonous sound of musketry. The town of Loos looked
gruesome with the spire of its church every now and then
emerging through smoke.

A line of men were walking up carrying rolled-up signal-
flags; they stopped not far from where I was, and I noticed
that the sergeant was referring to me as he said something
through his shaggy moustache. I at once showed the officer
the pass issued me by the corps. He told me that he was
from the Guards Division that were on their way to attack
Hill 70 in the IV Corps front, and showed me on the map
the way they were going. Shells exploding uncomfortably
near us cut short further conversation, and we dispersed.

Coming over the open ground back on my left were
columns of infantry moving up in perfect alignment
making towards Loos—their deployment kept a perfection
which only the discipline of the Guards could have attained
in such circumstances. When they got to the crest and met
the barrage, line after line walked into it at the same steady
pace and vanished behind the smoke, followed by the rest
steadily coming up.

With an unnerving "swish" a piece of ragged shell
thumped into the earth about a yard from where I lay;
the unburied part of it was like the raw edge of a saw and
as hot as a red-hot poker. As the German artillery was
increasing its attention to their old trenches, I had to move
further down the slope. It gave me a still better view on
to Hill 70. I made a drawing of Loos and the ridge behind
showing the ground as it appeared, marking with little
dots formations of lines which must have been the Guards.
Very severe fighting was also going on all the time on my
left. I longed to be in touch with things; I didn't know
where Brigade Headquarters were. Some aeroplanes came
flying low—passing over me, the observers may have wondered what I was doing all by myself in the company of
corpses lying at the bottom of the trench.

At last I got news from wounded men who were trailing
back. The badly hit ones had little to say. Those with
"cushy" wounds were more loquacious. One couldn't
always rely on a Tommy's report, however, for he would
generally only refer to his own particular experience, which
did not precisely convey an accurate appreciation of the
situation as a whole, but Hill 70 then was assuredly no
health resort.

Towards the end of the afternoon the weather gave indications of breaking up. The sky had turned a steely
grey; soon rain fell, blanketing the battlefield, plunging
the coal-pit area into a deep depression. It was the hour
when, in peace-time, miners would have been flocking back
to their homes, instead of which processions of wounded
were straggling down towards casualty clearing-stations,
followed by groups of prisoners on their way to cages, meeting battalions of fresh divisions going up to reinforce the
line. Guns were still hammering hard—Hill 70 could not
be taken. We had even been driven out of Fosse 8, and
only part of Hohenzollern Redoubt remained ours. All
the reinforcements arriving on the scene were, alas, too
late. Once more G.H.Q. had kept them too far back; the
element of surprise, our only chance of success, had now
gone. The falling rain seemed to emphasise the depression
caused by our failure. The constant bark from the French
seventy-fives on our right, who had also failed, added a
hopeless note.

It took nearly a fortnight for the battle to die down.
One after another pathetic remnants of shattered divisions
were relieved and marched back through the same villages,
which a short time before had seen them go up in full
strength. Very depleted battalions of that fine 9th Division
were marching behind their bagpipes.

After the battle I went back to see my friends of the
Flying Corps, wondering on the way which of them had
survived the attack. A look across the mess-table and I
knew that I was in the presence of entirely new faces.
The pathos was deepened by the fact that those to whom

Troops marching back from the Battle of Loos

I spoke didn't know anything about those who had gone—even their names conveyed nothing to them. . . . One of them did mention that a German plane had dropped the clothes of a missing aviator, but this in a casual way, and I had to find out from the office to whom they belonged.

During the attack on Loos I slept on the floor of a room in a miner's house. Having come in one day earlier than usual, I saw the miner return home, exhausted after his work in the mine. Out of his black face two red-rimmed shining eyes stared at the light inside as he stood at the door. Without a word he walked towards a chair where a basin of hot water awaited him. His daughter, a smart young woman, who had been waiting for him, sewing in silence, undressed her father as one would a child and proceeded, without speaking a word, to wash him before me without the least sign of self-consciousness. The miner, as his flesh became white again, seemed to revive, and turning to me said: "You did make a hell above the earth to-day."

.   .   .   .

After all these activities life at headquarters reverted into a dull routine. The trees were denuded again, gusts of wind were whirling the leaves along the road, rain had set in, another winter was rolling on us. Without any particular work to do there I spent my time going to and from the trenches: I simply couldn't bear the idea of remaining at headquarters. Fortunately a Captain Brody, of the Highland Light Infantry, came as a learner on our staff. Office life being pure torture to him, he took every chance of going up to the line, and I always joined him. He was a V.C. and a very experienced soldier. From him I learned a great deal about warfare. Coming home one night he told me a good story. His battalion was holding the line in front of Ypres. They had repulsed several German attacks, and his men, exhausted, had given up trying to restore the trench which was being continually destroyed by heavy shelling. Their casualties were lying all over the place, and everyone expected to be blown up

at any moment. Amongst some Germans lying dead in
front in the open was a wounded German who, unceasingly, kept imploring the "good Englishman" to put him
in the "grave," as he called it—"grave" being the literal
translation for German "Graben" (trench). Everybody
was bored with this fellow, who kept repeating the same
phrase over and over again in the same melancholy tone.
At last the Colour-Sergeant became fed up; leaning over
the trench, in a soft voice and the broadest Scotch, he said
to him: "A'richt, ma wee won; dinna fash; in a wee whiley
we will a' be in the grave.". . .

On one occasion as we were walking along the front-
line trench we came on to a group of men bending over
an officer who lay dead, shot through the head. His servant
stood dejectedly by, holding the valise of his officer whom
he was accompanying on leave to England. As he came to
a sniper's post he thought he would just fire a shot, and a
German sniper got him. I always wanted to believe that
had the German known the circumstances, he would not
have pulled the trigger of his gun.

From Vermelles, where men were at rest in cellars under
ruins, it would take an hour and a half wading through
mud to get to the front line. The weather made it impossible for the men to spend more than two days in the
line at a time. Clad in leather coats with waders up to
their waists, they looked like sewer inspectors rather than
soldiers.

The areas round Hohenzollern Redoubt were indeed
depressing. Hardly a night passed without a mine being
blown up, or a bombing attack or raid taking place.
Cemeteries behind the front line were steadily growing in
size, extending their little patterns of pathetic crosses in
the chaotic ground.

At times, when frozen snow lay on the ground, the blackness and dreariness of all these pits became emphasised.

Very early in the afternoon the light would fade—the
sun, which we seldom saw during the day, would sometimes appear like a red ball as it sank in a leaden sky. Men

would avail themselves of any ruin to make a home. As one passed one had a glimpse of lit-up faces sitting round braziers toasting bread for tea. . . . As darkness fell long lines of men would start moving like grey shadows plodding their way up to the line. Every day it was the same. . . .

CHAPTER XVII

MARCH, 1916

A LONG and cruel winter had passed.

During March the battle of Verdun reached its height . . . we all followed with anxiety this gigantic fight.

Early in the spring General Gough sent for me and instructed me to proceed to the 2nd Army in the north to make a series of drawings, taking in the battle fronts of Messines and Wytschaete. I was to get all the information and facilities for my work from Corps Headquarters at Bailleul.

I drove north in a comfortable staff car, looking forward to renewing my acquaintance with a part of the front I knew intimately from the days of 1914.

From Corps Headquarters I was sent on to one of the divisions holding the line. There I was put in the care of a Captain Nelson, of the Lothian and Border Horse, who had the control of all the observation on the line. He had under him observers recruited from a very fine lot of men in the Border country. His curly red-haired batman, with a strong Edinburgh accent, had found me a billet in a dilapidated house. After a good night's rest Captain Nelson and I set off for the line.

I noticed at once that he was exceptionally gifted for his work. The night before, he had planned our day's activities with the keenness of a sportsman who carefully organises his shoot. Knowing his sector intimately, he had every inch of the enemy's country espied the whole day by his men, posted in numerous stations, from which they sent in their reports. All these men were frightfully keen— many were stalkers.

The ground we held gave a good field of view on the German positions. Their front line ran parallel with ours in a valley, the support line winding round a small range of woods. Of the country we had fought through in 1914 I could scarcely see a trace—hardly a house was still standing, the place having been constantly ploughed up by everlasting shelling. Kemmel Hill, its windmills still standing, was a familiar landmark. Mont Noir and Mont Rouge had remained prominent in the landscape suggesting the typical background of Dutch scenery. Of Ypres, seen in the distance, only the ragged shell remained—still the walls of the Cloth Hall shone undaunted, ringed in smoke.

The line in this region lay in comparative tranquillity. To get to our first observation posts we entered a communication trench starting on the outskirts of the old town of Kemmel. It was not until I saw a board with "Kemmel" written on it that I realised I was walking through the grounds of the red château which had been the 2nd Cavalry Division Headquarters in 1914, and of which only a few piles of red bricks remained. The church hardly stood higher than the weeds in the churchyard. Of the actual park only the pond had survived, in which a solitary fish was rising. The cemetery adjoining the church had not been spared. A few scattered pieces of wood were all that remained of the crosses which had marked the graves of our soldiers buried there. Knowing that some of my Liverpool friends had been laid to rest in this ground, I looked at the inscriptions on the bits of rotten wood lying about and found the identification plate of my friend, T. B. Kendell. As I showed it to Nelson, he remarked that he knew him well, having once played against him for Scotland in an International match. He had never seen him since. I couldn't find where he lay now in that disturbed cemetery, and placed the metal riband bearing his name in a corner, hoping that at least it might be spared further desecration.

Meanwhile shells were flying past, following each other with the rumbling of a train entering an underground station. Their terrific explosions in rapid succession were shattering still further the already ruined houses by the

K

cross-roads. We had just missed being caught by one of
them as we had walked up. We had stopped to ask a man
the way, and the few seconds' delay had kept us on the
right side of a wall. One often owed one's life to a most
trivial incident of that sort.

At length we got on to a trench running down from a
ridge towards our front line which bore the name of Poppy
Lane. It had been very carefully built, and from it one
had an excellent view. I immediately thought of starting
my drawings there, but on being told that a German sniper
had made a speciality of three senior staff officers within a
month, I promptly changed my mind.

We went to the line every day. My work was most
interesting, Bit by bit we dissected the ground with our
field-glasses, and I made drawings from every possible
angle, marking every obstacle which could hinder the
advance of our troops. In order to show these more effectively, I imagined myself looking on to our own lines from
the German side. It all took time, and aerial photographs
were a great help.

The days were lengthening, and we could work until
late in the evening. We used to wait until the German
observation balloons had been hauled down and then go
home. Nelson always took their bearings on the map just
about that time. One evening it happened that he was
noting the position of the first balloon in the line. When
he looked up towards the others they were in flames,
collapsing towards the ground. Our aviators had shot them
down. He merely smiled and said: "I have never been so
interfered with in my work before."

We would ride all the way back to our billets, chatting
on the way. Nelson's judgment was very sound. Even then
he was concerned with the economic conditions after peace.
He foresaw all that we would go through. As a member
of a large and celebrated publishing firm, he had a great
deal of experience. He took a broad view of things and
made his assertions in such a humble way that he was
always charmingly persuasive. The war brought one in

contact with exceptional characters. He was one of them. At his age, with a large family, he might have been any- where away from danger. He had everything to lose by serving, yet, like many others, he was ready to give all, be- cause, as he constantly said: "We *must* win this war." He was a keen sportsman, and I loved to hear him talk of Scotland and of his fishing on the River Awe. His descrip- tions of certain pools were as vivid to me then as they are now after fishing them. Like a true Scotsman, he loved his country and all the sports of his own land. Often he would look up towards a wood and say: "Look, that's a good place for high pheasants." One day in Poppy Lane we were talking of shooting, and I remembered an occasion during the battle of Messines in '14 when I had taken a shot-gun and brought down a few scared pheasants in the wood of Wytschaete. I was telling Captain Nelson of the incident when at that very moment we both heard very distinctly the crow of a cock pheasant. It must have been the only survivor left in those woods, or perhaps merely a ghost.

.   .   .   .   .   .

I stayed in the north until the beginning of June. Then my work was over. I was informed that General Gough was at Regnières Ecluse, a small village near the old battle- field of Crécy, and also that he had been given the com- mand of a new army in process of formation. Putting two and two together, I thought that his new army would be employed on a fresh offensive over the ground which I had been surveying. I found him with only a skeleton staff that included Colonel Howard-Vyse, a delightful person, in charge of the Intelligence Department. I helped him with maps which covered an area that had nothing to do with the country I had come from. We were very busy.

The cavalry signals for the new army were in charge of Colonel Sadleir-Jackson. His sections were running cables everywhere in record time with a flourish and style which were the wonder and envy of every other signal unit, especially the French.

General Sir Neill Malcolm arrived as General Gough's Chief-of-Staff, coming from Gallipoli. I remember seeing him limp out of his car and greet me with his warm smile and a kindly expression in his eyes.

The staff gradually increased. We moved to Crécy into the comfort of a lovely château on the outskirts of a deep forest. It was a glorious spot, and the weather was lovely. We had great field-days with the cavalry all around us, for General Gough had also been made responsible for cavalry training. "Goughy"—as everyone called him—was in his element when ordering his cavalry brigades about. Keen and quick he spotted anything that went wrong. Once he sent me galloping after a troop to say that, to his knowledge, they had been dead for a considerable time. I shall never forget the look of surprise the officer gave me when I told him that the message came from the General. I think he wished then that he was!

A most distinguished French division from Verdun—La Division de fer—had come to rest near us. General Gough inspected it. Drawn up in the middle of a huge plain the regiments marched past to the playing of their band. General Balfourier, with his white hair and martial white beard, took the salute as companies went smartly by, headed by their officers who were caracoling, neat and proud, on their horses. It was a very fine sight. They all wore the red fourragers given to French troops as a distinction for some great action. The division had been granted this honour for its heroic conduct in the defence of Verdun.

.   .   .   .   .   .

I was responsible for organising a boar-hunt. One evening the head huntsman announced that a very big boar had been located, and at an unearthly hour the next morning hounds were baying underneath our windows. General Malcolm got out of bed, only to see the start from his window. A regular arsenal came out of the château. General and Colonels, covered in red tabs, were posted in a line along the wood; their rifles cocked, they waited for hours, shivering in the early morning chill. The boar had slipped through. I was looking for it, galloping about on my horse, a large revolver in my hand, when from an adjacent bush came a noise which I took to be from a boar. I was on the point of firing at random into the bush when slowly the red nose of General Sargent, our A.Q.M.G., emerged over the top. A cold shiver ran down my spine. There and then I gave up the boar-hunt and galloped off to bed, hearing the hounds still in full cry in the distance.

CHAPTER XVIII

THE BATTLE OF THE SOMME

SINCE May, the 4th Army had been busy preparing a big offensive on the Somme front. As the Reserve Army was to participate in it, I was sent by General Gough to make panorama drawings. I rode my horse all the way south, which took me through the Forest of Crécy. Now, in June, the foliage was green and fresh—flowers covered the ground everywhere, birds were twittering and singing in every bush. After the glare of the chalky battle-grounds of the north it was delicious. My mare, reflecting my happiness, ambled along on the soft moss of the paths, swishing her tail, bobbing her head up and down, playing with her bit. Everything around me spoke of new life—yet in the distance the faint noise of big explosions succeeding each other with a dull thud could be heard—the noise of death! It was difficult to imagine that this verdant way was leading me straight into the hell of the Somme battle.

From Gibraltar trench on the crest of a ridge south of Albert I got a perfect view of the future battle-ground which our big guns were already steadily hammering down. Strong points like Maple Redoubt showing black masses of wire were going up sky-high all day long. Circling planes above us, droning incessantly, directed the fire of our guns. The village of Fricourt and all the rising ground beyond it were also being ploughed up by our high explosives. Every house was obliterated by clouds of dirty yellowish smoke and brick-dust. With my field-glasses I scanned the ground and made my drawings. Trônes Wood and Bernafay were barely discernible through the haze on the horizon-line. Bazentin, Contalmaison and Pozières, which were nearer objectives, stood out plainly, stern and forbidding.

Not a living soul could be seen on the whole of this

expanse of ground, either on the German side or on ours. Everybody lay hidden in trenches. The offensive was being conceived on a gigantic scale in comparison with any previous attack. Preparation had gone on for weeks—there had never been so much artillery and infantry gathered in one area before. Ammunition-dumps had risen everywhere, shaping in with the form of the country by clever camouflage.

I made my last drawing from Bonté Redoubt, lying hidden in a bush looking right into the remains of Carnois village beneath me. It was late in the evening; the sun had set, but the light still lingered on the baked battle-field. The guns had eased off their firing and a fictitious peace was creeping over that immense stretch of ground broken up by the maze of trenches that the Tommies were to storm at dawn. Nature at that moment was overpowering everything with its beauty, the only sound that now and again would disturb the serenity of the scene being an occasional ticking noise as a bullet struck a tile on a roof in Carnois. It would echo like the distant shooting of clay pipes from the booths of a village fair.

I waited until the darkness had fallen to go home . . . multi-coloured Verey lights were illuminating the line as on some gala night.

The last battalions were moving up to their final assembly positions; the metallic clatter, made by the cavalry massing near at hand unseen in the dark, mingled with the sound of feet.

JULY 1ST.—I was awakened by a hurricane bombardment, shaking everything; already the divisions had gone over; daylight was just entering my room. Sudden detonations in the sky diverted my attention from the uproar coming from the line. I looked out of the window and saw, high up above, a tiny speck racing and buzzing through the air evading our shrapnel bursts, which, after flashing, broke into yellowish balls of smoke. I went on with my dressing when the sudden quick rattle of machine-guns made me

look out again—there the space of limpid blue was divided
as by a plummet-line by a vertical spiral of black smoke
which the fall of a plane in flames had left in its wake. . . .
The anti-aircraft guns had ceased firing—up above all was
peaceful again—the smoke from the shrapnel was expand-
ing into long filaments which floated across the sky. . . .

The Reserve Army and three divisions were waiting to
exploit the breach which the 4th Army had to make. As
General Gough was going to the 4th Army Headquarters
in Querrieu to keep in close touch with operations, he told
me to follow on, as he might need me with my motor-bike.
Though still quite early, it was already very hot. Waiting
outside in the château grounds I could see into the signal
office, where hands were busy at switchboards. Staff motors,
flying every description of little flags, were constantly
arriving and departing, adding to the dust that rose into a
thick white veil on the main road.

Ambulances had already started rolling by with their
first loads of wounded. The noise of guns was alarming.
The windows of the headquarters rattled from some heavy
guns hidden in the park, firing off their big shells. The
French, attacking simultaneously with us on the right,
were contributing to the uproar.

The first news received from the line was marked with
success and filled us all with hopeful expectations; the
right divisions had passed their first objectives and were
going on. However, it was not so definite about the left;
conflicting reports were coming in; the situation there did
not seem so clear. . . .

Formations of aeroplanes, continuously passing overhead
to and from the line, were adding to the excitement by
exchanging signals with tracer bullets. At the same time
the yellow nose of an observation balloon was looming in
sight, tossing awkwardly over the tops of houses as it
gathered height pulling on its tight cable anchoring it to
the ground. The light breeze was making ripples on the
big envelope, now reducing in size as it rose towards the
blue sky, the gondola swinging about as the observer in-

side reeled out his aerial and looked at the ground receding
under him.

Great tension was reigning in the office. I didn't envy
the Generals their responsibilities as they pored over maps
and messages, and faced at every moment the taking of
grave decisions.

At noon we knew that in front of Thiepval and Beaumont Hamel we had been severely checked. Of that, there
was no more doubt—the attacks on the whole of the left
front had failed. The casualties were very serious. The
Reserve Army stood awaiting further developments. . . .

I went at night to Albert, where I knew that from some
high ground I could look into La Boisselle and a wide
stretch of the battle-ground. The line kept emerging
from the darkness, illuminated by brilliant lights from a
constant succession of soaring rockets, bursting and spreading into vivid colours, momentarily revealing quivering
patches of the deep shade beyond.

Our men were then bombing the craters in front of La
Boisselle. Occasionally the light showed up little figures
crawling over broken ground. Behind me the town of
Albert was trembling with the shelling, as flashes from the
guns played hide-and-seek through the beams of its gaping
roofs and intermittently lit up as in daylight a white streak
of the Albert–Bapaume road. A batch of dejected prisoners
was being shepherded to a cage near-by, where their comrades packed in it were pressing their white faces against
the netting, peering with curiosity at their new surroundings.

Ambulances were taking away the wounded from the
casualty clearing-station in Albert. Lorries were packed
with the lighter casualties who waited their turn in big
groups, all labelled with the nature of their wounds.

Roads were crammed with marching troops and lorries.
Dust was rising everywhere. Lines of cavalry horses, con-
tentedly munching hay, covered the rolling plains as far as
Amiens, hidden in the darkness.

On July 2nd the Reserve Army came into the line,

having taken over the shattered 8th and 10th Corps from
the Fourth Army the previous evening. The orders for
renewing the attack were cancelled. Our headquarters
were advanced to Toutencourt, a typical Somme village
with its little church, a square called the Grande Place, a
château (only in name!) and farms with clay walls. We
had some difficulty in fitting in our daily-growing
establishment.

General Gough sent me to Ovillers and La Boisselle to
find out the conditions there; if possible I was to make a
sketch from a certain place. The Brigade Headquarters I
had first to report at were in the trenches of Marsh Valley.
Taking a short cut, I walked over the open across Usna
Hill. Scattered in pits all over the place our field-guns
were firing. I was nearly shaken out of my life. Terrified,
I ran down towards Marsh Valley, dodging about over the
rough ground as each sharp detonation displaced the air
around me. I was indeed relieved to find a communication-
trench, into which I jumped.

It led to a dug-out where, deep down in a tiny stuffy
room, a General was writing out his orders. When I explained what I had come to do, he at once detailed a man
to take me up to the front line. I stood watching my guide
putting on his kit, squeezing his head into his steel helmet,
grimacing as he tucked the strap under his chin. Picking
up his rifle he slung it over his shoulder, and without a
word started towards the front line. Along a monotonous,
dazzling, chalky trench we walked, seeing a streak of blue
sky above and the sandbags drifting past. As each corner
of a traverse eclipsed my companion for a second or two, I
had the illusion of following my own shadow. I screwed
up my neck looking for La Boisselle; all I could see of it
were more sandbags over which smoke was drifting, following a succession of violent reports.

We walked on; I could hear shells whining past through
the air, exploding ahead in a straight line towards the
direction we were making for.

I wanted to wait, but my guide strode on. I could still

follow the whistling rush of each shell bursting nearer and nearer, until one landed in the next traverse and made everything rock with the violence of its explosion. Covered in earth, my heart racing, I looked at my runner, who, doubled up, had his chin between his knees as if he had been trying to squeeze the whole of his body under his steel helmet. I was relieved when he moved, unhurt. We moved on again.

The firing, without easing off, lifted over our heads and followed a perfect course down the trench we had come up. A few yards further on mutilated bodies were lying amidst fallen earth and tumbled sandbags, directly where the parapet had been blown in. In the next traverse stood a group of wounded men, white and shaken, with blood oozing out of their riddled tunics. We helped some of them into a dug-out where others had been already carried to safety. The enemy had the range of every trench, and they shelled them day and night. By the time I had reached the front line my interest in La Boisselle had nearly gone.

Through a gap between two sandbags I was shown the village, where smoke was drifting across skeletons of trees on a torn-up mound. An uneven line of sandbags, stretching across piles of bricks and remnants of houses, faced our front trench. The enemy was there, a few yards away. His presence, so near and yet unseen, made upon me an uncanny impression.

The ground between our trench and the ruins beyond was merely a stretch of craters and burnt-up grass broken up by tangled wire, not unlike gorse-bushes. The dead were lying there in all conceivable attitudes, rotting in the sun. A veil of fumes from lachrymatory shells was rolling along the ground . . . with the heat the smell had become very trying.

A small attack was to be made on the place that night. As I intended to see it, I went back to Brigade Headquarters to rest. The General was still busy with his plans.

Late that night I followed a company going up to the

front line, making room all the way up for stretcher-
bearers moving down with their casualties. The trench
was narrow, and we had to squeeze past each man; in the
darkness no one spoke.

I found the battalion preparing for the attack. A heavy
dew had made the ground clammy and slippery. It grew
cold. . . .

Shells fired from Usna Hill were shrieking over our
heads, crashing one after the other a little way beyond in
that mysterious gap. After an anxious wait the men began
assembling round the scaling ladders and got ready to
climb on to the high parapet.

Amongst much older men a young Tommy was awaiting his turn. He seemed weighed down by his kit and
the loose belts of extra ammunition hanging from his
shoulders; his small head was buried beneath his tin
helmet. In a long nervous hand he held a rifle with fixed
bayonet, and looked anything but anxious to use it. Heavy
thoughts seemed to be in that boy's mind, and the lack of
enthusiasm displayed by the rest filled me with misgivings
as to the ultimate success of the attack. Vitality is low at
that hour. . . .

They were all moving slowly and in silence while the
officers, apparently keyed up, were now gazing at their
watches as the last seconds slipped away and guns from
the valley were angrily spitting fire. The first men
clambered up the steps, followed by the rest, who stumbled
forward into the night after the barrage—black figures
silhouetted against the flares, flooding the broken ground
with brilliant light.

Machine-guns raked the open space, shells tore the air,
bullets thumped against the parapet; wounded men were
crawling back to safety, helped by a few terrified German
prisoners. We waited—the waves hadn't got far. The few
men who had survived the stretch of No Man's Land were
scattered in shell-holes just on the edge of the village. Once
again they had failed to reach an objective, which had
already been obliterated.

When day broke, fresh forms, lying ominously still, showed the cost of the few craters we had gained. A sense of new life was rising from the earth with the freshness of the morning.

I followed the wounded who were crawling down to the aid-posts. The stretcher-bearers, climbing over the earth in places where the trench had been blown in, were obliged at times to expose their burdens to the merciless sniping from La Boisselle.

.   .   .   .   .   .

At Brigade Headquarters the General seemed rather disheartened with the result of the attack. When I left him to go back to the army, he said he was running a very tired brigade. I think he hoped I would mention it to them!

At length I came out of the communication-trench and faced the iron crucifix standing at the cross-ways with its arms extended parallel to the Albert–Authuille road. Troops passing it going up and down to the line made its position very significant. It came to be well known by all those fighting in that area. It stood there offering its message to thousands of men until almost the end of the war, when at last a shell shattered it.

Twisted bits of iron were all that remained on the road of a staff car which had been imprudent enough to drive up so far.

On the safe slope of a bank rising from the road an aid-post was receiving the wounded of the night. Further on a battalion in reserve was sheltering, as the enemy at the time were plastering with high explosives the village of Aveloy and the road leading to it. The men were casually watching the shells splash into the marshes down below and the shrapnel explode at the entrance to the village. A horse with a water-cart and no driver had bolted up the main street, whilst a party of men lay flat off the road waiting for a lull in the squall.

The French seventy-fives with us in this attack had also buried themselves under the bank and were shooting their gas-shells over the ridge at a terrific rate—the muzzles of their little blue guns, cocked up high, were recoiling with the smoothness of an engine.

I became anxious about my motor-bike, left in a block of houses now being shelled. As soon as the shelling eased off I took the opportunity of getting it. I found it covered with dust, but otherwise intact. Riding up the hill through the shattered village, I looked down upon a well-known bicycle factory where machinery and hundreds of bicycle parts were twisted up as if in a paroxysm of agony. The traffic on the road further on was creating a fearful dust; some of the infantry passing looked as if they had been fighting in flour.

From the high ground of Hennencourt the view was very impressive. Down below the valley of the Somme made a graceful loop towards the town of Albert, with all its roofs open to the sky. The high tower of the damaged cathedral was squarely facing the rising ground which was striped by a maze of chalky trenches which the artillery on both sides were thoroughly pulverising. Still holding the infant Jesus in her outstretched arms, the statue of the Virgin Mary, in spite of many hits, still held on top of the spire as if by a miracle. The precarious angle at which she now leaned forward gave her a despairing gesture, as though she were throwing the child into the battle.

La Boisselle, where I had come from, was like a volcano in eruption. To my left, on a promontory, the remains of Pozières were bouncing up and down with the bombardment.

CHAPTER XIX

MAMETZ RIDGE

THE next day I was sent off to see the newly conquered ground round Mametz Wood. I walked through what was left of the village of Bécourt, where, amongst dust and battered walls, French gunners had made a home and had hung out their washing. Their guns, hidden from German observation balloons, fired suddenly, making me jump.

Once over our old front lines I had to cut across No Man's Land to get to a mass of black tangled wire still lying in front of the original German front line. A good many of our men had been killed on their way across. Although the guns were barking loudly and the musketry in the line kept up a constant clatter, I had an impression of great tranquillity when I reached the German front line completely flattened out. Flies had already settled on the dead. A solitary private smoking a pipe was picking up souvenirs in an indescribable mess of blood-stained equipment. He moved from place to place as leisurely as a beachcomber steps from puddle to puddle in search of barnacles. The entire surroundings appeared to have been scraped by a gigantic rake.

Unable to trace the trenches leading to Carnois, I had some difficulty in finding my way there. It lay through many of the old German strong points and redoubts which, although shattered to pieces, had resisted to the last. From some of them I was able to look back towards our old lines, realising what targets our troops had been as they advanced in waves over the open. Every bullet from the enemy machine-guns must have found a mark; right down the slope motionless khaki figures dotted the ground.

Further along a working-party was leisurely sorting over some of the battle débris and making dumps. A few shells landing near made them run for cover into some shell-holes where, safely ensconced, they at once drew forth their cigarettes, glad of any excuse for a quiet smoke.

It was midday; the sun was beating fiercely down on my neck; it was an exertion to move. The light on the white crumpled ruins of Fricourt was dazzling to the eyes. Some men were pulling dead horses in an advanced stage of decomposition off the road, from which the heat rose as from a furnace. The smell was awful.

I saw a board indicating Brigade Headquarters, and watched heads of men popping in and out of an entrance as high explosives pitched near it. Rushing in between two bursts, I landed inside into pitch darkness. A smell of hot sweating humanity rose from a stifling atmosphere below as I groped my way down. Crumpled up in all attitudes men were asleep on every step of the stairway, leaving little room for anyone to pass, their unstrapped kit hanging loosely off their shoulders obstructing the way. A runner coming up had to scramble over me to get past, forcing me to collapse on to some slumbering forms which subsided under me without making a sound. I don't know how many steps I went down. Through a long corridor, completely blocked with sleeping men, I descended deeper into the airless gloom, towards the buzzing sound of the Morse.

At last in a small room I found a Brigadier facing a map spread on the table, dimly lit by candle-light, with un-appetising pieces of bully-beef and bread lying in a tin plate beside him. In the dark corners of the room I made out the shapes of men asleep on wire bedsteads. The flame of the two candles continuously flickered as the earth shook from the shelling, although down below one only heard a muffled sound. The dug-out, being damp, smelled strongly of mildew. I felt the sweat turning cold on my back.

The General having shown me on his map the best way to get up to the line and indicating places to avoid, I groped my way back through the dark passage and, at the bottom of the stairs, saw, high up against the speck of light of the entrance, the outline of recumbent forms blocking the way. Having extricated myself from this tangle of sweating humanity, I emerged again into the heat and blinding light.

Following my instructions, I slipped into a shattered communication-trench on my right and had a solitary walk as far as the junction of two trenches, where I found the way completely blocked. As I scrambled over the fallen earth, I felt half-buried bodies softly give under the weight of my hand. I went on, keeping to the open until voices, shouting to me to come down, made me drop into the trench. Looking over, I saw the head of a man bob over the earth, and, as he beckoned me to join him, I crawled towards him and was led safely to a trench which his battalion occupied. I was in one of the reserve lines; a little way ahead, where the earth was being flung up by shells, lay the front line.

I showed my pass to an officer, who led me to the Colonel. On hearing that I had come to make a drawing, he said: "I am afraid you won't find the landscape very inspiring." He instructed an officer to guide me, adding: "Don't show yourself, as we don't want to draw the enemy's fire."

We started plodding along towards the front line looking for a suitable place affording a good view and, if possible, shelter for my work. So far, except for khaki figures confused up in the chalky ground, and the tops of trees in Mametz Wood, which was still smouldering, there was very little to see. All the time enemy shells were searching the ground near us.

We had now reached an overcrowded trench, and found it hard work to push past all the men, scarlet from the fierce heat of the sun. Although they kept still, sweat could be seen pouring off them. The smell from dead bodies lying around the parapet was nauseating. Flies, keeping up an incessant buzzing, would rise from them as we passed and then immediately settle again.

L

We eventually reached the high ground and slipped into a machine-gun emplacement, where, in a hushed voice, an officer told us a good view could be obtained. In broken ground, advancing a yard or two more made all the difference; what had been completely hidden was suddenly revealed. I peeped over very carefully; northwards astride the top of a ridge, the village of Pozières, half obscured by smoke, suddenly loomed in sight, showing its ruins. Following the sloping ground with my eyes I saw, lying in the valley divided by the Albert–Bapaume road, then being heavily shelled, the two villages of Ovillers-La Boisselle and La Boisselle, still occupied by the Germans. The bursts of shells on our line of trenches indicated plainly a loop we were beginning to form round the enemy's position.

While sketching I could not help my attention being diverted towards the sound of musketry rising and dying down, coming from the south, where at that time the Fourth Army was attacking. As soon as I had finished I became conscious of a weird change creeping into the atmosphere. Indeed, beyond the ridge, big pink clouds had piled up, climbing high into the sky. The sun became gradually obscured, and an odd half-light that changed the aspect of everything crept over the landscape. Gun reports seemed to have a different resonance, the air was charged with electricity, as though something violent and terrific was imminent; the sky had turned blue-black. Realising what was going to happen, I quickly started to get back. The first big drops of rain began to riddle the dusty ground with grey holes as I was half-way down. Suddenly a streak of lightning tore across the black sky. The country vibrated under a most colossal thunder-crash, followed by torrential rain that blotted everything out in a second—the tension was broken.

I ran vainly seeking shelter, and overtook other men who were laughing and joking, welcoming the change as though the end of the war had come. The rain, falling down the shiny slopes, formed streams everywhere. Steam

rose from the hot ground. Drenched through, I kept pace
with the running water rushing into the road, where the
traffic had come to a complete standstill. I was glad to find
the car which had been waiting for me. The storm seemed
to have subdued everything—even gun-firing. The surprise
over, the movement of traffic soon restarted on the roads,
but the Somme dust had turned into liquid mud; lorries
rushed along plastering everybody with it. Drenched infantry and horse-lines were out in the open—everything
now looked miserable.

During the next three days the rain hardly ceased. Conditions became appalling. I went during that spell to our
front facing Thiepval, where we were back in the front
line from which our attack had started on July 1st, and
where the depression caused by our original failure still
hung about. The trenches had now crumbled down with
the rain, and water rushing down the slopes had invaded
every communication-trench. The mud was a soft yellow,
sticky paste that clung to one's boots and had to be kicked
away at every step. Men were slipping about, tripping over
duck-boards sunk into deep bogs at the bottom of trenches
which were being constantly shelled; no communication
route escaped.

The accumulated smoke from incessant shell-bursts
seemed unable to rise out of the Valley of the Somme. It
clung to the trees of Thiepval Wood, already oppressed by
a blanket of damp mist that gave the blurred branches an
appearance of submarine growths.

As the Germans looked down upon us, it was difficult
to get up to the front line without being seen, and more
so to find a place from where I could sketch without being
observed. No Man's Land ran upwards for fifty yards towards a line of sandbags defended by a thick line of rusty
wire that fringed the ruins of Thiepval. It formed a salient
on the high ground, on which stood the remains of a red
château encircled by the charred trees of a once lovely
park. The broken ground made an ideal nest for machine-
guns to infilade our waves. The casualties of July 1st were

still there, flattened out by the rain, which, dripping off their clothes, trickled away in little rills into the shell-holes.

As another attack was being launched on Ovillers that night, I thought I might get there by keeping to the front line, which would eventually lead to the village; but conditions made this impossible. In vain I paddled in slush, elbowing my way along a line of dripping mackintosh sheets covering the men. I had at last to turn back, go round by Authuille, then up again through communication-trenches. It was a very tiring walk.

General Gough had told me that the attacking brigade would be relieved the next day, and I thought it would cheer the men if I told them so, but even that prospect made little impression on their worn-out minds and bodies.

As the strength of battalions was considerably reduced, a fresh division on their right was co-operating in the attack.

The sloppy condition of the ground did not make it easy for those poor devils to assemble. However, after a very short bombardment, all struggled forward through mud and water.

The first news we had of the village being ours was when a German tumbled down from the top of the parapet with the rough help of his guards, quickly followed by a bunch of "Kamerads," who fell into the trench like a landslide. The first man seemed to have collapsed on the duck-boards. As the light of a torch was flashed on to his shaven skull he pulled himself together, drew himself up and clicked his heels, saying: "I am an officer. We have only given in because our machine-guns were put out of action and we had no more rifle ammunition." It was good, anyhow, to learn that. Our shelling had prevented reserves and supplies reaching them. At once the whole lot was marched down to Brigade Headquarters, both captors and captives caked in mud and dragging along like tired men. The General received the officer in his dug-out with great courtesy. He congratulated him on fighting like a soldier, made him sit down and offered him whisky, hoping he

would talk. He drank, but that only revived a true
Prussian spirit. Beyond stating that they had had a lot of
casualties, he would not utter a word: he sat white and
emaciated, gazing at his surroundings. As he was led out,
in walked an Intelligence officer attached to a prisoners'
cage. His interrogation of the prisoner was no more
successful. As he took this German officer's Iron Cross
and field-glasses the Colour-Sergeant who was standing by
rightly objected; "Let him keep his medal," he said, "but
I'll stick to the field-glasses, he won't have any use for them
now." The whole party thereupon filed down the communication-trench, red caps and grey uniforms showing up
in the light of star-shells that were spasmodically spinning
like silver streamers across a paling sky.

On my way back I passed many lorries lying in the
ditches into which they had skidded. Parties of men were
engaged in pulling them out. Labour battalions were busy
re-making the roads damaged by torrents of rain—steam-
rollers were crushing layers of newly-laid stones with a
heavy rumbling noise, lorry traffic going on all the time
bringing up more ammunition and supplies.

．　　．　　．　　．　　．　　．

The Australian Corps was coming to our army. I saw
them arrive one morning while out riding. I had been
galloping across fields behind Toutencourt, putting up
young coveys of partridges, constantly startled by hares
springing up from under my horse's feet and shooting off
at most unexpected angles.

It was foggy; I had come on to a broad spur and halted
to breathe my horse when, coming from the opposite slope,
rose the voice of a French peasant encouraging his horses
at a plough. A cloud of steam rose from their hot bodies
and the furrows fell away from the shining steel. I was
chatting with the peasant, who had stopped to mop his
brow, when both our heads turned towards the sound of
a brass band in the valley below. As we listened, the sun,
as though by magic, suddenly came out and lifted the mist

like a curtain. There on the road below were columns and columns of Australian regiments moving like long snakes. I waited until the sound of their tramping feet came up the hill. They passed, swaying under their heavy haversacks and singing tunes which for months afterwards were to be heard wherever they went. Endlessly, battalion after battalion went by, impressing me with the fine physique of the men, all tanned by the Gallipoli sun. The whole corps arrived. Anzacs swarmed all over the army area, marking their presence by the colour of some of their wild escapades. But they were soon to prove their worth in the line, for they were sent up to take over a new portion of the Fourth Army ground.

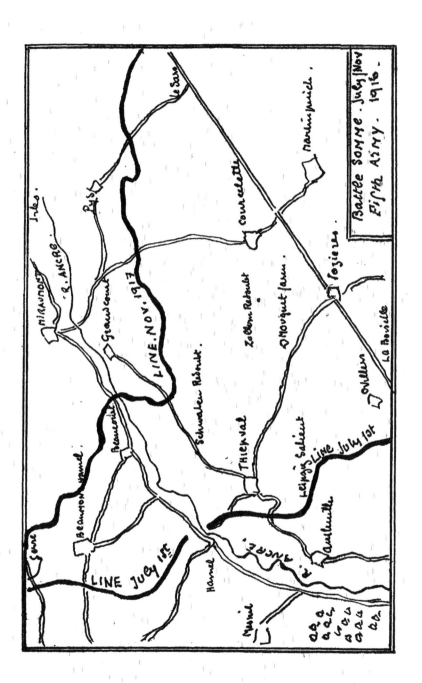

Battle SOMME . July/Nov
FIFTH ARMY - 1916 -

Looking towards Pozières and the ridge from "Black Watch Alley"

CHAPTER XX

(1)

THE Australian Corps was given the arduous task of capturing the spur on which stood the village of Pozières. The attack was fixed for July 22nd. To possess this ridge, very strongly held by the enemy, was of vital importance to us, for it commanded the ground over which we were attacking, and would in turn give us the entire observation on the reverse slope and the large stretch of ground rising from the valley of the Ancre towards Bapaume. But before we could reach the ridge a formidable system of trenches had to be stormed, and every German in those trenches knew the significance of holding on.

I was sent by General Gough to be of what assistance I could to General Sir H. Walker in command of the 2nd Australian Division which was making the attack. I was shown all the objectives on the map and their tactical points were explained. As all frontal attacks had failed so far, the enemy lines facing north were to be taken in enfilade and rolled up, so to speak. I was to stay with the division, go about and learn what I could of the lie of the land, make drawings and explain them to units concerned in the attack. Although I was to report all the information I collected to General Gough personally, he firmly instructed me to impart it first to the battalions and brigade in the line. I was also to keep in close touch with Division and Corps Headquarters, who were to give me every possible help.

Having obtained all the necessary passes to units holding the trenches, I set off eagerly and confidently for the line, satisfied that my General meant to make full use of me.

From Albert one followed the main Albert–Bapaume road across Usna Valley which, since the last advance, had become comparatively safe, not being under direct observation from the ridge. Immediately before the village of Ovillers, however, the road became exposed, ran like a taut tape through the untrodden ground of the battle zone right up to the ridge and, falling in a straight line on the other side, led to Bapaume.

The depression caused by the days of incessant rain had now given place to the discomforts of excessive heat. The communication-trench I followed had been recently dug through chaotic ground, showing traces of the gruesome fighting that had taken place.

After proceeding along this trench for a while I saw, over the parapet, the shattered branches of the cypress trees which hedged the cemetery of La Boisselle. Of the village nothing remained but a few blackened walls precariously still standing. The graveyard itself showed the wreckage of warfare in its weirdest aspect. Every tomb had either been blown up or slung aside; broken slabs of marble lay scattered in shell-holes, which exposed long-buried coffins. From a mess of mud-caked equipment, drab funereal ornaments, spent ammunition and unexploded shells, protruded shattered crosses with limbs of crucifixes hanging lamentably upon them. The head of a Christ severed from its body gazed contemplatively at the unburied soldiers who, in crawling attitudes, appeared to be escaping from the gaping earth on all sides. . . .

I left the cemetery and wandered on to the recently captured craters of Ovillers, originally made by months of mining and counter-mining by the enemy and the French. This place, like a huge ravine, had been very strongly fortified, and every crater was linked by subterranean tunnels which subsequently joined on to a maze of trenches. It had cost hundreds of lives to take, and the enemy may well have thought the position impregnable. From the edge of one of these craters I looked down the sides, covered with rusty barbed wire, where clusters of corpses grilled in the hot sun, khaki and grey uniforms indiscriminately mixed. To shelter from the glare rising off the chalky, tortured ground, I scrambled down into this hecatomb, where, like the dead staring at the roof of blue sky, I felt separated from the world.

I toiled my way up again, following the paths made by the footmarks of troops and, with the help of newly erected direction-posts, wended my way over the broken ground. Here and there the shelling had ploughed up vestiges of earlier French occupation. The trenches were all shot in, dug-outs were destroyed, many of the entrances being blocked with bodies, mingled with earth and sandbags. . . . There was no shade anywhere; the earth glared with light.

At the junction of two collapsed trenches the clean-shaven head of a stout German, his eyes open, was perched on a heap of earth, sticking out like a head out of a Turkish bath. The protruding hands and feet of other insufficiently buried comrades appeared all to belong to him and gave him a peculiarly diabolical significance. As I clambered past him, the earth giving way made him lean over to one side with a horrible semblance of life. For days I had to pass this place. I don't know whether it was worse in broad daylight or at night. Every time I neared it I wondered, and hoped that at last he had somehow been buried, but for some unknown reason he remained conspicuously pivoted, the smell around him growing ever more intolerable. Once I thought my runner and I had successfully hidden him by shoving earth over him, but days later his fair moustache was waving again in the breeze; with many others he had worked his way through again, the area having been constantly shelled.

It seemed appropriate that the front line should be called "Black Watch Alley," running as it did through ground studded with crosses bearing the names of so many of the Black Watch regiments. From the southern part of Pozières the line rose with the ground into a half-moon curve towards a trench called O.G.1, which the enemy shared with our Fourth Army. The Australians at the time

were trying to link up their right with this trench, having
to bomb Germans out of a sap jutting out across the way.
The enemy front line stood out of the ground plainly
visible, and here and there the crest of the reserve lines
could be observed running astride the ridge. The reverse
slopes were equally well defended by a system of trenches
with deep dug-outs for the accommodation of their reserves. Pozières stood forlorn half-way up this crest, skirted
by a rough hedge over which peeped crumbled brick walls.
A double line of trees reduced to mere pegs divided the
village in the middle, forming the main street that went on
through a scraggy spur and past a windmill with its top
knocked off. A well-directed hit at its side had made a
gaping breach which, like an eye, stared for a long time at
the troops who vainly attempted to take the mill.

I looked carefully through my glasses, and showed on my
drawing, emphasising the smallest details, all I could see
of the ground leading to the objective. In order to facili-
tate the assault on the village it was necessary to push forward the part of the front line that formed a loop as near
as possible to the enemy line; it would give the attacking
troops a better springboard from which to attack. The
trench which eventually we were to dig would run along
the bottom of a valley hardly noticeable on the map, but
very important, as on the right, where the ground rose
abruptly, it became dead ground sheltered from cross-fire.
I made a small earth model showing this important
advantage. As I carried on with my work shells tore the
ground all round; often the views would remain blurred
with smoke, and I waited for it to drift away. Somehow the
shelling was concentrated more or less on the same places,
so that I took it for granted that I was safe where I was.

I liked these Australians. Every day I worked amongst
them and found them genial and ready to help. Days were
hot and long. Butter would spread over bread like liquid,
the bully-beef was black; everything was dried up; not a
single leaf on the trees; an incessant buzzing of flies and the
smell of decomposing bodies wafting across the atmosphere.

I used to walk home in the cool of the evening, meeting on my way endless files of men coming up to dig during the night. Everywhere our preparations for the attack were being actively pushed. As our new communication-trenches were made, the dead of former battles were gradually being buried—yet the smell persisted.

Day and night our artillery was increasing its activity, until a few days before the attack it turned into an incessant roar, every gun being engaged in the systematic destruction of every known enemy trench, stronghold and ammunition-dump. All this but served to increase the enemy retaliation.

General Birdwood commanded the corps. It was easy to understand the popularity he enjoyed amongst those Australians, who liked his friendly manner. They called him "Birdie," to which he played up very well. His corps staff had an atmosphere all their own. In an unconventional way they were very business-like and efficient. In General White, their Chief-of-Staff, they had one of the ablest and most charming personalities in the army.

On the eve of the attack General Gough gave me his final instructions. He wished me to remain in close touch with the forward troops, to help units on the spot with all the information I could glean, and according to developments, report the situation to him. He again emphasised the importance of giving that information first to the people directly concerned, who could immediately deal with the situation. I could feel his keenness as he was explaining things on the map. Much depended on the success of this attack; already I had made up my mind to attach myself to one of the attacking battalions and follow its evolution from the very start. It so often happened, when troops had gone over, that the difficulty of reaching them delayed the gathering of valuable information. I felt that this was for me a great opportunity to prove myself useful; the staff would then give me more of that kind of work which thrilled and interested me.

The attack was to be launched at midnight. Having

called at Corps Headquarters, I repaired to the Divisional
Headquarters in Albert, where General Walker and his staff
were feverishly engaged in last-minute preparations. The
day was drawing towards its close when I left for the line.

The sun still struck the parapet of the communication-
trench as I followed on the duckboards the footfalls of a
party of men a few traverses ahead of me. Undisturbed by
their passage, rats moved about in the shadow of the
trench, nibbling at the remnants in discarded bully-beef-
tins. Everything was burnt up by the sun; the light was
still very glaring, glistening on the blue bodies and silver
wings of flies as they buzzed in swarms from feast to feast.
The men carrying heavy loads leaned and rested against
the hot parapet, wiping the sweat off their flushed faces.

Having passed them I walked on alone, engrossed in my
thoughts. The approaching experience of "going over the
top" was steadily forcing itself on my mind. Although I
had seen fighting before, even courted trouble on many
occasions often out of pure curiosity, it had always happened on the spur of the moment without prior reflection.
Somehow this seemed an entirely different affair, and it
made me think; however, my mind kept reverting to the
necessities of the immediate present, and I trudged along
feeling very hot, peeping now and then at Pozières on the
ridge being steadily hammered down. There would soon
be nothing of it left to take.

Companies had already walked up and were stretched
out across the trench, awaiting the dark to proceed further
to their assembly positions. Shuffling past them I came
to our reserve positions, and found them packed with
Australians as far as the old front line. I managed to
squeeze myself along into the new front line, dug the previous night. The rays of the vanishing sun were glowing
on rows of scarlet faces. With shirt-sleeves rolled up, showing their big forearms, the men were busy having tea or
cleaning rifles, sliding the breech up and down in a
significant way. They certainly looked fit, all these Anzacs.
I had come to know a good many of them, who nodded as

I passed. One said to me: "Well, Captain, are you coming over with us to-night?"—somehow I was glad to say I was.

A continuous stream of shells was blowing up more and more of Pozières. Otherwise a perfectly lovely evening was settling down upon this mass of waiting men.

I went on picking my way over the feet of these Colonials until I came to a group attending to an officer visiting the line who, on looking too long over the parapet, had been shot through the head. One had to be careful; one could peep over the top once, for a second, but never twice from the same place.

I followed the trench right down to where we joined with the Forty-eighth Division on our left. They were going to attack the village simultaneously from the south. The sun had by then dipped behind the horizon, sharply defined against a mellow sky. Brilliant patches of sunlight which had lingered on the high ground were slipping into shade one after another, as lamps are switched off by the invisible man controlling the lighting of a scene from the wings of a stage.

A grey light had invaded the valley lying between us and Albert. The rushing past of shells or their resounding crash seemed completely detached for the time being from that peculiar stillness into which nature sinks after the sun has set. But the momentary sense of peace was tinged with apprehension.

Between two sandbags I looked over our wire across No Man's Land like a jockey inspecting the course before a race. I wondered what the going would be like. With the dew a freshness rose from the torn-up ground, and the growing darkness obliterated the unevenness of the surface.

A slow movement of troops had started all along the trenches. I retraced my steps to a battalion headquarters dug-out, where I had made arrangements to meet the Intelligence officer with whom I was to keep in touch. I picked my guide from several runners, a small and nippy man, in contrast perhaps to my height. From now onwards everything I did was well thought out, even to the minutest detail, as though it were a plan for a journey of indefinite length.

We were now engulfed in deep darkness. Men were merely moving shadows, barging into me with their kit. I felt exhausted and clambered on to an open space behind the trench to lie down, in spite of the heavy dew. Stars were twinkling out of the deep immensity; I was soon sound asleep. . . .

I woke out of a dream which had no relation to my surroundings. Guns were thundering, enemy shells whistled over my head on their way to our communication-trenches further down, or to our firing batteries in the valley below. Still men were coming up all along communication-trenches, moving like a dark silent stream that isolated me with my thoughts. As time advanced an apprehension crept in my mind and became acute as I weighed my chances of surviving the attack. No, I could not so easily give up life, so alluring and precarious at that moment. Its grip on me was tightening, and, more than ever I wanted to live. For the first time I was facing the great conflict. Possibly the swarm of men surrounding me were struggling with the same thought. None of them spoke, except to ask for room to move towards their fate. I heard something within me say: "You'll get through," and I clung to that as I slipped into the trench, shuffling my way along until I struck the battalion wearing the distinctive badge on their sleeves. The captain was waiting for me outside the dug-out entrance. All was now ready. The assembly trenches behind us were blocked with troops.

Units had crawled up between trenches and had squatted in shell-holes in perfect silence. As everybody found his right place and time crept on, the atmosphere became more tense. Except for a few runners still threading their way through with messages, movement had completely ceased. Even the guns on our front appeared to have eased off firing. A silence enveloped us, emphasised by the din coming from our right, where the Fourth Army was making a diversion attack.

The bombardment was timed for midnight—thirty minutes before zero. Time flies when you are facing eternity. We waited. Now and then a Verey light soared out of the village, and for a second groups of tin helmets here and there glinted out of the darkness. Suddenly a crash fell like a thunderbolt and the earth shuddered. Hundreds of guns had opened fire from the valley on our left. In hundreds, shells came shrieking and burst over Pozières, where now tongues of flames were rising, glaring on lines of waiting men mesmerised by this unprecedented burst of sound. Chromatically the German artillery retaliation swelled the row into a mad roar, and the general tac-tac of machine-guns became discernible like the beat of a steady pulse. I heard the clash of steel as men near me fixed their bayonets. The men were slipping out of the trench in single file to form the leading waves on No Man's Land. The time for the creeping barrage to open was near.

It dropped like a curtain. With a rush, every man went forward. Bullets hissed past as we followed. A man in front of me tottered and fell. I could hardly control my legs as I leapt to avoid his body. The ground seemed to quake under me. Everything appeared to be moving along with me, figures were popping up and down on either side over the convulsing ground, and I felt the rush of others coming on behind. The waves in front were merged in smoke, moving like animated figures projected on a glaring screen. Flashes made everything vacillate and wobble. Shells were pitching in front, behind, coming from every direction, crashing all round. I felt stunned and hardly conscious of anything. I caught stray words of company commanders urging the men forward. Where men had been near me I suddenly felt space, which immediately again was filled in by others. We went on. Down in the hollow a barrage of shrapnel shook us like leaves, many went down and remained; the flashes lit the ground, showing up the soles of boots of prostrate forms. I just caught glimpses of ghost-like faces as a group of Germans surged through us shout-

M

ing "Kamerad." We struggled on through a line of blown-
up barbed wire, to which I stuck as to a thorn-bush. As I
freed myself more men came on, and with them I came to a
trench where Germans and Australian wounded were tearing open white field-dressings and shouting for stretcher-
bearers. The noise was deafening.

Again we pushed forward and quickly made for the
second trench, our next objective. We tore again through
broken wire, where some of the company were re-forming,
and then went on. Suddenly I remembered something.
. . . We had now reached the outskirts of the village in
which were the remains of a blown-up railway-track. It
flashed through my mind that General Gough had asked
me to look out for a light railway. This was it. Everything seemed to be going up around us. We passed the
first crumbled walls of houses, against which bullets were
spattering like hailstones. Men were hardly discernible in
the darkness. Lashed by sprays of dust and broken brick,
we stumbled over stones and plunged into shell-holes. I
hopped from place to place, zigzagging with the shelling,
following first one man and then another. Everything was
blurred. My throat was parched, my eyes full of water. We
ran into a hail of bullets as we struck some cobble-stones,
which must have been the main road. The men staggered
across it, all lit up by the sudden glare from Verey lights.
I managed to scrape under the lee of an old capsized
ambulance-cart, though bullets were ripping through it as
though it had been brown paper. Then our progress
slowed down. Everything was swaying. Musketry firing
and machine-guns were making a terrific din to our right
and left; trees were falling across each other. Shells bursting on the ruined houses hurled the walls sky-high, filling
the vibrating air with more dust and smoke. The glaring
light from a burning dump lit up the smoke like a cloud.
I saw men advancing through it as through a screen.
Officers kept shouting: "This way."

I followed stumbling men shifting from shell-hole to
shell-hole as best I could. It was difficult to see. At last

we stopped in a shattered trench where several men had clustered. Bullets hissed past, coming from every possible angle. A short way in front on some higher ground one of our machine-guns rattled away, firing for all it was worth. Now and again I saw the silhouetted helmets of the machine-gunners, who were holding on to their gun as though it had been a runaway horse. Units had become very mixed up. Where was the front line?

From rifle-flashes coming from the rising ground it seemed that the right hadn't progressed far into the village. An officer left us to try to find out. We waited, packed together, protected by our dilapidated trench, the earth leaping all round us from bursting shells—some were coming from our side with the rumble of a train; a thing like a torpedo half buried itself a few feet from where we were. It failed to explode. The air stank of fumes.

Apparently some of the forward companies were about forty yards in front, but the officer, who had now returned, said they were not in touch with their right. Suddenly, for no apparent reason, the shelling eased off and a spray of flares inundated us with light for a moment. The lull from the firing was of short duration. With renewed violence it opened again, rolling down in a barrage from the crest and starting a general uproar of musketry. The Germans were attacking. Rifle-flashes were darting in front and to the side on our right. Every machine-gun was spouting tongues of flame. Bombs were hurled from both sides. I could see nothing but flashes and smoke, and expected any moment to be swept away by the rushing torrent. I thought sections of our troops were falling back, as out of the smoke grey German uniforms sprang forward, but, although their hands were upraised, they met a volley from our trench. Those who got through squatted at our feet. It was the enemy's first counter-attack. One of the prisoners said that our shelling had cut them up on the ridge.

Our reserves were coming up from behind all the time, appearing in stumbling groups. Men and prisoners now filled the trench. We sent the prisoners with an escort to

the back lines, and they started off as though they were
demented. We thought of having some of our wounded
carried down by the prisoners, but it was madness for
either to move.

We were told to keep away from the trenches, as they
were being shelled to blazes. There seemed to me no
difference anywhere else. We scattered away into shell-
holes. I followed an officer who had established a post on
the right. In a weird semi-darkness I crept along inhaling
the sulphur fumes which lurked on the ground, crawling
past bodies already still, feeling the wooden handles of
bombs still round the Germans' waists. At last I sank into
a deep hole which exposed the roots of a large tree. The
trunk split by a direct hit spread above like a palm-tree.
Providence had hurled a tin plate that had once been part
of a shelter across the hole. A company runner who
crouched at the bottom of the cavity said that the men had
gone to run a wire on to battalion headquarters. The light
from the moon, breaking at times through the smoke, cast
weird shadows about us, producing an unreal atmosphere.

We had lost sense of time. Hours must have slid by
since we started the attack, for already the freshness of
dawn could be felt and what we could see of the sky was
a dark greenish-blue, the colour which heralds the first daylight. Darkness was slipping away imperceptibly. Doubt-
ful forms were growing all round us and the most fantastic
indefinite shaped objects were appearing. Overhead we
had a roof of tangled branches that might have been the
stage scenery for a tropical forest. When daylight broke
on us it seemed as though we had suddenly opened our
eyes.

With the same untiring regularity explosion after explosion shook the ridge. I looked over the rim of our shelter
as shells turned the earth like rough seas, and saw bodies
lying about as though drifting after a wreck. Here and
there only hands could be seen, flung up with the final
gesture of drowning men.

As the sun came over the ridge we were dazzled by its

brilliant rays. Where were we? We were much farther
into the village than we at first thought. In front of us
earth was being rapidly shovelled out of a trench, and we
could see the heads of a few men busily consolidating the
position. No movement in the open ground seemed possible. The shelling had increased. The ground was so
thickly littered with broken bricks that the battle might
have been fought with them. Field-dressings were strewn
all over the place. Some German dead were still clasping
their hand grenades. Near us an Australian and a German,
killed at the moment they had come to grips, hung together
on the parapet like marionettes embracing each other.

The sun completely altered last night's scene. Aeroplanes swooped over our heads, blowing their klaxons as
they looked for us to signal our position to our artillery.
Our tin plate squeaked from splinters and stones. Bullets
thumped into the ground.

Strangely enough, precarious as our position was, we
felt protected. It became very hot. We grew thirsty. A
few men began to venture out into the open to gather up
ammunition that lay scattered all over the ground and
which was now needed. Some were crawling up, dragging
forward their ammunition boxes, panting at every yard,
everything flying about them.

We buzzed on our telephone buzzer, to try to get in
touch with Battalion Headquarters, but without success.
The wire was cut. Several times we sent our runner down.
We got a message from the front line. We knew now where
the front companies were and approximately put down
their positions on the plan we had of the village. The
battalion on our left had its headquarters in a dug-out,
where, close to a brick wall, a machine-gun we could just
see was firing. I started towards it, ducking at every crash
and swept about by the constant displacement of air. The
machine-gunners in their shell-holes were surrounded with
casualties. The men, as they always did, had grouped near
dug-outs for safety, although they knew they must naturally be shelled. I squeezed past two beams supporting the

entrance of the shelter, along which, in complete darkness, sweating men and kit were crowding the stairs leading
down to what seemed the bowels of the earth. I had to
force my way through; detonations shook the sides; grit
earth, and splinters swept the gallery, like swilling water
down the companion-way of a ship in a gale. Every burst
resounded at the bottom with a weird thud and the wall
rocked, like the side of a ship struck by consecutive waves.
At the end of the gallery, like a captain in the chart-room
of his ship in the grip of a hurricane, an officer was flashing a torch on to a map—otherwise it was dark, overcrowded
and stifling.

With the lights of our combined torches I managed to
put down the approximate positions of the companies. I
gave him the information I had about their right. All was
heat and tension inside, although it felt much safer than
above. It was a trying experience to scramble up those
stairs again and throw oneself once more into the boiling
cauldron outside. I endeavoured to make my way along
towards the left to get their position, but the smoke was
so thick I lost my sense of direction. I wandered about in
the remnants of trenches strewn with many German dead.
To help myself along I had to touch them as I bounced
and sprang, often having to lie side by side with them, remaining as still as they were, as though I clung on to a
raft. I couldn't see an Anzac anywhere about. It seemed
to me that I took hours to cover fifty yards.

Having at last seen some of our tin helmets move in
front, I rushed towards them and, as I did so, I thought that
one of the German bodies, propped up against a bank,
moved slightly as I passed. A succession of thunderous
crashes near me made me fling myself on the ground, and
as I did so there I faced, standing poised, revolver in hand,
the man whom I thought had moved. Before I had time
to realise him fully, a bursting shell had swept him out
of sight. I told the men I found further on what I had just
seen and they said they were being constantly shot at from
all sides. They were not in touch with anyone at the time,

and advised me not to proceed any further along their left, as they had tried to get into touch several times and the men they had sent had not come back.

I took their advice and started back towards my company shelter. I had to crawl, and for the best part of the way dragged with me some barbed wire that had caught on to my clothes, and which in my excitement it didn't occur to me to pull off.

Through the drifting smoke a party of German prisoners could be seen attempting to carry down our wounded. They stumbled and fell with their heavy loads, sometimes never to rise again. Two of them had fallen in an attitude of prayer over the body of an Anzac whom they were carrying.

As I plunged into our shelter one of our runners was half-way up the slope, also on his way towards it, taking his chance between every shell-burst. As he slithered down beneath our tin roof, the neat tick of a bullet finding its mark was distinctly heard. Hardly realising what had happened I looked at him, propped up against some roots, and saw his face turn white under his tin helmet and a thin scarlet streak of blood run slowly down his cheek. . . . Opening his mouth like a bird, he gasped. I cut with my knife the strap of his accoutrement to help his breathing, and his chest expanded for the last time. Death came quickly, simply. His body quivered—his eyelids fell like a curtain. He subsided gently, like a shot pigeon and there he remained, a silent and crumpled companion.

The enemy was now firing gas shells, which affected our eyes; the smell became trying and the heat increased. We were marooned in this inferno. I had to think of getting back to Army Headquarters. It was important to let them know the conditions. Just as I was about to leave, a shell pushed in the side of our refuge, partly burying us. The shock of the explosion made our dead Australian slip down to the bottom, as though he were seeking more shelter.

I took some messages for the Colonel of the battalion and quickly slipped down towards his dug-out. I had another long flight of stairs to struggle down, still chock-a-block with men. In contrast to the heat outside this dank dug-out was chilling, like a vault. Every sound from the fury above repercussed along the gallery in an infernal way. The Colonel had not received half the messages we had sent, but he had, however, the approximate position of his right companies.

I then made for home, working my way, through Brigade Headquarters, along communication-trenches, which were being blown up all the time. Everywhere men were held up on their way to the village, waiting all the time for the shelling to ease off; whole parties had been blown to pieces. It seemed unwise to push up reinforcements at that time. I took mental notes of everything as I went along.

From one place I had a glimpse of the previous night's No Man's Land pitted with fresh shell-holes, most of them rimmed with motionless human forms.

Men carrying ammunition and water in petrol tins were going up, wounded men hobbling down, while signalmen were attempting to lay down wires. I followed a stretcher and heard groans as the bearers stumbled and shook their limp load, of which I saw only a wobbling boot and an inert pale hand stained with dried blood.

From certain corners the tower of Albert Cathedral peered between the rising sprays of earth like a distant lighthouse. Every step towards it was a relief. To avoid the crowd I took to the open, entirely broken up with shell-holes. I suddenly became aware of a lovely sky; it was evening again and what a glorious one! The trees of Thiepval, standing on the ridge to the right, showed up against shining gold as the sun touched the horizon. It was twenty-four hours since I had wondered whether I should see it rise or set again. I was conscious of myself once more. I suddenly realised I was alive.

The area I was now crossing was comparatively safe, but still obsessed with the constant crash of explosions, I started at the "swish" of every shell passing well over my head fired at our back lines, and hurried on like a vessel struck aft by the wind in a storm. Running up and down the broken ground I had the sensation of riding waves, while the crest of our distant chalky trenches suggested white breakers rolling towards me; the stretch of black barbed wire might have been an oyster-bed on a strip of rocky shallow shore, and Albert and the hill beyond the solid coast-line.

I had reached the flat ground and found myself strangely walking between a row of houses in a street in Albert. Like a ship straightening on its keel on entering the shelter of a harbour, I felt my legs again and a new lease of life; the roll coming from the firing of our own guns near-by was as comforting as the welcome bustle of a port.

I turned to look back at Pozières on the distant crest, where it remained in continuous volcanic convulsions. Above it aeroplanes were circling like gulls. Tac-tac went machine-guns and an aeroplane spun and whirled like a falling leaf, catching the golden light at each turn until it fell to the ground.

Divisional Headquarters were busy locating the exact position of their troops from the many conflicting messages they had received. They were, however, hoping to push the Germans completely out of the village and were preparing for a fresh attack that night. I gave them all the information I had, and explained the reigning confusion in the line, where the necessary organisation required for a renewed attack would be difficult under the prevailing conditions. Units had to confer with each other—some were not even in touch. All wires were cut, messages took a long time to get through, many failed to be delivered at all. . . .

I wondered what they would do as I sank into the back seat of an army car and was whizzed through the cool evening air. We passed marching Anzacs singing along the road and endless convoys of lorries rolling up with supplies. After the noise of the line, even the grinding of wheels sounded smooth and regular and almost dreamlike, as though they weren't touching the ground. Houses in villages we passed through were still standing, complete with roofs. It all seemed strange. As my car sped towards the back areas I ran into peace.

At last we stopped in front of the Army Commander's house. The room I entered seemed to glare with light, but it was only in contrast with the darkness outside. The Army Commander and his staff were still at dinner. He jumped up and at once led me to a large desk, on which lay the outspread army map, and then I answered a regular bombardment of questions. Running his fingers over the map he would press and turn his thumb on certain spots, emphasising his meaning. I carefully weighed my answers, so as to convey as accurate a picture as I could of the actual facts. Sometimes I was unable to read my notes, so shaky was my writing. He was anxious to know how far I thought we were from the top of the ridge; he hoped the divisions would attack again that night. I laid stress again on the difficulties involved. Recalling the German prisoner's remark about their reserves having suffered from our shelling, I thought it important to mention how our bombardment of the ridge and immediately behind had been cutting up the Germans assembling there for their counter-attacks and how important it was to keep it up. This brought a smile of satisfaction from the Army Gunner, who was standing there with the Army Chief Engineer. They both questioned me in turn. The gunner, of course, wanted to know if his guns were shooting on the right places, whether they were reaching here and there, or any firing short, and where exactly were our men. What seemed a possibility on the map was, on the ground, often an impossibility, so that any indication as to this or that place observed on the spot would be of help.

The sapper wanted to know about the conditions of trenches and roads, the immediate use he could make of light railways, the state of dug-outs, dumps, etc. There were a lot of questions to answer in minute detail.

When my examination was over I was very tired. General Malcolm, Chief-of-Staff, who had so far said nothing, wound up my ordeal by a human enquiry about

the troops. His eyes sparkled when he heard how well they
had done, and I described various incidents.

It struck me then how on the map the ground won yard
by yard and at great cost was merely shown by a few inches
of red pencil marks—that was all; an incident, vital as it
was, in a great battle!

As I went down the dark road to my billet a plane was
droning high in the sky. Officers were leaving the mess and
going back to their work.

At the main cross-roads the man on point-duty wished
me "good night." As I snuggled up inside the sheets, the
rumble of guns and roll of traffic still in my ears, a cock
crowed in the village—he had mistaken the time. . . !

CHAPTER XXI

(II)

As I woke up in the morning the noise of movement from the village might have been the excitement of a populace flocking toward a fête. Even the boom of guns had a festive note. Although the day had barely started the heat could already be felt; the nails of boots that had marched since early dawn could be heard scraping and dragging on the hard road.

I went to the Army Commander's office to get my orders for the day. The enemy had made four counter-attacks on Pozières during the night and the position of the troops in the line was therefore still very indefinite. However, it appeared that the Anzacs had a footing in the cemetery, which lay on the high ground. I was to go and see where the line actually ran.

The army car in which I drove threaded through marching columns, ammunition convoys, and vegetable carts driven by peasants in their best clothes. It was market day in Amiens and the military police was controlling this hectic human movement as though it had been a crowd on the way to the Derby. Children were off to school, motor-bikes were scattering in all directions, planes droned through the air, observation balloons had taken their accustomed places in the sky. The plains between Amiens and Albert were like a gigantic camp. Lines and lines of horses shone in the sun, tents were stuck out everywhere, and where roads appeared troops could be seen on the move. It looked a gay and lively scene but for the ambulances streaming through the landscape, the staccato reports of machine-guns fired from aeroplanes and the increasing growl of the bombardment.

Seen from the high ground south of Albert the shining Virgin Mary on the Cathedral seemed to command the battle. The smoke from gun-fire rose into a thick cloud and partly screened the ridge, which was being hammered by the fury of both bombardments and where thousands of hidden men were being torn to pieces. A peasant who had pulled up his horse near my car turned towards me and said, "I cannot understand how anyone can survive over there. It's been going on like this for a week." I dared not tell him that I was going there. . . .

To satisfy my driver's curiosity I let him drive me into Contalmaison over a road on which no vehicle had so far ventured in the day-time. For his first real contact with the gruesome realities of war, it was a severe one, as his car bumped over the broken road, cutting across shell-pitted ground, and we manœuvred past human bodies and carcases of horses spreading their nauseating smell in the air. He pricked up his ears as shells swished over our heads and the remains of the village in front whirled into the sky.

I jumped out of the car and he immediately turned it round and went back down the road, jolting along with the precipitation of a made-up mind. He was a C3 man, or something that absolved him from stoicism.

I walked on alone in the sparkling sunlight until I found some Anzacs scattered in shell-holes, basking in the sun with the detachment troops have when waiting in reserve. I then entered a communication-trench where an arrow pointed to Pozières 1,500 yards away and fell into the peculiar isolation the sudden shade gives to one who has been walking in the glaring light. As I concentrated on what I had been sent to do, I gave the distant barrage a listening ear until fear, perhaps, made me climb on to the top of the parapet to look where I was going.

To my right, earth was being shovelled and thrown up by invisible men digging more strands to the web of trenches running up towards the spur. Shells were bursting all over the place, the sprays of earth rising high into

the sky and hiding at times the German balloons that
loomed placid and limp high in the distance above the crest.

Of Pozières I could see nothing. A steady barrage completely encircled it in smoke that turned from lightest
yellow to dark orange and through which blurred columns
of brown earth unceasingly rose like fountain spouts.

To my left, behind the remaining stumps of Contalmaison Wood, the valley and Albert seemed to have receded in the heat haze above which our balloons hung
like tiny specks.

A party of men with wounds freshly bandaged hobbled
past me smoking cigarettes, with the contentment of men
assured for the time being of their lives. I got a strong
whiff of ether and heard the snip and tinkle of scissors as
I went by a dug-out used as a dressing-station. Along the
bottom of the trench thereafter the little pools of black
blood that had dripped from the wounded men attracted
the flies that were humming from place to place. It was
hot; although I hadn't really walked far I felt my belt
cutting into my waist and the packet of sandwiches I carried
had now assumed the shape of a roly-poly.

The trench was very battered, although it had been reconstructed during the night and many of the previous
day's casualties had been removed to the open. Some of
them were hanging on the side of the parapet as though
they were looking at a show going on on the other side.
At every step my perception of sound grew more acute,
and the rising clamour seemed to be rolling towards me.
However, I was still outside that net of hell which I was
soon to enter, and therefore still able to control in my mind
every sound with perfect vividness. A few intermittent
shells crashed near-by, as though detached from the main
bombardment, and then the unbroken whirr of successive
swarms brought a calming rhythm over the whole fracas
as they passed over my head and landed further down. I
was now walking like a man who, waist-deep in rough
water, sees for a second the waves come up to swamp him.
There was a near crash and then an unheralded burst—I

was lying at the bottom of the trench with part of its side over me, half choked by sulphur fumes, my mind all confused in a nightmare of space, hurtling rockets and vibrations. I got up unhurt, and surprised. Knowing that I couldn't turn back I went on with measured bounds, feeling my fate controlled by anything except myself.

I was now within sight of a dug-out entrance that was receiving severe attention from a series of 5.9's. I sat crouched like a frightened rabbit within a leap of my hole of salvation, waiting for the lull that would give me my chance when, with the next crash, an Anzac swept round the traverse facing me and was flung against the sandbags. As soon as the smoke lifted, I saw lying at his feet a message he had been carrying. Promptly I picked it up, and as I raised his tin helmet which had slipped over his face to see if the man was alive, part of his brain slithered down his back.

It was no good carrying him into the dug-out, which faced the enemy shelling like an open window.

Below, men sat tense, obsessed by the ghastly consequences of the inevitable direct hit. Two guttering candles showed up the faces of the two officers I had left in exactly the same position the night before. Their unshaven faces looked more drawn. A loud snore rose from a broad man stretched out on the floor, fully equipped.

I handed over the message. Our conversation was punctuated by the shocks following each shell-burst. The message came from a company asking for ammunition and water. When the Colonel asked where the man was who had brought it, I explained—a shrug of his shoulders indicated that he understood.

I was told that the line was now held as thinly as possible, for the casualties from the shelling had been very heavy. Pozières had been uselessly overcrowded. Most of their officers had been killed. No telephone wires had survived the bombardment. All dumps were blown up. But for the runners who had succeeded in getting through, they were cut off from the front line.

I made for the stairs with the mechanical "good-luck" send-off one gets on such occasions, fully aware of what I was walking into. At the entrance I found the unfortunate runner now subsided over his rifle like a beggar over his crutches on the sun-baked porch of a Continental cathedral.

I was bent on working my way round, starting from our furthermost advance positions on the right and then on to the division linking with us on the left. Near the village the battered-down trench became very shallow. Every few yards one or more casualties lay stretched out. Just before reaching the road skirting the village, I came on a group of men looking green with exhaustion. They had been carrying up ammunition and as they had attempted to cross the road at the end of the trench they had lost three men. The road being higher than the trench they had to get up on to it and run the gauntlet, their only protection being the débris strewn about and the bodies of those caught by machine-gun bullets, fired from the windmill which enfiladed this open space. The derelict ambulance cart that I had felt such a protection during the night attack was still there, but a little more shattered. This, with a tangle of shelled barbed wire and an agglomeration of perforated petrol tins, acted as a screen. At all costs the ammunition had to be got across. There was nothing enticing about the prospect, nor indeed about entering the village, where clods of earth were being thrown up by the shells bursting, as though the end had come.

We first lifted a box on to the road and, remaining in the trench, pushed it lengthwise across the cobble-stones. Having placed another box-head against it, both were pushed a little further across, until the line stretched about three-quarters of the width of the road. We got several lines spread in this way and then managed to crawl between them into the trench on the other side, where we gathered the boxes within reach. How long it took, shaken and nerve-racked as we were by the infernal shelling, I cannot remember, but it seemed a lifetime.

After that I left the men and slipped into a trench curv-

ing off through the village towards the ridge. The sun,
shining through smoke and dust, was casting dazzling rays
like artificial light. I could hardly see beyond the few yards
immediately ahead. The trench lost itself amidst the shell-
holes, some of them huge cavities made by uprooted trees
lying on their sides. The earth clinging to the roots made
a parapet.

As I sidled along the crumpled walls of a house I caught
sight of ragged civilian garments, parts of a smashed um-
brella and a dead bird inside a cage. Whenever I saw the
tops of tin helmets I made for them. Often I plunged into
a hole and found it full of men I had not seen. A shell-
hole was a complete isolation, for once inside nobody
chanced looking out to see who wanted help.

I vainly tried to enter a dug-out chock-a-block with men.
The cellars of houses were also packed. Both were picked
targets for the enemy guns, judging by the casualties all
around. In the event of a counter-attack these men risked
being scuppered like rats in a trap, but for the moment
the predominating thought of every man was to escape the
incessant shower of bursting shells.

I was relieved when at last I came to a shell-hole and
found an officer whose company was scattered in front. He
gave me a very clear picture of the situation before him
and also on his right. They had managed to form a running line, which they held with as few men as possible,
relying mostly on their machine-guns. They were running
short of ammunition and the men were clamouring for
water. As I could have gathered no more information than
I was given, even if I had gone further on, I went to find
touch with the left.

I had another anxious crawl over what seemed a rabbit
warren, where unexploded shells, half buried in the earth,
showed up like crawling worms. At times I remained
pinned in the hollows of craters filled with lurking fumes,
unable to raise my head for the pieces of steel flying about,
striking death everywhere.

The spasmodic fusillade kept up by both sides guided me

N

somewhat as to the position of the forward posts, but at times I became more startled as rifle-fire broke out much nearer than I expected. I found out the reason when I fell on to a machine-gun post. The line there made a loop and the enemy was in the salient. I had to go right round it. The different markings on the men's arms showed how mixed up all battalions were.

Shells constantly smothered a mound of red bricks which I was told was the headquarters of the extreme left battalion. The entrance faced south and a few steps led into the cellar. At the first opportunity I dived into it, but the shock from another crash had put out the candle lighting the place before anyone had seen me enter. I remained in the dark smelling sweating men round me until a trembling hand relit the candle stuck in the neck of a bottle, in front of which sat a stout man in his shirt-sleeves, dripping with sweat. He stared as he suddenly caught sight of me, covering me instantly with his revolver. I put up my hands. I said I had come from the army. "That's all right, search him." Out of my pockets came a Mills bomb, a map and my pass. "Who made the different marks on your map?" he wanted to know. I satisfied him with my answers. Suddenly he relaxed and offered me a drink of whisky, adding with a nervous smile, "It's warm, but it's all we've got, and we have no water." The shaking of the place kept putting out the candle, which was immediately relit. Everybody seemed exhausted and jumpy.

I told the C.O. that I was making for the Warwicks on their left. He said that I must have a runner as the line was not continuous and the enemy in places were in between. He gave me the positions of his companies and machine-guns.

Looking through the bright opening I saw the ground I had to cover being raked by high explosives. My runner, all ready, stood by and said, "Be ready to follow me. Do as I do, mind you jump—it's the only way." He started boldly in a rush with me behind, my eye fixed on his alert little figure, bounding like an animal. He ran first one way, then

another, up and down. We dived headlong into shallow
places, making the most of the slightest shelter. Bullets
flicked past, thumping into the earth as if fired from the
air. I had suddenly a sense of fitness in every limb and felt
sure that nothing would touch me.

We eventually came to a thinly-held trench, which surprisingly escaped being bombarded, and followed it up to
where it jutted out into the cemetery, most of which was
still held by the enemy. Actually we had men right in the
churchyard in front. As the General had been very definite
as to the possibilities of observation from this high ground,
I clambered up a shallow sap leading to it. The ground
rose abruptly; as I looked up, the tops of shattered marble
pillars and bead wreaths appeared all round. The very
front post, unshelled in the midst of this wild bombardment, felt like a calm backwater of a whirling pool. Men
talked in hushed voices, as though they wanted to keep the
secret of their sanctuary. One of them whispered: "Fritz
is there in the old boneyard, about ten yards away; if you
look up you'll see some of them moving about the communication-trench that comes down from the top." For
the first time I was able to see the crest of the ridge. I
noted carefully all I could see and from the shattered bits
of railing showing above the earth I made out the exact
spots where now and again the butts of German rifles and
tin helmets slid past. The doubts entertained by the
artillery of both sides as to who was actually in the
cemetery accounted for this peaceful gap only a yard or
two from the enemy.

I relaxed then for the first time and wrote down all that
I could remember of value to the staff. I got safely across
another stretch on the left, linking on with a further post.
There I had a sweeping view of our trenches all the way
down, held by the other division. The German positions
facing Ovillers and Thiepval were also very plainly visible,
and I was happy to see how thoroughly they were being
shelled by our artillery.

I had now to find the 42nd Division. The trench we

were in suddenly faded out into a miniature mountain
chain, where along the rims of craters we followed the footmarks of a path similar to a switchback. I was running
behind my guide when he suddenly fell forward and I
tumbled over him. I just saw his face quiver with a spasm
and he never moved again. As I attempted to pull him
down into the shell-hole someone shouted to me to leave
him. After all, any place was as good as another. I was
now amongst the Warwicks, whom I had been looking for.
A bombing attack was going on in a sap near-by, where a
party of Germans had remained.

A Warwick man conducted me a little way back to a
deep shell-hole, where an elderly Colonel was placidly
smoking a pipe, sitting on a shooting-stick. Calmly he
asked me where I had sprung from. I showed him on my
map where I had been, and he gave me at once all possible
information about his line, explaining clearly what his
battalion was going to do. From where we were Pozières
looked like a burning furnace. "Look," said the Colonel,
"how well my men lob their bombs," as little things like
black eggs were being hurled and burst with the snap of
crackers. "Though the Germans have the high ground they
don't throw so far." I was ready to agree with him, when
two of their bombs exploded into the next hole. He didn't
move; like an old cricketer he watched every "over."

Every yard of the high ground we were now gaining was
most important. Little by little we were widening the loop
and encircling the enemy position south. It was easy to see
how the possession of the spur on both sides of Pozières
would ease at once our precarious position inside the
village.

I started on my way back. I was running down a communication-trench with the happy feeling of being alive,
my Mills bomb dangling against my hip-bone. Grasping
it, I ran on, when I suddenly felt the cold tickle of a piece
of steel in the palm of my hand. It took me a second to
realise that the safety-pin had snapped and I quickly threw
the bomb over the parapet. My ears were still ringing with

the report of the burst as I faced the Crucifix on the Aveloy cross-roads. I thanked Providence then for that quick reflex which had saved my life.

It was 8 o'clock. Light was already fading. Another day had passed. From the roads the rattle of evening traffic rose and more infantry could be seen tramping up to renew the attack. The army car was waiting for me at the place arranged and the chauffeur had almost given me up. It was very late when I left the Australian Divisional Headquarters. Lines of cavalry were streaming past on their way to back areas—once again not required. The silhouettes of Indian Lancers sitting up in their saddles looked magnificent, with right arms stretched out holding their lances, their long backs giving elegantly to the motion of native horses. As I came upon a cage full of prisoners it occurred to me how little the enemy is seen in a battle, however near you are to him.

CHAPTER XXII

THE FALL OF THIEPVAL

THE battle for the ridge went on. After ten days of the hardest fighting Pozières was well in our hands and the trench running on the sky-line called O.G.1 was now our front line. Costly had been all our attacks. We were now tackling O.G.2., the parallel trench running on the other face of the spur, but the nest of machine-guns posted about the windmill on the brow checked our troops each time. Most attacks were made at night; during the day we consolidated the ground won. My contact with Australian troops then brought me in touch with a Captain Bean, who was the official war correspondent for the Australian Commonwealth. He was a delightful person, who, in spite of short-sightedness, always roamed about the trenches after an attack in search of news. As a war correspondent he certainly gleaned first-hand information, for he was always on the spot. His tall figure was familiar to all the Anzacs, who loved him, for they well knew that he recorded their deeds. Once I came across him sitting with a row of men in a trench that was being heavily shelled; his glasses on the tip of his nose, he peered forward like a spectator in a front stall jotting down notes now and then, perfectly unperturbed. . . .

Every day the sun beat down relentlessly on the troops. The ground had become very hard. Going about the line became very exhausting. I went up every day and had the satisfaction each time of discovering new outlooks over the German positions. The smoke from our shells was whirling over the villages of Courcelette and Martinpuich. In the day-time all the roads winding across this stretch of land which the enemy had hitherto been able to use freely, were now under observed fire from our gunners.

We could see for miles, to where the windows in distant villages, still untouched by shells, flashed in the sunlight. When one looked back from this high ground the salient made by our advance into the enemy line was very noticeable. It encircled Thiepval, starting from Leipzig Salient, a small corner of the German position south of Thiepval, which was the only position of the enemy line that the Fourth Army had managed to seize on the left of their attack during the first day of the battle.

In that Salient, Mouquet Farm became the centre of German resistance. It was prominently situated half-way up a long slope, with Thiepval higher up and several strong redoubts, of which Schwaben was one, above and below. If the enemy was driven out he would have to straighten up his line and give up a good deal of ground. He had made use of the dry chalky soil by constructing deep dug-outs and tunnels, which securely sheltered his reserves. Day and night shells of every calibre unceasingly blew up the place. Everyone of our attacks met with a stiff resistance.

The II Corps, commanded by General Jacobs, held that sector. One day I was walking up a trench to find a position from which to make a sketch of Mouquet Farm. I carried a roll of paper tied with a red band; as with difficulty I was elbowing my way through the crowded trench I heard a man say, "For God's sake let him pass, it's a bloke with the Peace Treaty." To make a drawing from such a place was not easy. I had to climb on to the fire-step, and hold my board and head level with the tops of the sandbags, and peep over.

I was to get a rest. The strain of all these days was beginning to tell on me, when, on my way back one night I came past a quarry where a heavy bombardment with gas shells had caught the day casualties lying out in rows ready for transportation at night. The shouts and groans of the men made me give a hand in helping to get them away from the gas area. In doing this I became affected by gas fumes. I was feeling and presumably looking so sorry for

myself that a queerly-dressed, long-haired Salvation Army
enthusiast whom I met in Albert was moved to ask me
whether I was looking for Christ.

I was sent to a French hospital at Amiens, where I remained five weeks. It was in the middle of the town and
opened on to a wide square, where patients sat under the
shade of broad chestnut trees, watching the fluff fall off the
leaves. Some were hobbling about on one leg, others with
bandaged eyes felt their way hesitatingly in the yard. We
had so little to do that even the arrival of civilians, called
by their dying relatives, used to break the monotony of our
thoughts. They came up in small groups. Those prepared
for the worst were in black clothes. A man with a bunch
of keys led them to the lugubrious building with
"Mortuary" placarded in large letters over it. The
rumbling of distant guns sounded like a dirge as the drab
and awkward procession came out again and made for the
main gates that let them out into the merciless busy world,
detached from their individual burdens.

I was given leave as soon as I felt well enough to go. I
went at once to Normandy, where I spent some lovely
weeks that sped by all too quickly.

I received there a letter from General Gough telling
me that the Fifth Army had taken Thiepval. It sounded
very far away from my remote retreat—another world
altogether.

                                        27. 9. 16.
Dear Maze,

*Many thanks for photos of the old abbey. It all looks
perfectly charming. Would like you to escort my family
and me over Normandy—someday—when peace comes and
the Bosch is beaten and cowed.*

*We have given him two or three very bad days and have
taken Thiepval!*

                                    Yours,
                                    Hubert P. Gough.

I remember one funny incident of that leave. I was in the little town hall of the village to get my leave stamped by the Mayor, when a huge Norman peasant came in to get a pass for himself and his wife to proceed to Rouen. In those days no one could move from one place to another without a permit. He had to fill in a form giving a description of his features and those of his wife. The Mayor was able to make a written picture of *his* physiognomy, but when it came to the description of the wife the peasant was completely puzzled. At each question, whether it was about the shape of her mouth or of her nose, he scratched his head as though he couldn't remember. When it came to the colour of her eyes, "Ah!" he said, disclaiming any such knowledge, "I have never bothered to look at them."

It was the end of September when I departed, boarding the train at a little halt where the railway runs through a green glade. It was evening, and the country was at its best after a lovely day. The country carts of peasants who had driven up their sons or husbands going back to the front were hitched up to the railings of the little station. With haversacks bulging with food and bottles, the grey-clad soldiers stood in the midst of their friends like true Normans, none of them expressing any emotion as they waited for the train to go. Now and again the engine whistled as though urging them to make a gesture to depart. After an awkward embrace they settled in a carriage, and as though reluctant to get off, the train slowly puffed away. German prisoners, working on the railway, were respectfully watching this scene of departure, no doubt reminded of a similar moment in their village in Germany. A soldier who had got into my compartment at once opened up a haversack and spread delicious-looking food on the seat, insisting on my sharing it. We talked a little of the war; he referred to the hardships like a man devoid of any sensibility. I wondered whether he was capable of any emotions at all. He certainly showed little when he parted from his family, but perhaps he was only bottling it all up.

Two days later I was on my way to the line beyond
Thiepval, with visions of crops and orchards in peaceful
Normandy in my mind. It was a very hot afternoon.
I was surprised suddenly to find myself driving over
a reconstructed road, where only a few weeks earlier
not even the communication-trenches were safe. Everything had changed since then. I looked for familiar
things, but they had gone. Trenches had been filled
in and the dead buried. The battle-ground looked
like a shore when the tide has gone far out. Pozières, on
the ridge, showing only its charred tree-stumps against the
sky, looked much farther away than before. On my left
Thiepval, which I had left in the enemy's hands and which
for weeks had been the centre of explosions, looked as forlorn and neglected as the shattered hull of a stranded four-
master on some rock, now that it was no longer being
shelled.

Although our heavy guns were still firing from the
sheltered banks of the river, all field-guns had been pushed
forward and their fire sounded distant. This area was now
in comparative peace, both artilleries concentrating their
fire on the other face of the slope. A quantity of rusty unexploded shells lay about, contrasting vividly with the
pallor of the chalky ground flooded in brilliant sunlight.

But for a few men busy making dumps of the rifles and
equipment scattered all over the place, the plateau seemed
strangely deserted. The gradual progress of our advance
was plainly marked by the white crosses sticking up everywhere. We had paid dearly for every yard.

Some aeroplanes were gliding between fleecy white
clouds. Now and then a big shell sailed lazily through the
air, exploding far away, but suddenly I was shaken by the
burst of a whizz-bang not far from me. I still felt very weak.

Further on, on a squeaky light railway leading up to the
line, men were pushing along loads of barbed wire and
trench implements. Derelict tanks, brought into the battle
after I had gone, were sticking out of holes like lame
monsters, their noses pointing defiantly towards the ridge.

Water lay at the bottom of the shell-holes, in which long-legged insects were swimming round and round.

I was watching a man who had come down from the ridge tapping a small white bag against his knee as he hummed a tune. He was an Australian padre, bursting with health. "What a fine day it is," he remarked; "here's a good day's work," throwing up his bag full of identity discs he had been gathering from the dead. Every man had to find satisfaction in his work.

To be able to walk through Pozières and not to be shelled was an odd sensation. Nothing remained of the village; it had been pulverised. Somehow, something attached me to the place. Crosses were sticking out of the churned-up ground like daffodils in a wood in spring.

One had to take to communication-trenches again at the end of the high ground, for the reverse slope was under observation. The glaring sun on the sandbags made the zig-zag walk a strain to the eyes. The smell of decomposition everywhere was very trying. In places human remains appeared, gruesomely forming part of the parapets. A party of sweating men, fully equipped, walked slowly past me; their kit seemed to weigh them down in the heat.

I didn't feel the same tension about the line as had existed when I left it. Everything seemed to have settled down into a routine. The trenches named after known objectives constantly brought to my mind the cruel fighting of the previous months. As I went through a dusty brickyard it suddenly dawned on me that this was the remains of the windmill, which had cost us countless lives. As a consolation I could read as many German names as ours on the crosses standing round it. Seeing for the first time what a view the enemy had of us as we attacked on July 1st and after, I realised what spirit our men had shown in storming such a position. Every man who ventured out of a trench was a plain target. Yet I remembered how careless one became and how often I myself took a short cut over the open ground, thinking it was safe. They couldn't possibly kill all of us.

Our front line now ran off from Bembridge Post, a well-
known landmark on the beginning of the slope beyond
Pozières. Many unburied Germans were still lying in the
burnt-up grass of No Man's Land. Rifles planted in the
ground marked the bodies of others hurriedly buried. The
German front line was about 40 yards in front of ours. Its
thick line of barbed wire gave it an air of impregnability.
The infantry of both sides were quiet during the day, but
the usual shelling went on. We absolutely overlooked them
everywhere.

Our artillery had already holed most of the roofs of the
villages in the valley below. Shrapnel could be seen bursting over the reserve trenches, the fire corrected from time
to time by gunners directing from Bembridge Post. One
heard them phoning to the guns, "Over!" "Short!" and the
next shot would burst plumb at the right spot. There was
no excitement, everybody carried on in the peculiar business-like way the British have of "getting on with the job."

The Army Headquarters were still at Toutencourt and I
took up my old billet, which was too primitive for most
tastes. I soon became acquainted with the army front
again and my work dispelled the strange feeling of return
which every schoolboy experiences after a vacation. I had
now a set job; I had to go up to the line every day and
report on things I saw to General Gough. He was always
in the best of spirits, and instilled in one the wonderful
keenness that even in the worst days never left him. So
early every morning I was on the road on my motor-bike.
I got through the traffic better than I would have with a
car and wasted less time. I could also venture up much
further and, anyhow, the army staff were not keen on
losing their cars. Methodically, at the break of day, war
activities re-started. Troops and lorries all over the roads,
aeroplanes sailing towards the line, balloons going up. If
it was misty they waited, partly deflated, and lay wobbling
like monster jelly-fish on the ground.

Calling on the various brigades and making a round of
only a portion of the line meant a good five hours' walk

along the trenches. I got to know the men who clamoured for news when I came, and I never failed to tell them a good story when I had one. Some would ask when the war was going to stop, and although the question came from deep down, I could only avoid replying seriously by treating it as a joke. Tommies had their own way of telling you things—"You remember So-and-so, the guide who took you up yesterday? He didn't half cop it. There he is," pointing to a rifle stuck up in the ground with a helmet on it showing a jagged hole—"He was a good pal, he was."

The battle of the Somme had removed many of the older men and the new faces were very youthful. To come up to the Somme was a severe test for boys straight from England.

It was always night before I got back to Toutencourt and walked up the hill to my billet in the quiet, away from the traffic. Often it didn't seem right to sleep in a good bed when one had left men in the discomfort of trenches or just getting ready for an attack.

To show to what extent religious wars would still leave their mark, the two old people I lived with were known in the village as "the dirty Protestants." They were both darlings. He was a wood-cutter. Their small cottage was rather dilapidated, but opened on to a wood of tall chestnut trees, and roses climbed round its tiny windows. It had an air of peaceful seclusion which I liked. The inside was very bare indeed, but exquisitely clean. The main room was a large kitchen with an uneven floor of red brick and a large open fire, on which there was always something simmering in a pan. I had a bedroom with the simplest bed and though the sheets were rough they were spotlessly clean. The old folks were so mysterious about the room they slept in that I never attempted to look at it, but after a time I found out the source of the mysterious noise that I heard every time they opened the door. The old boy, being a poacher in his spare time, kept his ferrets under the bed. He was so afraid of being caught that he never overcame his suspicious manner.

Throughout the summer I had seen very little of them, but when autumn came I slept in more often. Always I found a good soup ready for me when I returned. With my rations they were living luxuriously. What a good "petite marmite" the old woman made—it simmered all day. If the morning was damp, the old boy, after calling me, would bring my clothes into the kitchen, and I would dress in the glow of a large faggot that soon warmed the place through.

CHAPTER XXIII

AUTUMN 1916. ATTACK ON BEAUMONT HAMEL

A STRENUOUS summer had passed; October had come. Days had shortened considerably and the weather broke suddenly with violent storms following one another swamping the country. There was an interval when two or three fine days brought us a reminiscence of summer, and then the actual depression finally closed in on us.

The battlefield had become a quagmire. Yet the war went on and every night men lined up in the mud to attack. Moving in the trenches had become a sore trial. One kept to the side, clutching at the face of the slippery parapet until, after slipping down several times, the cold water squelching through boots and puttees, one gave it up and just slushed through it. The mud had turned into a liquid paste and as one sank into it equipment of every description came to the surface; one picked it up and laid it to dry on the parapet. Corpses had also sunk into the mud. Gingerly one stepped over them.

At night rain fell heavily, and it was weird to watch the endless files of men going up and down during a relief, their heads bent under their dripping helmets, the shining mackintosh sheets over their equipment giving them odd shapes; they waded through without a murmur. It was so dark at times one could not see one's own hand in front. On windy nights at every corner one's mackintosh flapped like a jib. Sometimes the body of a man carried on a stretcher would loom up lit by gun-flashes, the bearers struggling with the mud for every step. A shell bursting near them made them duck, as we all did, and the weight of their load would force them to their knees. Yet in spite of these conditions, it was remarkable how rarely the good humour of the men forsook them. Their lurid descriptions

of what they went through at times were a source of
laughter for teller and listener.

Our line south of the Ancre now ran in front of Grandcourt. After many struggles the whole of Regina Trench
well down in the valley was in our hands. It was desirable
to bring up the line north of the river level with these
positions, and with this intention we were preparing for
an attack on Beaumont Hamel. It was the last offensive
on an important scale that could be contemplated before
next spring. It couldn't be delayed, we had to strike before the weather got worse. As it was, the weather hardly
gave us a chance—it went on pouring. Day after day we
bombarded the German positions, hoping for a dry day to
launch our attack.

At last frost set in for a short spell and on November
13th, 1916, the Fifth Army stormed Serre and Beaumont
Hamel.

It was foggy and drizzling when early that morning I
walked down the Mailly-Maillet road and over 5th Avenue
to get in touch with our troops in Beaumont Hamel, which
was supposed to be in our hands. I had a bad throat and
felt depressed as I slid along the thawing ground. The
mist seemed to soften the boom of guns and rattle of
machine-guns. A number of German prisoners with an
escort of Highlanders caked in mud appeared on the road.
All they could tell me was that parts only of Beaumont
Hamel were in our hands.

I crossed over our old front line, now deserted except
for the dead. Everyone had gone forward. A party of
stretcher-bearers went past with sallow-looking casualties.
It was all very depressing. On both sides of the Beaumont
Hamel road, cutting through No Man's Land, ran a deep
ditch fringed with willow trees, every branch hanging
loose, snapped by bullets, and the bark ripped off in
ribbons. The rain dripped off these trees on to a
"brochette" of dead Highlanders, caught as they bunched
together by their machine-guns.

After picking my way through belts of German wire, I

heard the bombing and firing more distinctly, especially from the left, where at times it seemed very near. I had so far found no one to tell me anything. As I held my map to locate our troops, my fingers trembled with the vibration caused by the firing of the big guns. I had never felt so lonely before on an errand into a battle; everything was vague and uncertain.

At last I came upon a company in reserve. I was told that we were only partly into Beaumont Hamel, and that we were held up in front of Serre. Of the right they could tell me nothing.

So I made towards Y Ravine through destroyed barbed wire over caved-in trenches, meeting here and there a wounded man hobbling back. The visibility couldn't have been worse. I reached a steep bank that rose before me and ascended to the top, from which I could barely see the bottom or the opposite side. I heard bombs exploding all along this blurred crevasse, and then from the rock some exuberant men loaded with loot and smoking German cigars emerged from a dug-out. They were "mopping up," they said, adding: "The bastards are still all over the place in between our troops." At another dug-out a group of German prisoners sat waiting in charge of one man. The rest of the escort had gone down below to inspect a tunnel that communicated with another big dug-out. I stepped down into the darkness.

The combined odours of dampness and dead bodies created a smell which only those who have experienced it can believe. Oddly enough, our own dug-outs somehow never smelt in the same way. My feet struck some limp forms as I went along a corridor. I flashed my torch on dead Germans stretched out over each other. Shouts of "Bill" and "Jock" came from a party of men inside a small room. As they had put on the helmets of their captives it was difficult at first to see which was which. We all went up together again, and when the prisoners saw our kilties wearing their helmets they couldn't suppress a laugh. Good-humouredly a few more bombs were thrown down the passage to make sure that the work was well done, and the whole party drifted off away from the battle.

A great deal of musketry fire came then from the right, some distance away, where I thought the Naval Division might be. I went on to find out how far they had reached. The visibility grew worse. At one time, enveloped in fog drifting over the ground, I was just able to see the dead lying within a few yards of me.

The crackle of spasmodic rifle-fire would break out in the most unexpected places, spread, and then die down. There were moments when the fighting was going on all round me. After wandering about for a long time I saw a party of worn-out Tommies from the Naval Division appearing through the fog. They had no idea where they were. I stretched out my map, and together we located as near as possible our position in front of Station Road between Beaucourt and Beaumont Hamel. Heavy firing continually came from there, as well as from Beaucourt village, lying lost in the fog about 1,000 yards away. It was evident that enemy troops and ours had got mixed up in this fog.

Taking these men with me, I went on in the hope of striking a certain trench by the village cemetery. Bullets whining by made us spread out. At last in a big quarry we found a section of infantry in support, from whom I received some definite information about the situation. It seemed that a brigade was held up by Station Road. The enemy was between them and parties that had gone on, so they were now trying to work their way round the Germans by the right to relieve the troops that were cut off. They had sent the information to their brigade and had asked for artillery support, which so far was not forthcoming. As I didn't know how to get to the Naval Division, I thought the wisest thing was to retrace my steps and get on their trail from their jumping-off place.

I wandered about a good deal before I found the old German front line, but, once I did, I followed in their wake, as I recognised their dead. Firing still persisted from the road I had just left, and from Beaucourt village rose the row of a severe scrap. Some odd shells were falling, aimed at nothing in particular; it was very obvious that neither artillery dared fire, not knowing where their infantry was.

Tired out, I sat down and took my lunch out of my haversack when my friend, Captain Nelson, who was now Intelligence Officer to the Corps, walked into me. He looked exhausted and dishevelled in contrast with the two carrier-pigeons he had in a basket, whose eyes glittered with eagerness. He asked me what the devil I was doing there all by myself, and if I knew what was happening; he himself couldn't understand the situation at all. He had seen some sections of a brigade of the Naval Division held up by Beaucourt, but on his way back he had been constantly fired at by scattered groups of Germans. It seemed useless going on into the fog and confusion as we had both been doing. We tried in vain to find Brigade Headquarters, and then made up our minds to walk back to Divisional Headquarters, where perhaps they would have news. When we arrived there we heard that a carrier-pigeon had happily come in with a message from a Naval Brigade at Beaucourt, and reinforcements had been ordered to fight their way to them. This pigeon must have been released by one of Nelson's men. However, the situation was still very obscure. In front of Serre we were back in our front line, but Beaumont Hamel was practically in our hands.

As we walked back to Corps Headquarters we both felt very depressed. The bursts of bombs from "mopping-up" parties could be heard, together with the desultory firing of isolated groups. The firing from our guns sounded rather hopeless. All my miserable wanderings hadn't been of any use to anyone, except perhaps the sympathy I had brought to a poor devil of a German whom I had found mortally wounded.

Yet, surprisingly, from all accounts the day had been a great success. We had taken over 5,000 prisoners and even guns, and the staff, as a whole, seemed quite pleased. . . .

The advance was followed up during the next few days.

We pushed on beyond Beaumont Hamel and Grandcourt, and this last progress brought the Somme offensive to a close. Since July we had gained a great deal of ground and taken many guns, but the flower of British manhood lay beneath the sodden earth.

PART III

1917

*Winter on the Somme—Summer at Ypres—
Passchendæle, and the return to
the Somme*

CHAPTER XXIV

SOMME. THE COLD SPELL. WINTER 1917.
FLANDERS—PASSCHENDAELE.

WE dug ourselves in for the winter and made things
as comfortable as the rain would permit. Fortunately,
we had inherited the enemy's deep and large dug-outs,
which, in spite of their foul smell, were a great asset to
the troops.

During those winter months my billet at Toutencourt
was a great comfort. I used to long for the evenings by
the fire and my quiet browse over *The Times*. The wind
always rose at sunset and whistled round the house. When
my old wood-cutter came in from his day's chopping in the
forest the leaves whirled round him as he opened the door.
He would hang his hatchet on a nail and make for his chair
by the fire, where he would remain for hours staring into
the flames. Sometimes he would burst out with questions
about the day's activity, and ask about the conditions in the
line. His concern was always for the comfort of the troops,
and he would watch the weather and comment upon its
probable effect upon the men. "Anyhow, to-day," he would
say, "it will be dry for them." He had three sons at the war,
but he seldom referred to them. The letters that came from
them had to be handed to his wife, who, alone of the two,
could read. If she was in a bad mood she would read them
to herself, quietly torturing him. But he seldom showed
impatience, and would wait until she had quite finished
before he even ventured a question. If she was in a good
temper, not only the precious letters, but even the news-
papers would be read to him by the old lady through a
pair of steel-rimmed spectacles, awkwardly balanced on the
tip of her nose. "It's always the same," the old boy would
say, "we are always winning, and still the war goes on."

When the soup was served, we sat round a clean, bare

table. The wood-cutter carved the bread with great respect. He ate quickly without uttering a word, eager to get back to his place by the fire, which he kept on poking and arranging. He hated his wife to interfere with that; it was his affair, as he gathered the wood. He would point out the different kinds of wood burning in the fire, and their various properties, but he harked back always to what he described as the "catastrophe" of the war. Trying perhaps to find some justification at least for us, he would talk sometimes, but without conviction, of the enemy's vices. In his heart he hated nobody.

He deeply resented seeing or hearing of British soldiers undergoing field punishment. He became livid at the idea of their being tied to the wheel. "We are not in the Middle Ages," he would say. He admired President Wilson because he said: "He was the only man who had the sense to talk of Peace."

So the time would pass till 8 o'clock, and as that hour approached he would turn every minute or two to look at the clock. When the first chime struck he would straighten his old back, reach for the candle on the high mantelshelf and disappear, saying: "This is the best moment of the day."

His wife never joined in our talks; she was always preoccupied and bustled about, the clatter of her clogs making a comfortable accompaniment to our conversation. One stormy evening after her man had gone to bed, she sat opposite me at the fire darning her thin stockings. The flames lit up her old face, and were the only light she would have for her work. The bare twigs of the roses rattled against the windows and the trees beyond groaned and creaked. After a long silence she said: "Sometimes when it blows like that, I feel uneasy . . . j'ai presque peur . . . To-night one would think that the bon Dieu wants to end everything." She brought her chair round near mine as though she must be within physical reach of another human being, and after a deep sigh she looked at me and said: "You are very quiet to-night, Monsieur. Often you look as though you thought too much. You must not do that. Thoughts can go too far."

Often I made drawings of them both; their perfect immobility by the fire made them ideal sitters.

The old man's day of rest was Sunday. He would get up early and pull from under his bed the box in which he kept his ferrets. Well muffled up and with one tell-tale hand in his pocket, he would start out with obvious satisfaction in his forbidden but fascinating occupation. He was a poacher to the very core. When the time came for his return, his wife would wait impatiently for him at the window; there was always a chance of his being caught. When he was safely back in the house, he first assured himself that he had not been followed, and then pulled out the rabbit by its ears and handed it over with great pride to be cooked. She had the pan ready, and the delicious smell of cooking butter, onions and fresh herbs spread through the house. The dissection of the little victim of these nefarious activities was the affair of a moment, and the old man's eyes glistened with pleasurable anticipation as it was dropped into the pan.

A son came on leave from the front. He looked awkward about the house, like a man who has lost touch. I don't know where they put him to sleep. On that Sunday, the wood-cutter dressed up in his best to accompany his son to the village. He was made to sit in a chair, while his wife struggled to harness his poor neck into the unaccustomed collar and stud. And then the two set off, slightly embarrassed, the old man pathetically stiff in his uncomfortable clothes. But his return was even more pathetic; his eyes were watery and there was a false gaiety both in his face and walk. He sneaked into bed before his wife saw him to try to conceal the all too obvious effects of this unusual Sunday "walk."

One day General Malcolm came to tea. The *bûcheron* sat and watched while he spoke a language he did not understand. When the General had gone, I said to him: "Eh bien, c'est un Général, vous savez." "Ah," he replied,

"Ca, peut-être: but he also has goodness written all over his face." On another occasion a light-hearted French southerner came to see me. He was a chauffeur from the French G.H.Q., dressed elegantly in light blue like a General. In the few minutes he was there he talked so much that his departure was a relief. As the door closed behind him my wood-cutter said: "He ought to have been in a fair, to pull teeth out, like a charlatan."

He told me that he had once been to a theatre, the only time in his life. "I shall never forget the lovely words I heard," he said.

As I put on my kit every morning, preparatory to starting for the line, he would watch me from the corner of his eye. He hated to see me go. Once they were both asleep when I left, and I peeped into their room to say good-bye. They lay in bed exactly like the marble statues of an ancient knight and his lady on a church tomb, only they had white cotton night-caps on their heads!

I would always try to get a message through to them if I couldn't get back at night. During a certain cold spell I stayed away three weeks. The old lady wrote to me in a hand so shaky and a spelling so very much her own that the letter was difficult to read. The old man had put a cross at the bottom. They were darlings, that old couple.

After a time I found it less tiring to live with the brigades in the line than to go up every day. General Higginson's brigade, with whom I stayed for a long period, had comfortable quarters cut into the bank on Nab Road not far from the ruins of Mouquet Farm. Somehow I grew to like the desolation of the surroundings, and I became very much attached to the brigade staff and the battalions holding the front. I slept in a cubicle where I kept my clothes, and had an oil-stove going all the time, as the dampness filtered through the earth and covered everything with mildew.

One day was very much like another at that time. I came in from the line in the evening and changed my clothes. Dinner was always a relaxation, and was generally a lively affair. We discussed everything. There were many alert minds on this staff, and all callings and professions were represented. Our Brigade Major was a meticulous person with a brilliant University record. He always kept the conversation alive. He wore an eyeglass and had un-impeachable manners. Once on a cold night we found him wandering about lost in our wire. He apologised and thanked us for finding him, like a polite stranger who had lost his way in Piccadilly Circus. The Staff Captain was a future padre, very young, able and brave. Our Signal Officer was a Civil Engineer.

All had their original point of view, and as an artist I had mine. They looked to me to keep them amused, and I did my best. They all coped with their work with the calmness inspired by their able and delightful Brigadier. All these civilians had now become most efficient staff officers.

At 11 o'clock at night, if we hadn't to go up to the line again, we turned in and soon fell into a sound sleep. Some-times the shelling would waken us. One's sense of percep-tion was very clear at night, and I could diagnose by the sound exactly what was happening. It was either the barrage for a raid, or a bombardment on a neighbouring division, or passing shells which exploded a few seconds later in some part of the back area. One turned over and slept again with a sense of comparative security and com-fort. If the shelling persisted and grew into a hurricane bombardment, the battalion phones got going at once. We attended to urgent calls in our night attire; the reserve battalion would be ordered to stand by; batteries were asked to put down a counter-barrage; the division had to be informed. In a moment the active business of war was set in motion, every department tackling its own job. Some of us would dress and go out into the night to find out what was happening—as often as not nothing was happen-ing. Probably a company had opened fire, the company alongside it had done the same, and so it spread along the line till the enemy started his reprisals. The German staff had reacted in the same way as ours, and after such an alarm an unfortunate officer on night duty at headquarters would come in grousing loudly for having been disturbed for nothing.

Days went by; the line was quiet. I made panorama sketches from all our positions. We were tired of the persistent rain.

One night, however, it cleared, and as I walked up the slope away from Regina Trench the moon shone straight into the communication-trench and lit up my path; clouds were racing from the north across a clear sky. I stepped briskly along humming the gramophone tune I had heard in the company dug-out from which I had just come. As I passed Zollern Redoubt I looked over the top and saw through the barbed wire the valley below glinting with light. Only an occasional explosion disturbed the lovely night. By Mouquet Farm convoys of lorries were unloading supplies. Near Brigade Headquarters a battalion had halted for a rest, before resuming their way up to the slope where they entered the communication-trenches. But for a small light always burning in the office, all was dark inside headquarters. I felt a delicious sense of comfort as I rolled into my Jaeger blanket, and the wire mattress gave pleasantly under me with a friendly creak. The noise of the rats scampering across the corridor became fainter and fainter, and I heard only vaguely the heavy steps of a runner coming in with a message, while the phone-buzzer sounded like Chinese music as I dozed off.

My next conscious sensation was a hot mug of tea placed in my hands by my batman in the morning. Sitting up in my bunk, I felt an icy draught on my back. From the scraping noise of shovels on the ground outside, I could tell that the earth was hard with frost. A grey and desolate view met my eyes when I looked out of the dug-out. It was cold; the men were blowing on their fingers and stamping on the ground.

Thiepval that morning looked sad and derelict. Pozières seemed silenced by a warning. The few shells that were coming over crashed sharply far back behind the lines. As the men coming from the line in the valley on the other side of the ridge appeared on the sky-line one could see them muffled up in greatcoats.

Towards evening snowflakes like feathers began whirling round our faces and settled on the frozen ground. The fall at first seemed hesitant, but it increased quickly and developed into a blizzard that blurred the landscape with a cinematic motion. Aeroplanes were cutting through the drift like birds seeking the shelter of the woods, hurrying to their aerodromes and flying dangerously low. A battalion was marching up the road, the heads of the men all turned against the blizzard. They were already so snow-covered that they looked like a white tape and left a brown trail of footmarks on the ground. Winter had come.

After two days of bitter winds the sun came out, the sky was green and cloudless, and purple shadows stretched on the sparkling snow. Everything had changed, even the aspect of the men who now wore woollen flaps, sheepskins and sandbags on their feet to prevent their slipping on the duckboards. Braziers were put into all the trenches.

The parapets sheltered us from the sharp wind, but the dug-outs were almost unbearable with the stifling fumes of the braziers. I preferred to keep out of them and to walk about in the brisk air. The views from certain places had become really beautiful; in the direction of the River Ancre a white panorama unrolled towards a distant hill. Only when our artillery was firing could the position of the enemy trenches be detected; the shells made brown patches that showed approximately where they lay. At times the small black figures of German parties could be seen moving openly about in the distance; this would be immediately reported by telephone to the artillery, and batteries would get to work scattering the little groups like frightened rabbits.

I couldn't make sketches, for my brush froze as I laid it on the paper. For days the temperature kept at 18 and 20

degrees below freezing-point. The ground was too hard for
digging, and the men had little to do except to try to keep
warm, huddled round a glowing brazier and waiting for
their soup.

A certain animation always started at night; working-
parties, strung out in long files, carried queer-shaped loads
along the duckboards leading to the line. They reminded
me of Chinese silhouettes in a Hiroshige print.

There were company dug-outs in the valley below
Regina Trench; coming out of one of these into the fresh
air you felt dazed and choked with the heat-fumes. We
held a line of posts 400 yards beyond the front line; the
enemy did the same. There was no means of communicat-
ing with our outposts during the day-time; they could only
be approached at night. I often went with the Intelligence
officer of the brigade or joined a patrol on its round
sometimes an exciting experience. We always started when
night had really settled down, and looked for the footmarks that led to the first post lost in the haze. The snow
crunched under our feet, as in single file we searched for
the helmet-tops protruding somewhere out of the ground.
The powdery snow whirling off the frozen surface chilled
our hands and faces. If the moon shone behind us our
long shadows would crawl in front of us like guides. When
we had crept up to the post a challenge would ring out,
and we gave the counter-sign. The four men in the hole
had stood all day in dreary vigil hardly able to move. Nor
until they were relieved would they get anything hot to
drink. It was wonderful how they stood that cold
monotony, with nothing to do but to watch a few
suspicious black patches here and there in front of them.
They were always glad to see us, although they hardly
spoke more than to answer our questions. Sometimes they
would ask if the relieving party was on the way.

On to the next post we would go roaming about again in
the white space, and watched not only by a full-orbed
moon, but also probably by the German patrols going the
round of their own posts; they were at times difficult to

detect when they wore long white coats. If we were sniped at, we lay down and waited or, crept along the ground to the safety of the next post. The last of them was in "Stump Road." There was nothing more weird on the whole of the front than this road. It wound along a deep hollow between two banks hedged with the stumps of trees torn into the queerest shapes. The remains of old German gunpits burrowed into the banks. The surface of the road was broken by rocks and big holes hardened and sharpened by frost. As we moved about this sinister valley we often felt unnerved and crept along furtively, hiding behind the stumps, peering at the smallest details of the mysterious gully and oppressed by a strangely ominous silence. Our imagination would play us strange tricks; suddenly shadows would change places, giving an uncanny sense of movement to immobile objects. As often as not, however, we would detect distinctly other forms than our own moving up from the blackness of the road and lurking among the tree-stumps further on; as they vanished down the bank the enemy's steel helmets would be recognised. We would stick behind the trees, stiff with fright and cold, and with revolvers cocked, our only comfort being that we had probably alarmed the enemy as much as he frightened us.

The posts in Stump Road were even more difficult to find than others; we had to grope our way right up to them before they became visible. Once we had a fortunate escape. As we were walking up we were followed, without knowing it, by another of our patrols, who had seen a party of Germans working their way from tree to tree trying to surround us. Only when our protecting patrol suddenly opened fire did we realise what had happened. We had heard and seen nothing. The enemy, so we learned, had been after us for some time, but little knew that they themselves were being watched in their turn.

Such was life at night in Stump Road, where the cracking of a shot, the bursting of a shell or the movement of a shadow was more unnerving than anywhere else.

There was, however, a certain type of man who fortunately felt nothing. Once we stood motionless, our hearts beating, when two men appeared as if by magic right in the middle of the road and apparently from the German side. To our surprise we heard them engaged in the broadest Cockney conversation, as they dragged their blanket along the ground. We hailed them in a hoarse whisper. They did not show any fright or surprise as they walked up to us, and were cursed for going about unarmed. What the hell were they doing? Simply shifting . . . they had found a better spot! "Don't you know that the Germans keep patrolling this road?" we asked them. "Can't we see the bastards moving about all night like rats," they replied. Such was the nerve of some of our warriors, especially when they were full of rum, as, judging by their breath, they were that night.

On another occasion I came on a lonely sentry left in a dreary spot. I asked him if he was all right, and in a queer dialect, pointing to his Lewis gun, he said: "Am I not as good as ten men with this here musket?"

I often wondered what they were thinking about when I saw their pensive faces silhouetted in the moonlight gazing into the night.

When a north wind blew and cut our faces, or when the snow was falling, we missed the foot-tracks showing the way to the outposts. This meant nerve-racking wandering, for it was easy to get lost. We were squatting in a shell-hole on one such night trying to get our bearings when four Germans on patrol suddenly emerged through the blizzard. They were bent forward, for they were slipping about and didn't see us, though they were making straight for our hole. They passed within a few yards of us and disappeared like a vision into the grey as they had come, swearing at the weather in their deep guttural tongue. We had waited breathless, uncertain until they were well out of sight and hearing whether to shoot or not.

After a night spent in such fashion, the return to Brigade Headquarters in the early dawn was often the worst part, for we were tired and there was a long way to walk. We had to call at Battalion Headquarters and, limbs numb with cold, we would feel our way down the dark stairs and along the passage to the stuffy, candle-lit room. Officers snored in their bunks; without waking them we would pour ourselves out a drink, leave a note, and start again up those innumerable stairs, bidding the silent sentry a good night. Then we had the unending communication-trenches to climb as far up as Stuff and Zollern Redoubts on very slippery duckboards. The frost had made the parapets as hard as cement. The dead of both sides still lay in frozen pools at the bottom of trenches. Some of them seemed to watch us as we slid over the cracking ice, others formed a solid block with the trench. Occasionally a signal-wire was supported by a frozen hand or twisted round a limb; a use could be found even for a corpse in the business of war.

But for an odd whizz-bang which stirred the frozen snow and scraped up the brown earth, the line was relatively quiet. The beauty of those clear moonlight nights gripped me. Colours were almost as bright as in day-time. The moon seemed to watch placidly all this white waste, like the silent sentries whose helmets could be seen above the trench. I loved my wanderings under the stars. I liked being with all these men dumbly enduring the hardships of cold and war, while civilians grumbled at their petty inconveniences and found the papers dull because armies didn't move and the western front was quiet.

Boom Ravine was another odd place. It lay in front of Petit Mireaumont at the bottom of a long sharp slope that always struck me as an ideal place for ski-ing. Death Valley, it was called, and it lived up to its name in a mysterious way, for although it didn't look a dangerous place, death lurked in it everywhere. The enemy could fire from the high ground by Grandcourt and catch our working parties as they went up and down, so no one loitered there; the silent crosses dotted about were a warning to which everybody paid attention. A German officer lay there for a long

P

time on a broken stretcher, frozen in death. The moon and
stars shining straight on him lent him the quiet dignity of
a corpse lying in state. He remained there all through the
cold spell.

Boom Ravine was a bit of an old quarried road about
half a mile long just off the Mireaumont Road. I never
knew what it was really like, for I only saw it at night, and
the weird appearance of its shape and shadows was probably the distortion of my imagination. The enemy occupied half of it. We had posts along it, and one of our
companies occupied a deep dug-out in a smashed-up old
barn. The enemy constantly attempted to raid us out of
it, and consequently the men's nerves were always on edge.
Some of the posts were perched up on the rocky banks,
while others were hidden down in the gully; when flares
went up the whole place rose at once from pitch darkness
into quivering silver light; you could then see our watchers
like sailors in a crow's nest, the muzzle of their Lewis guns
facing the enemy.

In the old barn everybody moved about knocking their
rifles against the ground, challenging each other in the
dark corners where the moonlight could not penetrate.
We had a sentry at each entrance—one of them facing the
German side; he stood for the most part hidden behind the
old beams, his bayonet glinting in the dark. Above him
rose the long sticks of rockets covered in frozen sacking
that hung like the pennant of an Oriental chief. If the
sentry moved from his hiding-place before the glare of
Verey lights had completely died down, rifle-shots would
inevitably ring out and bullets would thump into the barn.
Two bodies already lay there, his predecessors at the post.

I couldn't possibly make a sketch of the ravine in the day-
time, so I took my chance on a bright night. Accompanied
by a Tommy, I progressed unnoticed, scraping along with
my back to the rocks. We were passing the silent watchers
of our No. 1 post when my guide whispered to them in
his gruff voice: "It's all right, it's a bloke that wants to
do a drawing!" At once we were sniped at from the other

side. The post above us retaliated with a Lewis gun; I
had to shout to them to stop, and the gully once more
plunged into silence. We went on slowly, following the
diabolical shapes of our shadows as we twisted and turned
round the face of the quarry. At last we were within a
yard of a single line of wire that separated us from the
German side. My guide, breathing heavily like an engine,
had become a perfect nuisance. I unfolded my small
board and started a charcoal drawing leaning against a
sharp-edged rock—everything before me was grey and
vague. Suddenly a shot rang out from the other bank,
followed by a groan at my side; my companion had a
bullet in his foot.

Flares had all at once soared up—S O S's were being
sent by both sides, and the quarry shone like quicksilver.
I laid my face to the ground, imagining I was making myself invisible by shutting my eyes to the brightness. In
answer to the artillery call a shell came with a swish and
burst in the ravine, quickly followed by others—our guns
immediately retaliated; shells were now landing in twos
and fours, coming over in coveys, shaking the rocks and
filling the gully with thick smoke—it really saved us.

I hurried my limping guide back to the barn; unfortunately one of my sandbagged feet caught on a nail in a
piece of wood, and I fell flat with my equipment entangled
over my head. It was an uncomfortable moment; shells
were boring through the ravine like express trains through
a tunnel. I finally managed to free myself, and we stag-
gered into the barn. Everybody was moving to his fighting station, expecting a raid. "Halt! who goes there?"
"Your Brigadier," answered General Higginson, who was
inspecting his line. I shall always remember Boom Ravine
at 3 o'clock in the morning!

CHAPTER XXV

ONE night in February, as the Naval Division were forcing their way along the valley of the Ancre, our brigade participated in the attack by storming a small trench called Folly Trench, which jutted out from the main German line towards our post, and was supposed to be thinly held. Our attack was therefore in the form of a glorified raid with a short-gun barrage, just like the whiff of ether to a patient before a minor operation. It was perhaps the coldest night of the winter. At the prescribed time the barrage fell like a starter's flag. Shells crashed for a few minutes, and the men went to their fate, the moon shining on them like searchlights at a tattoo.

I had followed the attack walking behind the waves with the Intelligence officer. Somehow in the smoke from the retaliating barrage and the confusion, we overran the captured trench and found ourselves amongst the shell-holes of No Man's Land within a few yards of the German barbed wire in front of Grandcourt trench, their main defence. The enemy at the time was raking the open with machine-guns, putting an end to the wanderings of a few of our men who, like spectral figures, still staggered between shell-bursts, lost as we had been ourselves.

One of these whom we had hailed ran to us and flung himself into our hole trembling and petrified; it was his first attack. We had to wait where we were. I could see the bodies of some of our men lying on the frozen snow, their rigidity intensified by the cold, their uniforms, torn to rags by shrapnel, that made the khaki cloth look poor and shoddy.

By good fortune we were near a fallen aeroplane, which lay like a lame bird in No Man's Land. We were able to crawl into the shelter of its frozen snow-coated wings and then under a screen of smoke rush into Folly Trench. As we walked along the trench which the men were busy consolidating, I passed a young officer in charge of a section who was so nervy and incompetent that the sergeant-major had calmly taken over charge. It was pathetic to see the helplessness of this young man, while the few German prisoners who were there looked on.

As we had to find touch with the Naval Division somewhere in the ravine along the river-bank of the Ancre, the Intelligence officer and I struck along a very bare exposed slope, punctuated in places by enemy posts. Walking with our feet sandbagged, we gripped our revolvers in our frozen hands and stared suspiciously at every object on our way, giving a wide berth to the many apparently abandoned gun-pits which lay in our path. Several times we heard the whistle of a bullet carefully aimed by a sniper who could see us as well as if it were broad daylight. We learned afterwards from the Naval Division that those pits were almost without exception occupied by the enemy.

We had finished our round. The attack was over. The enemy retaliation had ceased. It was early morning; time to return to Brigade Headquarters. We walked in the wake of relieved companies hobbling along in the open like convalescents who are not sure of their legs, the result of being in the trenches for days without exercise. It was a long and stiff climb, but as soon as the tired men reached the brow of the hill and looked down towards Mouquet Farm in the wind-swept valley, they were cheered when they saw what might have been the wooden shack of a Canadian rancher in the prairie. Men coming from or going to the line got there some warmth, and a cup of tea or cocoa. How comforting was the burning mug as the heat worked through the mittens and how cold became the steam as it froze on your face. There were always men standing around the hut in the snow with all their equipment and loads, looking like Arctic explorers. The helpless tanks lying on their sides near-by might have been

walruses on ice-floes, with their dripping icicles the shape
of enormous tusks. In an old abandoned gun-pit the man
in charge of the gas-alarm had made his home. He was
always to be seen toasting large pieces of bread at his
brazier on the end of a bayonet. His many layers of cloth-
ing increased his size, and he overflowed on each side of
whatever he sat on. His woollen bonnet was pulled well
down over his eyes and rested on his weather-beaten nose;
his ragged moustache was adorned with pearls from his
freezing breath. He moved about his shed like a sea-lion.
All he had to do was to sound the alarm by striking a
shell-case suspended on a string. I once made a drawing
of him, but he kept asking me to do another one: "A
proper one, mind," which he could send to his missus.
He was rather a pet. One day I found his gun-pit shattered by a shell—and a few yards beyond a new cross had
sprung up.

The cold could not continue indefinitely. The temperature rose one day and one's feet sank into snow, now slowly
turning yellow. Soon footmarks showed up brown on the
wet earth underneath. Gradually everything that had
been hidden for over six weeks became visible again.
Trenches reappeared with their thick belts of wire, red
with rust—the whole panorama assumed its former aspect,
until there remained only small sheltered patches of dirty
snow, which the first rain would wash away. The change
was all to the bad—the ground became slushy—within a
few days we were sprawling about in the mud again.

.   .   .   .   .   .

Throughout February, 1917, our aeroplanes detected
signs of the enemy's preparation for a general retirement
in front of the Fifth British Army and the French further
south. They had also traced the building of a new system
of defence lines stretching for about seventy miles from
Arras down to Soissons, which was to become famous later
as the Hindenburg line. All this activity excited suspicion. It soon became obvious that the enemy con-

templated the evacuation of the salient formed by their
present line. To hide their design from us the enemy increased their activity, especially at night when they lit the
line continuously with their flares and kept up a constant
machine-gun and rifle fire. One night one of our patrols
succeeded in getting through the German front line and
boldly wandered about beyond it for a considerable time
without finding a trace of occupation. This confirmed all
our conjectures.

The Army Commander who had decided on a general
forward movement to probe the situation, allotted me to
a battalion that was to take part in the attack, and whose
first objective was a trench called Ten-Tree Alley. We
were, if possible, to continue to advance, occupy the high
ground beyond—take the village of Serre in our stride, and
if no serious opposition were encountered push on to
Puisieux, a village on the way to Bapaume. Both the
right and left divisions were to attack simultaneously.

The ground over which the attack was to be made was
a waterlogged area of shell-holes as near to each other as
the holes of a tapestry canvas. It had been incessantly
shelled by both sides since October, 1914. Looking at an
aerial photograph, one would have wondered how troops
could move at all in such a pitted morass, the only prominent features of which were a few ruins of Serre on the
left, and on the right the dozen tall branchless stumps of
Pendant Copse. Since the battle of Beaumont Hamel,
when the village had passed into our hands, we occupied
the enemy's old defence line which we had shot and
blasted to pieces prior to our occupation, leaving little
comfort for our troops to live in. Incessant rain had com-
pleted the destruction. Communication-trenches could
not be made, as the water draining from the shell-holes
turned them into streams. We had to move about exposed
on slippery duckboards laid over the old trenches and
shell-holes, many of which were five or six feet deep, and
if one slipped in one got a muddy ducking up to the neck.

It was in this morass that the battalions had to deploy

at night to get ready for the advance. My battalion was
to form up in three waves, supplied by three companies,
and two platoons were to follow behind in reserve. Strong
patrols were to precede the waves immediately after the
barrage.

Heavy-headed by the smell and smoke of our subterranean shelter, I woke to see the Colonel getting ready,
his runner standing by loaded with kit. I always remember the moment when officers, ready to leave their
dug-outs for an attack, gazed wistfully round their stuffy
little home as if it were the dearest place on earth.
Already the bunks had been cleared by the servants;
valises were being sent back with the baggage, and there
only remained at the table the leavings of a meal.

Water was oozing from the sides of the long gallery
which led up to the muddy steps from which we plunged,
dazed, into the darkest night ever known. Above the noise
of few but regular explosions rose the voices of N.C.O.s
cursing the men to come on, as haltingly they felt their
way along the duck-boards. We had to stand and wait
until we had become accustomed to the darkness, the
flickering gun-flashes lighting with a glitter the ripples
made by the mud falling off our boots into the water-
filled shell-holes. All was darkness in front.

Holding a torch very low, we picked our slippery way
along the duck-boards. Suddenly we all stopped. Two
men in front had fallen into the muddy water and were
being hauled out. At a snail's pace the march was resumed, everyone trying to be even more careful of his
foothold.

At last we came to the rendezvous and waited, as
arranged, for the adjutant who was superintending the
forming of the waves. A rising mist was enveloping us
with gripping melancholy. The attack had to be directed
by compass; each company took its bearings on definite
objectives, which only with God's help could they hope
ever to find. The second-in-command having returned to
say that everything was ready, I went forward with him

to await the five-minutes' bombardment that was to precede a barrage which no human being in that mud could
have followed up. A few rockets were making holes of
whitish light in the clinging mist in the near distance.

It was now exactly 5.30 a.m.—we were very tired. As
the barrage crept up the rising ground in front, a slow
movement from the forward men launched the rest into
the fog. Picking our way in the dark, we stumbled on and
eventually slid down a steep greasy bank, landing, to our
great relief and surprise, in Ten-Tree Alley itself, the object
of our attack. The trench was battered—amongst dirty
straw like a midden, British ground-sheets and used
rockets, sprawled the corpses of a few Germans. Everything showed signs of recent occupation, but, strangely
enough, we had made no prisoners and the front waves
had gone on. One enthusiast picked up an empty Verey
light pistol as a souvenir. We advanced again, wondering
if we were marching into a trap. The fog grew thicker;
the cold and damp increased.

We were now directed entirely by compass, the visibility
being about fifteen or twenty yards, sometimes less. The
men kept very quiet; the ground rose gently and was
strewn everywhere with German equipment; there was
no sound of shooting. We gazed curiously at another dead
German with arms spread out like wings as though he had
dropped from a height as we slowly passed by.

Word was received from the patrol in front that there
was no opposition to their advance, so we trudged forward. Now and again I got a glimpse of men in the first
wave, apprehensively clustered together; the voice of the
second-in-command was constantly heard bawling at them
to spread out—they separated reluctantly as though their
safety depended on physical contact with each other.

A report came through that we were in touch with the
battalion on the right—that was something. Nothing
stirred before us as we went on. Not a shot had been
fired. Suddenly we came on the first wave halted in an
abandoned trench. Which was it?—no one could locate

it. There was an acute divergence of opinion between
company commanders as to our direction. We stared at
the indicator pointing north, but whichever way we
looked we saw no landmark. As we bent intently over
our outspread maps the first shot whizzed past.

Men were sent off to the left to find contact with the
Manchesters, who should have been walking alongside us,
elbowing on Serre. We had to wait until they came back.
We had then advanced about 600 yards.

The waves had then to be re-formed, as the men had
again grouped together; the first wave led the way. We
were steering north-north-east towards a trench. A slight
wind made local holes in the fog, and groups of men
appeared before us, vague and individually indistinguish-
able, mere patches of khaki on a yellow background.

As an enemy machine-gun opened fire and bullets span
round us fired from the right, everybody crawled like rats
into shell-holes, and our bayonets faced all sides. Although
we couldn't have been seen coming up, already four men
were hit. The advance was resumed. Feet dragged through
the slush and sank at every step. A known shirker, covered
in mud, his puttees all undone, persisted in hanging behind, although several times the second-in-command had
cursed him and threatened him with his revolver, which
hadn't increased his enthusiasm. I suggested that he
should be sent back, as he was setting a bad example to the
other men. So with a parting kick in the direction of the
starting-line the dejected figure disappeared into the fog.
Little did we know that he would walk straight into the
arms of the enemy, who were behind us all the time.

A company of men appeared out of the fog walking
across our line. Who were they? The Manchesters! If
their direction was right, ours was wrong. As they were
not in touch with anyone, we made them spread out and
extend our line, and we all started forward again, forming
a line heading north. We could see no one but the men
in our immediate vicinity. Some were expressing in
chosen terms their opinion of the uncertainty of the direc-

tion as well as the condition of the ground. I seemed to recognise some of our freshly made footmarks, which inclined me to believe that we were going round in circles. Some German shrapnel had so far only torn the fog above our heads, and we had taken little notice until some of the soldiers lay groaning in the mud and shouts for stretcher-bearers went up. By then our barrage was rolling away well beyond us, probably where we were expected to have been at the time. Again we came on a new deserted German trench. This was Pendant Trench. As no one was in it, we began to wonder if the first waves had missed it. No word had come from them. We passed an old German gun position completely smashed up by our guns, where near-by three dead Germans lay facing their line, probably hit as they were running back. To the belt of one of them was attached a new water-bottle which was an irresistible temptation to one of our Tommies.

The fog having thinned, our missing wave was suddenly seen halted in the open out of touch with their right and left. Something had to be done. I took a man with me, and within fifty yards I was swallowed up in the uncertainty of the opaque mist in search of a trench parallel with Serre, which the battalion on our left should then have reached.

We walked on a while and approached some gaunt, shapeless trees rising above dismal ruins. We were on the outskirts of Serre. We went on carefully and came to a dug-out. I looked down through its gaping entrance and saw clods of mud freshly dropped from boots on every step. A smell of mildew rose from the bottom. All was still. Further on, we came to a shattered house, where I peeped through a broken window. Roof, bricks and furniture were as one. There was not a sound except the dripping of water from a beam punctuating the oppressive silence with a melancholy regularity. I had to pull myself together to advance a short way inside the village. I hated the look of it, and so did my guide. Something was urging me to get out of the place, and quickly. Every yard I took

forward marked a moment. Was I walking into a trap? I
felt the enemy must be watching us all the time. As a
matter of fact, nobody at that time was in Serre. Anyway,
after a nerve-racking time I turned back; the fog lifted at
that moment, and for a second or two I was able to define
the shapes of some objects in the village before the fog
closed in on me again. A burst of musketry opened
from the ridge, and we hastened our steps back to the
battalion.

By pure chance we struck Maxim Trench. No one was
in it, but it obviously had been recently occupied; fresh
footmarks were all around it, but whether these belonged
to our men or the enemy, I couldn't tell. After a while
from the right the welcome sound of English voices
coming from our advancing waves reached us.

I joined them as they were debouching over the brow
of the spur and found the second-in-command in a shell-
hole near-by. A volley brought everyone to a sudden
standstill. Except for the stretcher-bearers, who were unfolding their stretchers and picking up the wounded,
everyone was flat on the ground. The enemy was now
obviously waiting for us. Was it wise to go on? The
second-in-command then suggested that I should go to the
Colonel and report, but on second thoughts he got up to
come with me as I left. He was an old ranker and rather
afraid of blundering, but he had iron nerves. So off we
went together, followed by a runner. We were busy talking and had not left the waves more than a few minutes
when suddenly we saw a patrol of a dozen or more
Germans spring out of the fog. Amazed, we immediately
fell into a shell-hole, having automatically fired our revolvers. We saw over the rim the tops of their black
helmets and the steel of their bayonets emerging from the
shell-holes into which they, too, had flung themselves.
Probably out of sheer fright I shouted: "Advance company, don't show yourselves." I said it distinctly and
slowly so that the Germans might understand. Fat and
fit, his finger on the trigger of his revolver, the Major

stared before him, while the runner, still as a statue, pointed his rifle at the enemy. A long silence followed, and then we saw the Germans get up quickly, and holding their rifles low along the ground, they bent down and slipped away like shadows. Were they working their way round us? Back to back we watched all sides, my hand grasping a suddenly-remembered Mills bomb with the relish of a thirsty man who finds in his pocket a forgotten pear. Then a plaintive call of "Kamerad" came from the hole they had just left. "Look out!" said the Major, "there are more of them." Speaking in German, I called out to the "Kamerad" to show himself alone and come forward. Eagerly he obeyed, scampering out of his hole lamenting and holding a limp arm. He was followed by a fat fellow who promptly side-stepped as he saw my revolver pointed straight at him. "Now then, quickly, how many are you? Where have you come from?" In a moment I knew all that I wanted. I was right; Serre had been evacuated by the enemy, and there were only strong German rear-guards with a few machine-guns between us and Puisieux, held by two companies. We had to find the Colonel. We hurried the two prisoners on, one of whom said: "We took one of your men a little while back. He was lost like us. He was walking alone. We sent him back through Serre in charge of a man." . . . It couldn't have been anybody else but the poor devil we had sent back.

At that moment shots rang out as when a hare crosses a line of guns. It must have been the rest of the enemy patrol filtering back to their line through our waves. "We ought to have scuppered the bloody lot of them," growled the Major as we went on. "Yes," I said. "You can say that now that we are temporarily safe ourselves."

We then met one of the reserve platoons ordered forward by the Colonel. They at once detailed a man who led us to him, and we found him alone following up the trail of his battalion, having sent his adjutant forward to clear up the situation, which we discussed and which I

hurried to Brigade Headquarters to report. I had to
splash through mud before I found again the broken trees
of Pendant Copse standing on their isolated knoll. Then
I knew exactly where to go to strike our front line. I went
towards it, and to my surprise came on a new untrained
battalion of a newly arrived division still there, who
should have been, of course, right up alongside our waves.
I couldn't help being snappy with the Colonel, who said
they had been unable to advance at all owing to fog and
machine-guns. He was such a sympathetic, incompetent
old dear, however, that I soon changed my tone; the
situation seemed utterly beyond him. Perturbed, he
apologised, saying: "Yes, sir," to everything I said. As I
pointed out to him on the map how the advance of his
battalion was secured by us on the left and how he could
move forward over ground already reconnoitred behind a
screen of patrols, he said "Capital!" and immediately blew
on a whistle like an old keeper summoning his beaters at
the end of a drive. Shells had been landing round us, but
being swallowed up with a sucking sound by the waterlogged earth, most of them failed to explode. We took
notice, however, when a group of men were laid out by a
salvo, which exploded and covered us with mud.

It was pathetic to see this oddly assorted battalion comprising all sorts and conditions of men which constituted
this new division, so different from the older and more
seasoned divisions who, alas, were already largely reduced.
It was unlucky for them in one way that conditions should
be so deplorable for their first show, but, on the other
hand, they were fortunate in having so few Germans to
cope with and the fog to screen their mistakes. They
gained experience in time, but not till many of their
superior officers had been sent back to England. They
went back without a word of complaint. They were really
gallant and keen, those old boys.

As the fog lifted a lively fusillade started from the line.
I was then scrambling back over the net of trenches of
"White City," which once had been a model factory

village and was now nothing but a mass of crumpled plaster, which acted as a screen for our field-guns, with a few shattered chimneys standing like the pillars of a ruined Roman amphitheatre.

As I reached the brewery in Mailly-Maillet, which was used for Brigade Headquarters, an aeroplane, quick to take advantage of the improved visibility, skimmed the roof-tops of the village and darted towards the line. It was now noon.

The General commanding the brigade, who had offered me whisky and biscuits, did not appear convinced when I suggested the possibility of pushing on the attack. He preserved a lethargic calm. He said he had given his troops definite objectives and he wasn't going to rush them into the blue. I knew what General Gough's views were, so I left for the corps, where he told me he would be. I met him on the way walking up with General Fanshawe, who commanded the V Corps. I gave him the news, and as he was going to Brigade Headquarters, I knew he would quickly find out for himself the state of mind in which I had left the Brigadier. He hurried to the office, and in a moment the atmosphere changed. Unfortunately, the cavalry, which was at hand, could not be used owing to the state of the ground, and for the next few days the infantry had to plod on fighting German rearguards who held strong posts with picked men. Nevertheless, we advanced along the whole front. We took Puisieux, Mireaumont and then Pys, where we made 700 prisoners.

As the army advanced the enemy retirement appeared to have been admirably prepared. Not a house was left standing; every tree was cut down; wells were rendered useless; we found mines laid everywhere. A tornado could not have worked more destruction. The havoc was thorough and methodical. Anything that might have been of the slightest use to us had been blown up. Villages and towns, even those which the war had so far spared, were razed to the ground. Orchards had been neatly felled; no cattle had been left. From the forward villages inhabitants had been sent away. The army was advancing into utter devastation, which roused the anger of the men. The population of Bapaume welcomed our troops with flags. Old men were crying for joy, children were frightened at the sight of strange uniforms. The Mayor delivered a speech from the Town Hall, which some days later blew up sky-high with a delay-action fuse, killing many people, including their Député, who had rushed back from Paris.

Unfortunately, neither the artillery nor supplies could follow the pace of the advance. No wheel traffic could get over the blown-up roads, so mules and pack-horses had to carry every supply over the broken ground. The time came when it was unwise to push the army too far forward from its supplies. We dared not risk a counter-attack with provision unmade. So the advance slackened until the roads were repaired and the army could systematically resume its pursuit.

On March 20th, 1917, the armies encountered the Hindenburg line, and were immediately brought to a standstill. The enemy had abandoned his dangerous salient and fallen back securely on the heavily fortified new line, leaving us nothing but desolation on a front of seventy miles.

CHAPTER XXVI

ALTHOUGH April had come, the land failed to respond to the call of spring; the army was now spread out on its new position, and separated from civilisation by a stretch of waste, which gripped me with melancholy as every day I went through it on the way to and from the line. Not a bloom adorned shrub or tree. Larks were twittering in vain to wake up the land which seemed dead. The gay notes of their song sounded almost ironical.

The devastation robbed one of hope. Once only during that period, I remember, was the urge to live revived in me—and that was when, on riding through a devastated village, I saw standing amongst their scattered belongings, and framed in the radiance of the setting sun, a French poilu and his wife clasping each other in a close embrace.

The Army Headquarters finding Toutencourt too far away from the front, moved to Albert, where the houses, patched up with sacking and boards, were made habitable. Quickly the work of reconstruction had been taken in hand all over the devastated area by swarms of working parties from the labour battalions. Wooden villages were springing up to accommodate troops; the destroyed ones were beyond repair. The weather remained bad throughout the spring. The influenza epidemic was at its height, and the hospitals were full.

The Third Army on our left attacked then in front of Arras; my friend Nelson was killed going forward with his tanks. It was a great blow to me.

Albert was a ghostly place at night, so people said. One night a strong unimaginative Scotsman walked into the mess, pale and nervous, and asked me to go with him to a house where he had just seen a ghost. The whole front of the house had collapsed, so that we could see into every room standing just as the people had left it. As we started our explorations a shell exploded in the house next door, bringing down the plaster about us and with it a fully dressed mannequin that rolled at our feet. I thought this was a good enough explanation for my friend's delusion, but he wouldn't have it. "No," he said, "it was a woman, of that I feel sure, and she was in her night-dress." "Well then," I replied, "of what have you to complain? and in these days, too . . . !" This same man, on returning from leave in Edinburgh, was asked if he had enjoyed himself, and said: "Oh yes, I spent it straightening things out in the office; there was a good deal of my work all behind-hand." This conscientious fellow went back to his battalion and was killed soon after.

Wilson's "Fourteen Points" began to impress the men at that time. Even if peace was not immediately within sight, at least they embodied a new ideal. We had fought till then and drifted on, simply because, having begun the war, we had to win it. Go on the same as before? Would a new mentality be created in the world? What, after all, was it all about? Most of us by then saw through the war propaganda, and certainly Wilson, whatever he may have been responsible for afterwards, dreamed that this should be the last war. His timely definition of a new idealism revived amongst the Allies the belief with which most of us had started—that future generations, of friend and foe alike, would benefit as a result of these ghastly experiences. This ideal helped many a poor devil to face death with the feeling that he was not giving his life in vain. I do not believe that without this the majority of us could have stuck it for so long—whatever the alleged excitement and drive of the war feeling itself. God knows that those of us, who like myself lived through and beyond it, have realised since how illusory these ideals were.

I generally heard all the sensational news from my batman as he laid out my clothes to change into at night. One evening I was told that the Fifth Army was ordered north.

As a matter of fact, I already knew that our next scene of action was to be Belgium, where a big offensive was on foot. The contemplated change came as a relief.

One morning all the baggage of the army was put on to lorries and sent north to Belgium. It was extraordinarily quickly done. In a few hours a place that had been humming with life was empty but for a few men left behind to burn the rubbish and papers. My particular moving job was always a problem. Each mess was allotted a certain number of lorries, and as my private circus consisted of a horse, motor-bike, baggage, library and painting materials, I had to use great diplomacy with the Camp Commandant.

The Fifth Army arrived in Belgium on June 1st, 1917, and made their headquarters in La Lovie Château, south of Poperinghe. It was an ugly red building, redeemed by its lovely grounds. A large pond made an ideal landmark for enemy aviation. The general staff was housed in the château, and all round under the trees Niessen huts were put up for offices, and tents for the officers' sleeping accommodation.

The operation and Q staff departments began at once on the work of preparation, everyone keeping secret his particular activities. Gradually the work involved all departments, and the atmosphere of the Army H.Q. became obviously charged with tension.

As I lay in my tent at night, I could hear the rattle of lines of men trailing howitzers to their positions, and the incessant roar of lorries driving slowly with heavy loads of ammunition. Dumps cropped up everywhere and disappeared again under clever camouflage. The movement on the road increased nightly. But during the day the atmosphere about the salient relaxed into peace. We didn't wish to excite the enemy's curiosity too far, although the construction of new aerodromes could not be hidden and the growing number of casualty clearing-stations that were being erected ominously emphasised the purpose of our work. Whether the enemy knew of our intentions or not, he gave the salient little peace, and what

was left of Ypres was being blown up sky-high, fired at
from three different directions.

From the very first I was sent to the line to study the
ground section by section and make drawings of the positions we were to storm. It was June. The weather was
hot. I would lie hidden among the poppies growing between the trenches, and peer at Passchendaele Ridge, the
extreme right of our army. There the German trenches
ran just below the top of a broad spur and looked down
on to a valley where our front line wound through marshy
ground. This ridge extended snakewise through Polygon
Wood towards the town of Passchendaele, one of our most
coveted ultimate objectives. On the near slope which
faced our lines stood Stirling Castle, its forbidding ruins
of red bricks showing up against a background of the
shattered trees of Inverness Copse. These places were soon
to acquire a deadly and significant familiarity for all of us.

Although our heavy shells landed on Stirling Castle
with clockwork regularity, parties of Germans could be
seen sneaking round its ruins; some work was obviously
going on. Every morning as I looked up the slope with
fresh eyes I detected an increase of white patches amidst
the piled-up brick-dust. Our aerial photographs soon revealed the enemy's new scheme of defence, which took the
form of pill-boxes made of concrete, a new and unexpected obstacle. Our artillery had to deal with them one
by one. The photographs showed how well the work was
being done. Our planes were out all the time correct-
ing our artillery fire, but the enemy aviation began to
interfere. Often our machines were brought down.
Richthofen, the famous German ace, had arrived with
his "circus" of daring flyers. He himself could be recognised by his small, devilish-looking machine, and also by
the way he banked and swerved; his flying had great distinction. He hovered like a hawk in search of prey. Sometimes he would fly low following our trenches, and every
rifle would have a crack at him. Negligently he would
swerve from side to side, then suddenly climb into the sky,

pursued by our bursting shrapnel—he had seen a prey. In a sequence of dexterous movements the work was done— one of our planes would be seen in flames whirling down like a leaf unwinding a tape of black smoke behind it. We learned to cope with his ways, however. Our photographing or registering planes were guarded by strong patrols flying above them. If they were attacked they turned for home, leaving the fighting planes to take up the challenge. However, Richthofen daily added to his record. He fell at last, after winning the unqualified admiration of friend and foe alike.

The volume of fire from our artillery was increasing daily. More and more guns took up position close to each other. The enemy retaliated. Our impending attack was no longer unknown to them.

To avoid the drudgery of going backwards and forwards to the line every day, I settled in a dug-out on the outskirts of the village of St. Jean, north of Ypres. It wasn't really a dug-out, but a large shell-hole covered with a corrugated tin plate. I managed to make it quite comfortable. My batman preferred the comforts of headquarters, so after attending to my requirements he went back at night. The staff knew where I was and could get at me, and I was in touch with the divisions holding the line. In time I knew every yard of the line and every communication-trench. I knew when to turn, and instinctively felt where places were, though they could not be seen. From my retreat nook I had a very good view of the heroic remnants of Ypres. The Cloth Hall looked like a birthday cake after the guests had had their share. The shell of the cathedral rose above the flat land, still a favourite target for the enemy guns, although it had long been out of bounds for the troops. What was left of the town appeared impressively strong and undaunted. Its aspect constantly changed with the varying light. Sometimes it would be a grey mass of walls, like a huge crypt; at other times every house took on a prominence and came out with a distinctness that threw the surrounding land-

scape into secondary place. Shells fired at Ypres would sail
over my head as sometimes I lay reading. As they bored
through the air I could tell approximately the quarter of
the town they were destined for. There seemed no hurry
about the big shells, as though they had all their time to
get there and were used to the journey.

One day a storm swept over the salient. The sky turned
blue-black. The Cloth Hall towering above Ypres came
out a creamy white as a ray behind the cloud lit up every
rugged detail of its destruction. Swept by a galloping
wind, a big brownish cloud rolled over the salient, absorbing Ypres in its stride. In a moment the country was
swamped. Every gun was subdued until the storm abated
as suddenly as it had come. The Cloth Hall and then the
town reappeared through a heavy steam. A rainbow behind was stretching across the sky. . . .

Sundown always brought a sense of repose. Through
the warm grass where poppies had grown to the height
of the wooden crosses mingled with them, I would walk
to Ypres, where I roamed about the cathedral, recon-
structing it in my mind as I had once known it—but now
the nave was roofed only by the sky. Sundry pieces of
carved wood still lay about, but all the remains of the
lovely choir had been used for fuel when fires were needed
to keep out the bitter cold. If I burrowed in the dust I
found odd bits of vestry garments or leaves of Prayer
Books. Once I found a fine carved headstone, which I
managed to keep until, in a shift, it was lost. Ever since
1914 souvenir-hunters had picked up all that was of
interest—the ruins had been ransacked.

The place that drew me most was the Cloth Hall, for
some of its green stone pillars and arches were still intact.
The view of the town, seen through their openings, was
indeed inspiring. The spirit of its past glory still hovered
here. Grass had grown in between the cobblestones of the
streets, making a neat pattern, and on either side of the
roads all the fine Renaissance houses were now nothing
but a heap of ruins.

When the town received its daily "strafe," pigeons flew away from the cathedral and circled round and round until the shelling ceased. They seemed to sense the lapse between every crash, for with the last, they swept back in a body, flapping the tips of their transparent wings. Their little pink legs hopped along the borders scattering plaster and dust until they settled into their accustomed places, to resume their cooing, keeping vigil over a dying town. But still Ypres retained its soul, which no amount of torture could ever kill.

One night I heard someone playing a piece by Debussy on an old piano which had somehow escaped destruction. To my surprise I recognised the Provost-Marshal, in whose charge I had been during the retreat in '14. He turned out to be a charming fellow, very different from the impression I had formed of him when I had been his prisoner, which shows how often we are apt to judge people through our moods. I hadn't come across him since.

Although the evening breeze carried with it a smell of putrefaction, I was glad of the rest it brought after walking the whole day in the trenches in the trying heat, enclosed between two parapets, dodging the feet of hundreds of men crouched in the shade, hardly seeing their faces buried under their tin helmets. At tea-time, when the day was at its hottest, the sight of food was anything but appetising, the dixies of tea thick with dark tea-leaves which were constantly offered, and which I drank without relish. We had warm and lovely nights in July, and sometimes the place settled into perfect peace. Stretched out in my little bunk I looked at the stars through the aperture just as I had done in the tropics through the hatch of my sailing ship. My mind wandered back to those days; the ecstasy of the transient peace of evenings before a storm; the gentle flapping of a top-sail or jib; the easy rolling of the ship on an almost imperceptible swell. The squeak of a block would make me conscious of where I was, just as now a whining shell or a distant crash or even a shout of command would bring me back to reality.

These clear nights were, of course, favourable for flying. Aeroplanes constantly droned overhead. Every sound was clear. I could hear the rumble of wheels on the cobble-stones of St. Jean village a little way off. It was easy to guess what was happening—transport going through; working parties or troops tramping to the line. Sometimes it was only a single word heard from a solitary man looking for something he couldn't find—it sounded doubly expressive in the night!

If a shell crashed in the village, as transport or artillery went through, the horses would stampede. I could hear the rush and the shouting, and feel the weight of the short silence which fell on everything as it ceased—I could follow every detail as shouts for stretcher-bearers went up, and wagon-chains were pulled about and disentangled from the dead or wounded horses caught between the shafts. I would hear the softened voice of a man who having caught his horse was reassuring him, being now, himself, more composed. The march would be renewed, and eventually the clatter of hoofs would die down. I fell asleep at last, generally to dream of happier things.

In the morning I would walk to the village to see the night's destruction. The sun shone on horses stretched out alongside their shattered wagons and dead drivers. Pools of blood stained the cobble-stones, running from the bodies beneath the overcoats which had been hastily thrown over them. A pathetic stiff white hand or an army boot often was enough evidence to suggest a certain personality.

The salient at night was a wicked place for transport— not a road escaped—there was no shelter of any description.

I had been told by the division that an Intelligence officer lived somewhere near me, but I had never been able to find him, until one evening when I struck a patch of fresh vegetables and flowers in the middle of a desolate shelled area. This was enterprising. I found him sitting up in bed, a shelf full of books beside him. He had built up for himself a life completely detached from the war, and to this he returned every evening after his work. He was a delightful fellow—we quickly made friends. His pride was his vegetable garden, which until then had had a charmed existence. He was perhaps the only man who supplemented his rations within the line with "home-grown" fresh vegetables. We would meet at night, and while we talked we would watch the salient being shelled and the everlasting fireworks over the distant line. His mind always wandered back to Spain, where he had lived before the war and whither he longed to return. His descriptions of wild Spanish country with snow-topped mountain ranges defined against an everlasting blue sky contrasted with our surroundings, and would refresh the mind.

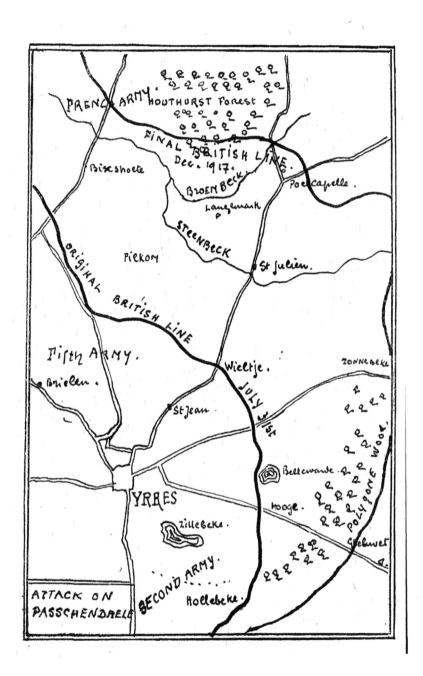

CHAPTER XXVII

THE ATTACK ON PASSCHENDAELE

HEADQUARTERS in the meanwhile grew daily more absorbed in their preparations. The atmosphere had become hectic. Alongside us on our left the 20th French Corps had come into the line, and the blue of their uniforms mingled in with our khaki. The rhythmic sound of their guns intensified the roll from our daily increasing bombardment. The weather kept fine. Often in the evening I walked over to our adjoining aerodrome to watch the aeroplanes taking off and circling over the hop-fields, or returning from the line like seagulls to a shore.

The XVIII Corps headquarters were near us, and General Maxse, their commander, could often be seen walking about, his cap low over his eyes, always smoking a cigar from a papier-mâché holder. It was difficult for anyone who didn't know him to tell who or what he was, for he wore no badge of rank, and sentries were often puzzled as to what salute they should give him. But they would know at once when the General fixed his little black eyes upon them and asked with sham severity if they didn't know their Corps Commander; his kind smile, however, for those who managed to see it, would always relieve their embarrassment. He was a strict disciplinarian, and left his mark on every division that came under his command.

I was neither a General nor an officer, but I, too, puzzled them, for I wore no stripes; at the same time my accoutrement had a distinction of its own; but sentries and men who saw me going in and out of the General's office, on friendly terms with everyone, were puzzled about my position. I myself put our new sentries at their ease. One day, however, as I was entering the Army Commander's house, I heard the sentry slap his rifle firmly in salute, and then the voice of a staff servant saying: "Don't bother about him, he's only a private." As it happened, the guard that week was supplied by a battalion well known to me, and the man had recognised me. "I salute whom I bloody well please," he retorted.

The day for the offensive grew near—the most important man on the staff became the "weather man," as we called him—the officer in charge of the meteorological station. As fine weather was essential for the success of the coming operations, our hopes fell when, a week or more before the planned attack, the rain started and continued for days. However, a few days before the battle the weather improved, and again it became scorchingly hot. More and more troops had marched up to the line, and the troops of reserve divisions were swarming in the back areas. By the middle of July the enemy could easily observe all our preparations.

As on my way up to the line one morning, I rode slowly alongside a marching battalion, I heard the regular sound of an engine, and saw puffs of smoke shooting up from a house on the road. A steam saw was cutting rhythmically through wood, working at high pressure with a tearing sound. Seeing the yard in front of the house piled high with wooden crosses and thinking to spare the men this ominous sight, I hurried in to have them removed. The Belgians engaged in the work threw up their arms in despair and pointed through the window at the back, where there was a still bigger pile. Nothing could be done; I watched the men as they passed by—some smiled, others passed a joke, some wouldn't look. But I knew they all saw and understood.

A few days before the attack I visited the II Corps. I remember seeing their commander, General Jacobs, standing on a little path fringed with white boulders in front of his Niessen hut. He looked like a man relieved of a strain. "Well, Maze," he said to me. "All our work

is finished now. It lies with the men. The work is out of
our hands. We have thought of every possible thing. (Even
to the crosses I remembered!) We have prepared this attack
with infinite care and on a scale never before conceived.
If we don't succeed, it won't be our fault."

General Jacobs' confidence was reflected in the spirit of
the attacking army who knew the stern task it was facing,
for we were not taking the enemy by surprise. Yet his
corps failed. It is true its job was a difficult one. His
three divisions had the hardest nut to crack. It is too easy
perhaps to criticise now, when one sees the whole thing in
retrospect, but it is clear that the work of the Fifth Army
attacking from the salient would have been easier if the
Second Army on their right had postponed until that day
the blowing up of the Messines Ridge, which had been
successfully accomplished some time before. As it was,
the German staff had had these weeks in which to draw
conclusions as to our next move and prepare their defence.
If this titanic explosion had been the immediate prelude
to our attack from the salient, undeniably General Jacobs'
II Corps, close on the left of the Messines Ridge, would
have attacked under cover of the German demoralisation
instead of being exposed to their carefully prepared
defence.

Two nights prior to the attack I had slept in the
trenches, where I still had some work to do. I was out
early. The morning of July 30th broke in brilliant sunshine. Already at 7 o'clock it felt warm. No Man's Land
was brown and the hills beyond it were casting long, soft
shadows before them. I was thinking what I would be
doing on a day like this in peace-time, when I had to
realise that we were making our big attack that night. I
had slept badly, thinking all the time about it.

For the attack I had arranged to be with a brigade
placed in the centre of the battle. I had been in battle
with the Brigadier on several previous occasions on the
Somme. He always said that I brought him good luck.
I received his instructions for zero day, which, though

couched in nebulous terms, guided me admirably.

July 25th, '17.
Dear Maze,
Will you join me on the afternoon of Y (?) day at what used to be the Gloucester Pioneer Batt. Hd. Qrs. about 300x north of where you met me last on the west bank of the Canal. If you have any difficulty in finding it, ask at my old Hd. Qrs. and they will know there. Only bring just what is necessary. I will arrange about food.
Your ever,
G. A. Armitage.

I had had three motor-bikes brought up at different places as near as possible to the line, so that I could reach one as quickly from wherever I happened to be. On previous occasions this arrangement, extravagant as it may appear, had proved a great saving of time. Although I was not officially on the establishment of the army, I never had any difficulty with the Ordnance stores.—"A special case" always covered my requirements, and when the motor-bikes didn't turn up again, as often happened, the words "Destroyed by shell-fire" shelved the matter for ever. Besides, the Army Commander's wish moved mountains of red-tape in those days. So, on the evening of July 30th, I found myself following a stream of troops making their way to the line for the great attack.

I had gone back to headquarters to "put my house in order" and get my final instructions from General Gough. He was ready and, as usual, keen and confident. In the event of certain things happening, I was to report to him at once, otherwise I was to help units on the spot, wherever I was, where help was most needed according to the immediate developments of the battle. I felt rather like an over-trained boxer just before his big fight. I had got keyed up for the battle days before, and now that the day had come I was tired out. I had fought it too often in my imagination before. I went on, however, my mind full of many thoughts, nervous fear prevailing. The hot day was over. The sun had set majestically in a glorious sky. The curving distant hills bounding the salient stood out a dark blue. A few walls of Ypres were still lit up from the reflected sky, but the town was gradually sinking into a grey vagueness, preparing itself for its deliverance that night. Somehow the skies were always beautiful before an attack.

I went round to say good-bye to my gardening friend at St. Jean. The cabbage patch was no more—a crater was there instead. The shelter was all smashed in—some cherished books were scattered about. I hardly dared look underneath the débris, but my friend was not there. I learned afterwards that he had been wounded and taken away.

General Armitage's brigade had already left its rendezvous, so I wended my way through trenches towards its reserve battle station, feeling more absorbed in the beauty of the evening than in the coming offensive. Enemy balloons were still peering into our line, facing the fading sunlight. Suddenly one balloon, then another, and then others went up in flames and collapsed towards the ground. Our flying-machines had cleared the sky of all enemy balloons with the exception of one which was being hurriedly hauled down. A line of parachutes had unfurled from the little black parcel I had seen drop like a stone from every balloon. They now formed a line of bubbles drifting gracefully to the ground. It was like a conjuring trick.

I had now some difficulty in getting along, as every trench was crammed with troops waiting for the dark to move up to their assembly positions. It was vital that every unit should start at its proper scheduled time—the least deviation from plan would have brought about delay and confusion.

As soon as it was dark every communication-trench became a moving platform. I found my Brigadier sharing a dug-out with another Brigadier of our division. As we had time, we looked again at the objectives on the map.

It all seemed simple enough; every yard we had to take
had now been studied both on the ground and from aerial
photographs; every battalion had rehearsed the attack on
ground models made to scale—everyone knew by heart
what he had to do. We had every chance of success. Our
orders were as follows:

Attack of the 39th Division—July 31st, 1917.
> *Brigades:* 117th on the left.
> 116th on the right.
> 152nd (51st Division, on left).

Objectives of the 117th.
> (1) Capture the German Line system.
> (2) Kitchener system.
> (3) Secure the crossing of Steenbeck.

118th Brigade will pass through the brigade at 0+6
hours 20 minutes and capture the Langemarck system.
The 16th Battalion, Sherwood Foresters, on the right
and 17th King's Royal Rifles on the left will capture
the German front line system.

(*a*) The 17th Battalion Sherwood Foresters on right
and the 16th Rifle Brigade on left will capture Kitchener
system and secure the crossing over Steenbeck.

Each battalion will attack on a two-company frontage
and each company on a two-platoon frontage.

First wave will capture the red line; 2nd wave the
yellow line; 3rd and 4th waves will pass through 1st and
2nd waves, capture blue line, including Civilisation
Farm, and make good blotted blue line, including
Camphor Support.
Hampshire Farm, Canadian Farm, Kultur Farm and
Civilisation Farm are each to be made the objectives of
a definite body of troops, who will not continue the

advance until the farm has been cleared of the enemy.

A. Attack on Kitchener Wood as follows:

The 1st and 2nd waves will pass through, capture and consolidate Canoe Trench, clear Kitchener Wood and consolidate a general line 100 yards in front of it.

The 3rd and 4th waves will pass through the 1st and 2nd waves, capture the enemy's strong points at Alberta, Hugel Hollow, Regina Cross and the usual C.11.A.75.45 and secure the crossing of Steenbeck.

I lay down for a little and tried vainly to sleep, but the phone-buzzer and messengers rushing in and out made it difficult. An officer came to synchronise our watches. After a while I walked up the steps out of the dug-out to get some fresh air. I was dazed by the intense darkness— a few stars were out—the bombardment had died down; the unexpected silence was impressive.

The infantry had vanished, packed together in the trenches that led to the front line and No Man's Land. Now and then a solitary gun fired. At that moment nobody could have foretold the intensity of the impending bombardment, where along eight miles of front sixteen divisions—about one hundred thousand infantry—stood ready for assault.

I went back to the dug-out, where everyone waited in suspense. A bottle of white wine stood uncorked on the table. We constantly asked each other the time. Soon the hour for the barrage would strike—we had nothing to do now but wait for the gong. We became hysterically nervous and made silly jokes and remarks to cloak our thoughts. When the barrage finally opened, its violence was such that we looked at one another aghast.

I climbed up the stairs into the night. The wind caused by the displacement of air was terrific—I might have been standing on the bridge of a ship during a typhoon and held on to the side of the trench like to a weather rail. Gun-flashes were holing the sky as though thousands of signal-lamp shutters were flashing messages. Field batteries placed in position immediately above our dug-out opened fire and rent the air with a deafening row. At every re-port I felt as though my scalp were being removed. An uninterrupted succession of shells of every calibre was whirling through the air. This bombardment exceeded anything I had ever witnessed before. The enemy retalia-tion was hardly noticeable, although some of their shells were bursting near-by.

Suddenly I imagined I was seeing things when the top of our parapet seemed to move. But it was only the terri-fied rats fleeing in an army of their own.

A few minutes before zero hour hundreds of machine-guns mingled their rattle with the roar of the bombard-ment. The shelling, as though not to be outdone, rose into fiercer intensity. Men, grimly facing death, had only a few seconds more—if only all their thoughts then could have been recorded!

My Brigadier came out of his dug-out, saying: "They've gone over now, Maze. Come on." Our brigade was fol-lowing on. We scrambled down the slopes towards the front line, Verey lights showing up troops all round, who went down in a land-slide after our creeping barrage, like a crowd rushing for a refuge. As we went through our own wire the waves in front were disappearing behind a screen of smoke with stretcher-bearers holding their stretchers as though they had been crucifixes. As we stag-gered through the gas and smoke of the enemy's bursting salvoes the earth was turning up in convulsions all round as if mined. There was a sign of dawn. I tore my breeches as I got through the enemy wire, endeavouring to catch up the brigade staff which were haring towards their report centre. There were only a few German dead in the enemy front line, but further on they became more numerous; evidently they had kept out of their forward trenches during our bombardment. We could hardly see for smoke. I stopped a second with a wounded soldier who had held out a hand from a shell-hole, while troops streamed past me climbing the rising slope and prisoners with hands up were scrambling down with a throng of wounded all hastening to the back lines. "It's all right, chum, I've got it in the chest," he said to me as I gave him my water-bottle. He had cast off his equipment and laid his kit neatly by his side as though he had prepared for death.

Daylight had broken through. We found a pill-box that was to be our report centre. We cleared it of its dead, made ourselves comfortable in it, and felt very sheltered. Through the growing light the sun suddenly showed itself by a gash of red, as though the bombardment had set the sky on fire. The heavy smoke from the barrage rested heavily like a long cloud on the misty ground, which was soaked with dew.

All the waves had gone on out of sight. The ridge which the troops had attacked was deserted but for stretcher-bearers and some batches of prisoners running down. The sound of our barrage had grown fainter as it now crept along in the distance following the schedule of its programme. We had now to wait for news. A battery of artillery slipped down the slope behind us, swerved into position as if on muffled wheels, unlimbered, and at once started firing. As its horse-teams were galloping up the high ground towards cover, enemy shrapnel burst plumb amongst them. I saw some black objects whirl in smoke above the commotion, and turned away.

More field artillery came up and took up new positions; that was a good thing, but they drew fire. The enemy were now pitching their shells all over the place, but, fortunately, all our reserves had gone forward. After long suspense, a runner was seen scrambling down making for our pill-box. His message confirmed our hopes. Our brigade had successfully gone through the leading brigade which had reached its objectives.

A terrific roar from musketry came then from the

distant right in the direction of Stirling Castle on the
II Corps front. Things seemed very hot over there. Our
aeroplanes were now all over us, searching the ground like
vultures. German machines were doing the same, some
passing very low, sprinkling the ground with bullets and
getting a splendid view on to our batteries' new position.
The Brigadier was getting anxious for more news; his
brigade major had already gone forward to the right, so
I went to the left to see how secure our flank was there.
So far we hadn't heard. We must have been by that time
beyond the River Steenbeck. I climbed on to the ridge
and saw the country stretched away round me like a
panorama. Layers of smoke blurred the distance where
violent battles were going on.

Now that the barrage had ceased, the place had an
appearance of deserted calm, with smoke rising from the
shell-holes as if from abandoned camps. Stretcher-bearers
were picking up the wounded. Here and there the figure
of a runner could be seen rushing to the rear with a
message, or a party laying down fresh wire as though employed in some peaceful occupation. Apart from this, no
troops were to be seen.

The German wounded lying in the open were patiently
waiting their turn to be picked up, watching our own men
being taken away first. I walked up to one who was moaning and stroked his cold forehead—it seemed so absurd to
be comforting a man whom for days you had been preparing to kill.

I reached Civilisation Farm. Its defenders had obviously
made a gallant stand. They were dead now, lying among
piles of empty cartridge-belts with many of our men alongside. I clambered on to a prominent knoll and looked in
vain for Oblong Farm. I was able to pick out Racecourse
Farm, Ascot Cottage, Kempton Park and Hurst Park on
my left, names which recalled better days. I had a commanding view on a wide stretch of the battle-field which
in parts was completely blurred by smoke. Kitchener
Wood stretched away about 300 yards in front of me, and

I could see the steel helmets of our infantry moving along the trenches skirting it.

Suddenly a very heavy barrage opened and rolled up along the flat ground on the left of the wood; the earth behind it suddenly sprang to life with waves and waves of Highlanders advancing with *élan* and spreading out in the open. Through my glasses every man was distinct, I could see every individual movement. Their kilts swayed in rhythm until balls of black smoke started pirouetting over them and scattered death with shattering bursts. Simultaneously the waves closed in to fill the gaps which gave a side movement to the advancing lines. I followed them until they rounded the end of a spur and saw the whole division vanish into the smoke and fracas.

The fight had now definitely developed into a new phase. I felt the pressure of German counter-attacks coming from several quarters, where obviously the progress of our troops was checked, particularly round St. Julien, where the fighting was most severe.

I eventually found Alberta Farm, where sections of forward battalions I was looking for were in reserve. The whole area towards the Steenbeck was enveloped in smoke, with a growling and persistent artillery barrage, while the thunder of musketry and machine-gun-fire increased.

As the area immediately behind the battle was also being raked by explosives, I thought it wise to wait before going on. I watched a small figure struggle through the barrage, coming our way. He was the bringer of bad news. The Hertfordshires had been thrown back on our side of the river, badly cut up; the Cambridgeshires were on their way to reinforce them. I moved towards a section of men who had fallen back and were visibly hurrying to get their machine-guns into position. The whole thing didn't look too good. From there I bore towards our left to see how the 51st Division had fared. During my rush the sound of battle had grown more and more confusing; and I was pleased to find a battalion of the Black Watch happily resting on their objectives, the rest of their brigade having gone through them and forward. As they had sent an officer forward to find out how they had got on, I waited until he returned to get his report. The situation there seemed quite clear. I hastened back to our brigade. The atmosphere was then oppressive; the sky had turned dull and threatening—I was wet through with perspiration.

Drops of rain began to fall, and soon it was pouring. I ran on as fast as I could, my course directed mostly by my involuntary reactions to the shells which, at times, were bursting uncomfortably near. Running some distance behind me a man was also struggling over the uneven ground, ducking as I was. After a time I failed to see him. He could not have gone far in that open space. Thinking that something might have happened to him and knowing that he must have been carrying a message, I made a search for him. But in vain; I couldn't look into every shell-hole.

The depression in the ground I was following led into the valley, where my eyes searched for our shelter. After a short halt in a pill-box to recover my breath, I started running again, when something happened. . . .

CHAPTER XXVIII

ALL I recollect is coming to, as one does after chloroform, when dim noises drum in the ears and one is only faintly in contact with one's own body. Daylight was a surprise as I opened my eyes. Soaked and cold, I was lying in a shell-hole and heard above me the loud drone of a plane flying low—there was a nasty smell of lyddite or wet gunpowder about me.

My behind felt quite numb, as though anæsthetised. I put my hand there; and felt blood. I looked round—my vast surroundings seemed impregnated with melancholy—rain was pelting down.

I crawled on slowly, feeling very shaken, and finally reached the headquarters, where I found the Brigadier and gave him my news. The rain had flooded the staff out of their shelter. They were putting boards across the floor, which compelled them to stoop if they stayed inside. I got a field-dressing put on my wound and walked to an aid-post to get it properly dressed. Great numbers of wounded men had drifted there, and stretcher-bearers were carrying in wet dejected loads with limp white hands swaying over the sides of the stretchers. Faces appearing from under the muddy greatcoats were sallow. Ambulances had come up quite close. They were splashing through the mud, taking away all they could manage.

As I had to go to Division and Corps Headquarters, I looked for one of my motor-bikes, and found it. I just managed to stick on the seat, and skidded about in the slush, feeling very sore and as though I were in a dream. The blood had worked through my dressing. How quickly the aspect of the battle had turned dramatic. I gave the Division and Corps Headquarters all the information I

had and hurried to Army Headquarters, meeting the up-
ward movement of troops and traffic.

After I had seen General Gough, our army doctor
packed me into an ambulance for the nearest casualty-
station. It was still pouring. My ambulance had to take
its turn behind a long line of ambulances slowly creeping
up inside the hospital grounds. From every ambulance
five pairs of inert muddy feet protruded through blankets,
and the mud-covered equipment of the men was piled up
on the floor. I got out to walk up the neat path edged
with whitewashed stone that ran all round the big tents
of the casualty clearing-station. Shining white trains like
yachts were waiting on a siding close by, with nurses in
attendance, looking spotlessly clean and refreshing in contrast to the bandaged men who hung about smoking
cigarettes. The red cross on the white trains, the blood-
stains on the men's dressings made a picture against the
background of green trees.

I was soon lying in a bed between nice clean sheets. I
was washed. Being too tired to eat, I implored the nurse
to let me sleep as long as I could without the cruel call
in the morning, the despair of every patient in the war.
She was kind and kept her word.

It was 5 o'clock the following afternoon when I woke
up. I had slept nearly twenty-four hours without waking.
I looked around. Every bed in the ward was occupied.
On the floor in the space between each bed lay a wounded
man on a stretcher. I could recognise no one who was
there when I came in yesterday. I wondered where they
had all gone. It was dismal and dark inside, for the wet
tent allowed no light through. But for the groans coming
from several beds and the guns booming in the distance,
it felt very still and isolated from everything. The heavy
rain was still drumming on the canvas, dripping off
regularly into little streams, gurgling along the gutters
outside. Nurses were quietly moving about, keeping an
eye on every bed that constantly required their attention.
I had had some food brought me. The strong smell of

The Sodden Front

ether and dampness in the air didn't stimulate my
appetite. Stretcher-bearers were coming in to take away
the wounded who could stand the journey to the base—
their badly needed beds were immediately prepared for
those waiting outside. Some, who came in straight from
the operating-rooms, appeared to be dead until they
groaned and shouted hysterically as they came out of the
chloroform. By a very silent bed the tall figures of some
Guards officers were watching over their dying priest, who
couldn't recognise any of them.

The wheels of the ambulances could be heard slushing
over the wet road bringing more cases in all the time.

An army A.D.C. came to see me, and I heard all about
the battle. The right of the attack had certainly failed,
but the whole of the left had gained all its objectives
and many prisoners had been taken. The rain was now
hampering operations, but the attack was going to be renewed—meanwhile the Germans were counter-attacking
all along the line.

I could see through the opened flaps of the tent, and
caught glimpses of the surgeons with blood-stained aprons
smoking cigarettes between operations. I also saw the top-
boots and the grey of some German prisoners mingling
with the khaki of our men.

Every night when I fell asleep and heard the everlasting
patter made by the rain on our tent, I wondered when it
would ever stop. Stretcher-bearers bringing in fresh
wounded throughout the night brought the smell of the
muddy battle-field in with them. They constantly woke
me. The wounded were soaked to the skin. Their uniforms had to be cut off them with scissors and thrown
away.

  .   .   .   .   .   .

It is the tenth day of continuous rain. I awake one
morning and everything feels still, as though I were in a
ship moored to the quay after a night passage. A few
drops of water are dripping as they might off a ship when

the decks have been washed—the drops falling at longer
intervals make each time a bigger and more resounding
splash. The sun is out, and there is an increasing glow
inside the ward as the tent turns yellow and dries.—But
the dampness of the heat turns it into a hot-house. This
change has brought a sensation of new life, even to this
ward, where death is lurking round so many beds. Aeroplanes, which had been silent, are droning outside and the
sound of the guns firing is clearer, sharper and more
vigorous. All the men in the ward, with the exception of
myself, are bad cases; they have been here some days, and
I have watched them with the eye of a man who observes
but cannot feel—I can feel no more; I am not callous—I
am merely immune from reaction to wounds, blood,
bandages, suffering, even to death; it is not selfishness—
the surgeons and nurses must feel the same, but they help,
and I can't—my insensibility to my surroundings is akin
to a pain. There is now a routine in the ward as each
case is dealt with. I see how nervous they become,
those whom the nurses prepare for the surgeon's visit.
They have now a horror of the pain which daily they
have to endure, as a long sharp needle is inserted into
their back and the fluid inside their lungs has to be drawn
out by an instrument like a bicycle-pump. They sit up
one after another for their turn, supported by a nurse,
and give that hopeless howl of a weak man who can resist no more. Some have to be anæsthetised to have their
wounds dressed. They all come back from the ordeal,
heavier to carry as they lie inert and yellow under their
deep artificial sleep. There is a man with gangrene who
every second day has to be carried out to have a bit more
of his leg cut off. One boy has both his legs off, and the
nurse watches over him constantly—he smells terribly of
decomposition, poor fellow, and infects the ward. I notice
the nurse put a screen round his bed and attend him as if
she were making him comfortable—I have not understood
that he has died, until I see a stretcher slip out of the side
door, a blanket covering his pitiably short body. . . .

It is very hot—the heat is accentuated by the dampness rising from the ground. There comes a diversion; one young fellow, a very bad case, shouts: "Nursie darling—don't leave me." Throughout his delirium he makes love to her. She responds sweetly. He is so lively that I cannot believe death is so near him, but he is shot in the head, and there is no hope, so the nurse tells me. She has to leave him for a minute, an orderly watching him from the door—several times he has attempted to get up. This time the orderly is too far off to catch him before he has nipped out of bed and slipped out through an open flap of the tent, where for a few seconds he sprawls and shouts, making diabolical gesticulations among the ropes and pegs. Like a truant child he is carried gently back, and, with one last shout, which rings in my ears for days afterwards, he falls into eternal silence.

Every day there seemed to be a critical moment for bad cases to survive. Just as shipwrecked people clinging to a raft let go one after the other, often at the moment that rescue is near, so sometimes a wounded man will die, although his condition shows an improvement, as if he were too tired to make the slightly greater voluntary effort required. A charming fellow in the bed next to mine seemed so much better. As he woke from his sleep the doctor on duty, the Harrow school doctor, was waiting by his bed with a letter for him. "Would he like it read to him?" I remember how gentle that voice sounded that read aloud to the young man the words of his mother who, with little bits of home news, tried to hide her anxiety. I saw the letter lying between two white hands as the doctor walked away to the other side—then suddenly two arms went up despairingly, like a drowning man unable to shout for help—he never uttered a sound. His white face moved once or twice on the pillow, and within a few moments he was dressed for the last time and carried outside. . . .

We had very clear nights when hovering enemy planes hummed like bees above us all the time. Against the

canvas of the tent I watched the gesticulations of big arms
of light from our searchlights following the droning
planes and the flash from our bursting shrapnel. Pinned
to our beds we waited, fearing the crash of the inevitable
bomb. One night it came. We recovered our senses in
the silence which followed the last crash. Our ears ringing, choked with dust and powder and gasping for air, we
lay under the shattered tent which had collapsed over us.
Those who could, crawled through the dark, pushing the
canvas away from their faces. Outside men were groaning,
but there was no panic. We heard reassuring voices and
saw the friendly flash of torches. The tent next to ours
was a gaping crater. Of the German wounded who had
been in it hardly one had escaped. Our anti-aircraft guns
had ceased firing; the roar of the engine from the enemy
planes was now faint in the far distance. By the mercy of
God the hospital trains were intact, and all cases capable
of standing the journey were packed in and the trains
moved away.

I was transferred to a French hospital attached to the
French corps on our left, and from there sent to Dunkirk.
I had visions of recuperating at the seaside, but I was
wrong. After the most uncomfortable drive in an
ambulance that rocked about the road, I emerged at my
destination feeling sick and on the verge of collapse; the
label tied on me read: "Buttock wound and nervously
depressed," so I was put into a ward that dealt with every
conceivable nervous disease. The hospital was like a huge
prison. Although the weather was lovely and the sea
within a mile of us, no one was allowed to go out. The
recreation-ground was a treeless, hot, asphalt yard into
which our feet sank as we strolled about and smoked our
pipes. We were a curious hotchpot of men and uniforms;
there was the ordinary poilu; some sailors; a number of
Arabs with burnous, and a good many Senegalese.

I wrote to General Gough to ask him to get me out of
the place at once. He sent his A.D.C. to General Antoine
who commanded a French army on our left, for I was

now in the clutches of French red-tape from which it was not easy to escape. I heard afterwards how they laughed at the descriptions I gave in my letter.

It was August, when the days are long and the evenings cool and beautiful; we were made to come in at 4 o'clock in the afternoon and we had dinner at 5 p.m.! From then until 6 o'clock the next morning was an agony of bored endurance.

I had never seen anybody in an epileptic fit before. However, I became used to them, for they were my nightly entertainments. When a man had a fit at night there was a rush for the bell to fetch the orderly who was supposed to be on duty. I can hear now the rope scraping the wall and the tinkle of the little bell in some far-away passage, but nobody came. At last, after continuous ringing and when the fit was well over, a French poilu would suddenly awake and come in rubbing his eyes, hurriedly tying up the tapes of a white apron round his waist. His exclamations never varied: "Nom de Dieu, what is the matter?" He would look at the patient, turn to the others and say, "Vous savez, moi je n'y comprends rien." "Perhaps cold water might be a good thing?" he would tentatively suggest, or other equally ineffectual remedies. Fortunately for the patient the fit was over before he reached the top of the stairs. Of course, the orderlies were not trained men; their only qualification was their age, which in those days fitted them for any sort of job away from the battle line.

The bed next to mine was occupied by a Senegalese who might have been a huge tame baboon. When he spoke to me from his bed the whites of his eyes rolled in my direction. He expressed himself childishly but, nevertheless, his descriptions were very vivid. He would imitate the noise of a bursting shell, get very excited, ducking and flinging himself under the blankets and emit the weirdest shouts as if he were in a trance; then slowly his head would reappear, his lips parted in a huge grin displaying his glinting teeth. Whenever we teased him and, as often happened, things were thrown at him, he would spring out of bed in a fury. I would bring him back and he followed me like a tame gorilla.

His last fight had certainly made an impression on his mind. When everything was dark and silent in the ward, I would hear him murmur, "No bon, la guerre; couper le cou Boches." He was really anything but bloodthirsty and felt things in his own way as we all did. Once he was sitting up in bed crying and handling a small piece of dirty cloth on which he had spread some sand that he had brought with him all the way from Senegal. He kept repeating, "Me had many wives and small children . . . Senegal good." Tears were rolling down his broad cheeks. . . .

When a man played the fool to entertain us, all the patients got up in their night-shirts and formed a circle round him. Sometimes the Senegalese would dance and the projected shadows of the company in its long white shirts were diabolical. I was cooped up in that place for ten days, hardly a tonic for one who was nervously prostrated.

I was thankful to leave Dunkirk. The hot wind, like a sirocco, constantly blowing over the town had torn our shattered nerves. I heard afterwards that such hospitals were purposely made as unattractive as possible so that the men should ask for leave and then be sent up to the line again; it was one way of keeping up the strength of the army, of course, but not the enthusiasm of the men.

CHAPTER XXIX

THE FIFTH ARMY MOVES AGAIN TO THE SOMME

I REJOINED the Fifth Army at the end of September. It was still fighting a gruelling battle in the mud. The memory of every yard of my first walk in our forward position will everlastingly remain in my mind. We had occupied at great cost the Passchendaele plateau and had advanced beyond Poelcapelle, leaving behind a sea of mud in which the army had to live. The road had been so trodden down by horses and men that they were now turned into liquid tracks. Wheel transport was out of the question. Feet clogged with mud, we waded through. Ammunition had to be brought up by carriers on mules. Batteries were up to their axles in mud, protected from enemy observation by a thin veil of autumn leaves spread on wire. The troops could find no dry comforts. The ground smelled of decomposition and filled the soul with an indescribable feeling of despondency and hopelessness. Every bit of space was ploughed up; mud kept shooting up in high columns all around; the enemy barrage was incessant. Against the leaden sky the silhouettes of stretcher-bearers could be seen carrying their still burdens, having long distances to go to the nearest place where an ambulance could venture. The enemy harried all our lines of communication. There was no shelter from the artillery.

Passchendaele! What mud, what desolation;—and what heroism was recorded by those thousands of crosses emerging from the ground. The summer passed out in rain and storms, which swept the leaves off the trees behind the lines preparing us for an early winter. We couldn't keep up a proper front line. Where there was least water we held what posts we could. Often when an attack had

been ordered the men couldn't even line up in the mud,
so the barrage rolled on without them. They were shot
down, but they always tried. Only the most disciplined
and patient troops could have endured the ordeal of that
autumn.

Around our Army Headquarters the poles of the hop-
fields were now stripped, opening views on to flat fields.
The leaves from the trees of our park had carpeted the
ground and the tall green trunks of the beeches stood
bare. The wind came in gusts and shook our Niessen huts.

At night it was very dark going from the office to the
mess and back to one's tent to sleep. The lights carried
by every one wandering about looked, from a distance,
like a procession of glow-worms. All windows were
covered up so as not to let any light through on account
of German bombing raids. We were being constantly
bombed and also shelled by long-range guns. We had
to make underground tunnels and trenches, where it
became a regular thing for the staff to meet in pyjamas
and spend part of the night waiting until the humming
planes had gone.

Night raids were nerve-racking. I infinitely preferred
to be in the line. Those who had never been exposed to
severe shell-fire were very nervous. We knew what to
expect when the searchlights crossed each other in great
sweeps searching the black night for that roaring little
object flying somewhere high up evading our anti-aircraft
shells. Sometimes the enemy plane was spotted like a
silver beetle, very high, flying at great speed. Guns fired
at it until it was out of range, then the batteries of other
anti-aircraft stations echeloned all the way to the coast
would engage it as it passed over their sky area.

We would read the next day in army routine orders
that a certain place had been bombed—St. Omer, Dunkirk
or Calais—the news left us unmoved after our disturbed
night. But we had several casualties among the staff one
night. We were all in our tents asleep when it happened.
The search for the killed and wounded in that wood

among the shattered tents, choking from gunpowder fumes, was a ghastly affair! I ran to the mess and brought out the brandy; lots of us slept soundly after that. . . .

G.H.Q. at that time had sent us an officer whose age and training made his employment difficult. They got rid of him by sending him to our Intelligence Department. He was a man of the world who had lived well and enjoyed his comforts. Although he had sportingly taken a commission he hated being in the d——d war and openly said so. But he was a great asset, for he kept us all amused, and in those days this alone justified his presence. The job he liked was being sent to Paris to get our provisions. Booted and spurred he would climb into a car and set off as though he had the peace terms in his pocket. He was an imposing figure. As a mackintosh always hid his 2nd lieutenant "pip" every sentry gave him a General's salute, for he looked the part. His tent was as full of bottles as a barber's shop. He was used to every luxury and the discomforts of Army Headquarters in the end proved too much for him; the air raids finished him completely. He gave us a banquet and went back to G.H.Q., where before his friends he sheathed his sword, standing dramatically on the ramparts of St. Omer. No one ever saw or heard of him again after the War Office gave him his discharge.

Our town was Poperinghe, a really dull hole. Neville Talbot sowed there the first seeds of Toc H. He was full of life, wandering all over the place and running wild like a good-humoured Newfoundland dog—everybody liked him.

The prospects of hibernating in Belgium were not inspiring. Oil-stoves in our hut at night smelt abominable, choking us. I preferred the cold outside. To look through the window at the misty morning was getting daily more depressing. God alone knows what the troops in the line felt like. But quite unexpectedly came the news that we were leaving the sector; never did I pack up with less regret.

As I was in no hurry I rode my horse all the way down
to the Somme. I wanted to see certain places again. The
areas I went through were given over entirely to billets.
Every house was occupied by troops at rest; horses had
left their mark on every field. The army spread everywhere from the line to the sea. The French inhabitants
were really patient, for it can't have been fun to have
troops billeted on them all the time. There were houses
that for four years had been occupied without a break.
As soon as one unit went a new one took its place. It
meant that every room was occupied except the few
allocated to the owners. Of course they were paid, but
it was small compensation, especially to those who didn't
need the money and whose house, on account of its size
and comfort, was most suitable for a Headquarters staff.
Like rats the troops nibbled at everything—inevitably
things were destroyed.

Amiens was all lit up when I arrived at the end of my
journey. It was alive with the traffic of people departing
and coming back from leave. The expression on their
faces showed who was going and who had returned. The
restaurants were then doing a roaring trade. Josephine
was still surpassing herself with her tender chicken and
excellent lobsters. Men still fell in love with Marguerite
at the Restaurant of the Cathedral—and the hotels and
shops were full. Nothing had changed; Amiens was still
the centre of life and the haven of every soldier who pined
for some comfort and distraction. Painters had come from
England to make war pictures—Augustus John with his
wry air looked like an officer of high rank in the Salvation
Army.

I recall seeing in broad daylight about 200 French
soldiers handcuffed to each other as they were marched off
to the station under a strong escort of gendarmes. They
were mostly soldiers who had overstayed their leave—
perhaps there were also some deserters—but many wore
decorations. Although they laughed and pretended not
to mind, it was obvious that they felt the degradation of

being paraded through the streets before a staring crowd, a big part of which was their British comrades. The authorities could surely have chosen a more suitable time to entrain them, wherever they were to go.

On one occasion when I was in Amiens I happened to be following two overfed gendarmes who had charge of a tiny fellow dressed in a new civilian blue suit. The gendarmes looked so self-satisfied, so sure of their prisoner, who marched with bowed head, that I hated them. At a corner of the street he suddenly nipped away like an escaping butterfly, leaving the gendarmes standing alone and shouting to everybody to help in the pursuit. I wouldn't move. The little fellow by then had dodged most of the crowd, running like a "threequarters" dashing for the goal-post. Liberty seemed in sight when, to my dismay, I perceived a broad-shouldered Highlander blocking his path, whose natural atavism forbade the refusal of a tackle. I knew it was all up with the fugitive when the Highlander dived at him like a full-back intent on saving his side. The prisoner, now safely handcuffed between the gendarmes, walked to the prison, with his new trousers all ripped open from his fall and his shirt hanging out. Those few inches of shirt won my heart and the sympathy of the crowd.

The Headquarters went to Dury, a village at the end of a long hill running out of Amiens. It had the advantage of being only two hours from Paris. As the army had not yet taken over the line, I often took the opportunity of going there on leave. Paris was a mixture of brilliant life and despair in those days. English officers who went there with plenty of money to spend in a very short time, moved in a circle of gaiety which didn't represent the true picture of Paris life; they saw nothing of the French families who stoically bore the burden of war. Paris at all times offers to the foreigner such gaiety and variety of entertainment that it is difficult to realise the existence of a large industrial humdrum population who never see any of the "night-life" with which the English or

American visitor is familiar. Paris intoxicated all these
English officers who didn't see the stern side of the picture
at all. I had my friends and I saw both sides—families
with the father already killed, had their sons at the front
while the younger children were at school. The mother
of such a family had her work cut out, and the lights and
festivities of the capital never shed their flash and glory
on such homes. There were other tragic homes. I recall
that of a Scotch doctor, a real pacifist whose convictions,
backed by great idealism and humanity, were full of good
sense—what that family endured! Finally he was im-
prisoned for an article he had written, and his small
children would ride down to the prison on their bicycles
to see him. Undaunted, he accepted everything with
philosophy. "Christ was crucified for his convictions," he
said, "why shouldn't I go to prison for mine?"

A great character was the concierge of a large building
in the Place Vendôme. He embodied the very heart and
soul of France. Broad-shouldered, with a white moustache
like one of Napoleon's Guard, he was always to be found
in a long blue apron either in his lodge or on the big
staircase striking the bannisters as he brushed the marble
steps. What a welcome that man gave you! He had two
sons and a son-in-law at the war. Wife and daughter
worked and kept house. There was a healthy atmosphere
of family life in the one room that comprised their Paris
home; one was struck by a sense of reality and perman-
ence. He had a garden in the suburbs, and a pipe always
in his mouth and he enjoyed life frankly and simply. He
was not tiresomely patriotic; he was simply a part of the
country, strong, confident and naturally a stoic. Often I
came in at meal-times and with joy accepted their invitation to share their delicious food. Sometimes when I
would be talking to him he would be called away and I
was left in charge of his recess. People constantly came
to ask what floor certain residents occupied without
looking to see if I was the concierge, so I sent them up
to any floor that came to my lips and they came back

cursing. This made the old boy laugh. "I wish I could do that," he said. He is still there. Life for him has not changed. There is still dust on the stairs for him to sweep and the bannister bars still ring vigorously from his broom, although he is very old now.

PART IV

1918

*The Great Retreat of the Fifth Army. The Fourth Army
Breaks the German Front. The End.*

CHAPTER XXX

VILLERS-BRETONNEUX

Towards the end of November, 1917, the Fifth Army went into the line and took over twelve miles of front from the Third Army constituting the extreme right wing of the British Army. The VII Corps and the Cavalry Corps held the line, linking with the French on their right. Later the Fifth Army began to relieve the French, and by January 14th, 1918, the front of the Army was stretching a length of 42 miles as far south as Barisis. The Headquarters had moved to Villers-Bretonneux, to be in the centre of its front.

Although the process of extending our line was gradual, the work of immediate reorganisation it involved was arduous, for the sectors we had taken over had been quiet fronts and were in a neglected state. A tenant who knows that his lease is up does not bother to repaint his house or install new bathrooms, and so the French Third Army had left the line with little evidence of defensive preparations for their successors—all the work remained for the Fifth Army to do. This must, however, not be taken as a criticism of the French or the British Third Army. Every division and battalion were apt to do exactly the same thing to each other when they were going to be relieved, although they would not care to admit it.

In ordinary circumstances we would not have needed to build elaborate defences in that part of the line which lay along the River Oise. But owing to an exceptionally dry winter the river was low, and its natural defensive power on which the French had relied no longer existed. This applied as well to large stretches of marshland which became completely dried up and passable for infantry. Here we had to constitute entirely new

defences. In addition to this labour we had to rebuild
all the lines of communication and make habitable for
troops the vast stretch of land between the front line
and the back areas which the enemy had previously
abandoned and wilfully laid waste.

This was a serious state of affairs and our anxiety grew
when, little by little, we ascertained that the enemy was
contemplating a break-through on a grand scale, judging
from the work they were doing behind their lines. By
the middle of February the staff entertained no further
doubts on the matter.

I had spent part of December and January with the
troops in the areas we were taking over from the French,
roaming all over our new sectors, then very quiet. On
enquiring about casualties I was amused to learn that
they were mostly, due to the persistence of the men in
fishing in the River Oise; otherwise hardly a man had
been lost.

The Fifth Army had set to work on an elaborate plan
of defences, the principle of which was the distribution
of the troops in depth. Three defensive belts of defences
sited at a considerable distance from each other were
being constructed in the forward area. The most advance
line was built on a system of lightly held outpost screens
covering our main position.

I was kept busy making drawings of our front for
General Gough. As time went on I became familiar with
every spur and ridge and every piece of ground in our
scheme of defence. All the advantages that the country
gave us for enfilading the enemy advance were used to full
purpose. Machine-gun emplacements were being constructed, field-gun positions were also made right up in
forward positions so that they could fire point-blank into
some of the gulleys which the enemy would use to penetrate into our battle line. My work was intensely interesting. I was learning the strategy of defence.

When I got back each night the General would look at
my drawings and I would explain the lie of the land which

he followed on his map. He himself would visit the places and see that what he wanted done was carried out. I worked mostly with the construction of the forward line and what we called the "battle zone," where he hoped to hold the enemy once they had broken through our front lines.

Meanwhile, behind, a whole army of labour was engaged in the laying out of intermediate lines on which the army might be forced to fall back under pressure from the enemy. Although at first labour came up sparingly, in February as many as 45,000 men were employed on this work; labour battalions, Indians, Chinese and Italians and a great number of prisoners. But even all this army of labour who had to cover the vast front of 42 miles was inadequate when time was a vital consideration.

Invariably I set off for the line every day, sometimes by car but mostly on my motor-bike which I preferred, for in most places I was able to take it much nearer to the line than a car. My daily ride became a monotonous routine, for it took me across an immense stretch of desolate, weather-beaten and war-worn country. Here and there were a few derelict huts or the ruins of villages. Miles of straight road slipped under my bike as I pressed on the throttle and sped towards Péronne or Noyon—names that became an obsession, for every signpost in that abandoned waste gave the same direction. My bike pounded and rattled over pot-holes and often I left pieces of it behind. It was a relief when the Labour Corps began mending the road and portions of it became rideable again.

The only indication of a village was its name written on a large board and a few ruins, hardly showing above the overgrown weeds. The pavé road through the village was banked on both sides by mere heaps of bricks. There was no life about; civilians were not allowed to return to their homes, although they implored us to let them; there were no homes left for them to go to. Labour battalions lived in the ruins, isolated from the world like men living in caves. We had days with grey leaden skies when the roads shone from the rain and telegraph poles stood out

darkly. Here and there were patches of acid-green grass;
the country looked drenched and hopeless.

There came a spell of very cold weather. Snow covered
the country and the roads were frozen tracks. It was
bitterly cold riding through that still land over which
rooks circled in the grey sky. In the distance German
prisoners could be seen working in their lonely wire camp.
Those poor devils led a miserable existence on that bleak
plain. I am sure both they and the shivering sentries
guarding them envied me as I passed them on the road.

The return journey at night was the worst part. I had
walked all day. My mud-clogged feet felt heavy and cold
on the foot-rests of my machine. I always had a ride of at
least 40 miles. Bent over the handle-bars, I rode in the
darkness, my eyes staring on the V-shaped ray of light
of my head-lamp which edged both sides of the road
with a silver streak. My machine roared on with the same
regularity, seldom letting me down. The darkness closed
in again over every village after I passed. I flashed my
light on many boards between Ham, Nesle, Chaulne. I
accelerated towards the end of the journey, splashing
through Lihons, Harbonnières—I knew them all without
seeing their names, although every shattered village looked
the same—the ghost of what it had once been. In places
there weren't even any telegraph poles to relieve the
monotony of an empty road—these, like all the trees, had
been cut down. At times I rode for miles in the silence
without encountering a soul, and then suddenly I would
cross an area in which there was movement. My lamp
would suddenly light up a marching battalion, and in a
cinematic motion it would slip past, oaths and curses
rising from the ranks because my lamp blinded them.
Or I would pass a column of lorries trailing up, every
vehicle displacing the air with a series of "whoofs," and
scattering mud and stones in every direction. The last
lorry left a sudden feeling of calm open space, making
the darkness deeper. Miles from anywhere I would meet
a solitary man on the road. Where had he been? Where

was he going, and what for? There wasn't a girl anywhere
within walking distance. A drink perhaps?

Towards the end the brilliance of my light dazzled and
strained my eyes. I had to dodge water-filled pot-holes
which, lit up, looked as though they might have been
craters on the moon seen through a telescope.

If a car came towards me, I saw its searchlights miles
ahead in the distance dividing the deep darkness with its
vivid rays—that road didn't deviate for 60 miles. If the
car drove up a hill the lights shot up and lit the sky, to
dip again on reaching the flat ground. Going downhill
the lights darted into what seemed a dark hole, the ground
above quivering from its glow. As it approached, the glare
of its lights increased and shot forward like a glittering
ripple creeping straight at me, until almost blinded I
found myself in the ditch off the road, as the car drove
past me like the wind. I could hear for a second the rasp
of the engine and then silence. Striking match after
match I looked for the scattered bits of my lamp which
had tinkled on the road. Sometimes I was lucky and
found them again.

For miles before I reached Brie I could see the blazing
fire of the 17th Lancers mess intermittently flash out like
a beacon whenever someone opened the door. I looked
for that light, anticipating an assured welcome from the
officers in the mess. I invariably came back through Brie,
and when there was time I stopped for tea and often
remained to dinner. The 17th Lancers quartered there
had built for themselves a most comfortable camp. I
remember how on windy nights, frozen by the cold winds,
I accelerated towards that light. Numb with cold I pushed
open the door to step into the brilliance of a well-lit room
where the flames of an unusually big fire leaped up the
chimney. If it was dinner-time Colonel Melville was there
surrounded by his officers dressed in blue mess kit. I can
never sufficiently express my gratitude for their kindness
to me and for those moments with them which warmed
my spirit and body for the remainder of my long journey

back to headquarters. The regiment was marked by a
spirit of cameraderie which Colonel Melville extended
to all his officers; they adored him and so did the men.
Their smartness and efficiency were exemplary.

They had a very amusing French interpreter, who, un-
intentionally, used to set the whole mess roaring with the
stories he told. He hated the war and didn't hesitate
to express his opinion of it, speaking always in a loud
voice, his English tinged with a slight accent. It wasn't
on humanitarian or philosophic grounds, but because of
the sheer discomfort and the disturbance it had made in
his hitherto pleasant life. Having once been an elegant
dragoon he spent his time caracoling on a white Arab or
seeking distraction in Amiens. He was very proud of being
interpreter to the 17th Lancers. "Le dix-septième, tu sais,
le meilleur régiment en Angleterre"—the smartest; what a
charming fellow the Colonel, he would say. Have you
noticed his riding-breeches? What a cut!

Georges was easily led on. On guest-night with champagne to wind him up there was no stopping him. He
would tell us all about his charming wife, describing her
to us in glowing terms, and would draw comparisons
between French and English life. For example, he would
exclaim, "I cannot understand why you English do not
build flats to live in. Look at me; for the amount I pay
I get everything, hot water, light, even my wife is centrally
heated by the concierge who does everything for me!"
The roof of the mess would shake from the roars of
laughter.

In the attack on Bullecourt Georges had followed the
regiment. Generally he made no bones about remaining
with the quartermaster and baggage, but this time he rode
by the Colonel as they came within view of the black wire
emerging from the snow in front of the Hindenburg line.
I will let him continue the story in his own words:—

"I saw some shells burst near one of our squadrons. . .
Gosh! . . . then more. . . . Horses and men were going
up in the air. I closed my eyes. . . . I said to the Colonel,

'But it's folly to remain where we are; let's go.' But these British are funny—he didn't answer. I said: 'If you wish to get killed, I don't.' So I turned my fat pony [he then explained which one it was!] and shouted for Michel, my batman, and we both galloped away. My pony jumped over trenches and over the dead like hurdles. My! he could jump. A General was coming up on his horse. 'Don't go there,' I said, 'you'll get killed; everybody is being killed.' Well, what do you think? That funny man spurred his horse to where I told him not to go."

When Georges was seen again he was asked what had happened to him. "But, my dear fellows, I don't know why you remained—it was silly to get killed—but did you see how well my fat pony jumped over those trenches?"

His story is to this day a classic in the regiment.

Georges was really splendid and everyone loved him. He was genuinely respected, as no one else would have been, for his thoroughly selfish point of view. No, he hated war. Had he not been happy at home with his nice wife? He had step-children of whom he had never spoken nor had he assumed any responsibility for them until the day when their existence worked in with his plans. An order had come out entitling every Frenchman who had five children to go back to the base. Georges having only two of his own, immediately claimed his two step-children and asked for leave, a certain plan having taken shape in his mind. He had calculated carefully how much longer he would spend in what he called "those filthy trenches" (where he never went). Soon there would be for Georges no more Niessen huts unfit for a human being in that wild valley of the Somme.

Months passed—Georges was smiling! "They won't see me much longer around here," he kept saying. For Madame Georges was expecting a child. When the baby arrived Georges waited expectantly for that little chit which would order him to the base. However nothing was forthcoming, but instead came March 21st, when the German barrage was falling on our trenches and the cavalry was urgently wanted. The regiment was lining up when Georges ran to the Colonel, waving in his hand his order to the base. "Good-bye," he said, "I don't think much of the British Army if they can't keep the infantry in front of those bloody Germans, instead of dragging out the poor miserable cavalry."

Refreshed by Georges and the spirit of the mess and strengthened by their excellent dinner, I would set off again on the remainder of my journey to headquarters—another 20 miles or so before I climbed that hill by War-fusée-Abancourt road, where lines of transport were echeloned as if asleep. I saw the glitter of a sentry's bayonet or perhaps my lamp would flash on a Tommy and a girl clasped in an embrace between two lorries. I was within reach of comparative civilisation. The elongated sheds of the aerodrome were in sight and I was in Villers-Bretonneux again.

As soon as I had seen General Gough I would turn in to my comfortable billet in the house of a schoolmaster who had gone to the war. If I was not too late I found the mother and two children sewing and reading round an oil lamp. The rooms were spotlessly clean. Although I was comfortable I could not be happy in a house where I felt impending tragedy; they always seemed to be waiting for it as if it were overdue—they even wore dark clothes. As usual one evening, Jean, who was a typical delicate overworked French child of nine, leaned over his exercise books while his sister solemnly sewed and the mother stirred a spoon in a hissing pan, preparing the savoury-smelling dinner. Outside the wind was shaking the door as though someone was knocking. Yes, someone was outside! The children didn't move. Through the partly opened door I saw a light held by a man who was covered in a wet dark cloak. A few words, of which I caught only fragments, were exchanged between him and the mother. The door was closed again. The tapping of the visitor's clogs on the road had died away. Without a word the mother went back to her stove and pushed into her pocket a slip of paper. Her shadow on the wall showed her right arm over her eyes, but the habitual tension in her room had somehow gone. The children got up to lay the oil-cloth for dinner. With red eyes the mother started to pour the hot soup into the plates. . . .

I thought she seemed relieved in a way. Had she not been expecting it every day for months? I think the children guessed. The only sound came from our spoons striking against the plate as we drank our soup. . . .

The distribution of bread to the inhabitants of the town took place in the evening. A long queue waited at the bakers' windows. The light coming from inside showed them all muffled up as they stood, sometimes for hours on end, their feet in melting snow. I often watched the distribution; the line of people growing smaller and smaller as every inhabitant reached his turn at the window and took the loaf handed to him from inside.

When the distribution was over the baker closed his window with a bang, the light was put out, the last served inhabitants could be seen surging into the grey street hurrying to their homes. The same thing happened every day, only very often the bread wouldn't be ready and the crowd had to wait long hours in the cold. They were mostly women, children and old men, for all the young men had gone. . . .

Villers-Bretonneux was exposed on all sides to the winds. It was a large village with a lot of ugly modern houses and a hideous church. One of the features of the town was a red château, in the wide park of which was caged a collection of rare exotic birds. They were out of place in these surroundings, and indeed they were soon set at liberty or died.

CHAPTER XXXI

By the end of February, 1918, the Army had very definite
information about the enemy's intentions. A warning cone of impending storm had been hoisted and
the whole energy of the army was now concentrated on
the speeding up of defence work. There was still a
great deal to be done; we knew by then that we were
fighting against time, and that in spite of the amount of
labour employed, we could hardly hope to complete our
elaborate plan of defence. We didn't know the exact
date of the attack, but we were sure that it would come
soon.

The all too few divisions holding the long line were
doing their best to deal with the improvement of the forward line, which was to be known as the red line. An
intermediate system of trenches, yellow and brown, came
into the battle zone. Every suitable position was used to
build up strong points and redoubts which were designed
to hold the enemy in the battle zone as long as possible.
Digging and wiring went on everywhere with the most
sustained energy. Guns were brought up into forward
positions and carefully hidden in order to be used only
on the day, to meet the enemy attack as it debouched
along the gullies in between the innumerable little spurs
in front of our line. The guns were intended eventually
to take on the tanks which would, we feared, assist the
enemy's infantry assault. We also prepared our eventual
retirement from the forward zone to our battle zone, and
on to our rear zone, the green line. Numberless things
had to be done; roads had to be made and perhaps as
many as two hundred and fifty bridges to be mined ready
to be blown up; dumps had to be made everywhere for

274

the artillery to fall back on, bridge-heads had to be fortified and organised.

From Gouzeaucourt, where we joined the Third Army, down to the beginning of the French lines the work was pushed on at double speed. Often the Army Commander was seen about, inspecting the ground. He sent me particularly to the left, where the system of defence was on a more extensive scale on account of our junction with the Third Army and also because of the lie of the land. From Gouzeaucourt down to Holnon by the St. Quentin Canal I was engaged in making sketches. The men were often amused and puzzled at my drawings; one rightly remarked that I drew in shorthand. I learnt in those days to take advantage of all possible short cuts. For instance, when colonels clamoured for wire and other materials urgently needed for their front line, I was in a position to drop a hint to the C.R.E. of the Army, who like a magician, had it immediately sent up without the delay of the usual red-tape formality.

Every man was working with the full knowledge of the pending event. By the middle of March every battalion in the line had rehearsed its part in the battle, and the companies in reserve, destined to counter-attack, had practised on the ground the part they were meant to play when called upon. No one in the Fifth Army was unacquainted with the stern facts.

General Gough was in close touch with the French all the time, as they were eventually to come in and help us out. We were firmly counting on them. The Army Headquarters had gone to Nesle to be nearer the line and more in the centre of the whole stretch of the battle front.

I spent March 19th in the sector facing the town of St. Quentin, which stood on a hill in the distance showing its red ruins. Through a telescope I had a good look at the town and searched for the museum where, before the war, all the pastels of Latour had hung, and wondered whether they formed part of the wreckage at which I was looking.

I had tea that day with General Neill Malcolm, who had left the Fifth Army headquarters staff to command the 66th Division. Though details of certain events immediately prior to March 21st have become a little vague, I remember a large room like a hall made of new wood where we had a long talk. The quarters struck me as being very temporary, as indeed they were. We had taken over from the French their sound-registering stations. It was very interesting to watch the daily increasing numbers of German guns which we were able to trace on these very ingenious recording machines, similar to a seismograph. A little indicator made either a spot or a line, according to the wave of sound made by firing batteries or guns. These sounds recorded from different stations formed diagrams from which, with certain calculations, the exact position of the batteries or guns could be determined. Daily the sensitive indicator would scrawl more and more strokes, which sometimes resembled Chinese puzzles and in which the positions of certain heavy guns would figure by a large blob which at once drew the attention of our own artillery. We were, therefore, under no illusion as to the concentration of the enemy artillery before our front.

On March 20th I roamed the whole day about the slopes of Chapel Hill within sight of the shattered roofs of Gouzeaucourt, which lay along a ridge. As I walked about I imagined Germans streaming down those slopes towards our forward lines, and thought how well they would be enfiladed by our ingeniously placed machine-guns. I looked at Gauche Wood, little thinking that twenty-four hours later its trees would make a place of glory for the division which held it. The day had been warm and spring-like. A little rain had fallen in the morning. I walked over for tea to the battalion holding the front line. Its headquarters were in a deep dug-out on the road to Vourcelette Farm, whose ruins looked up over the ridge in the middle of a system of strongly fortified positions. The farm itself had been turned into a bastion.

No one could have looked into the enemy ground without feeling confident that every German scrambling down the slope from his front line and ascending our ridge was bound to come at some time under a galling fire from our machine-guns and rifles. Every hidden gully was the target of some of our guns. We had specially marked the roads which their reserves would use; they were all to be dealt with by our heavy guns with block barrage—we had withheld firing on all these targets purposely to keep the effect of surprise for the day of the enemy onslaught.

We had a long-drawn-out tea; the Colonel commanding the battalion was very young and, I remember, came from Liverpool. We played the gramophone tunes then in vogue, and I made several sketches of the officers sitting round the table. No word of battle was mentioned, and no one could have been more gay and full of life than these men, conscious of the doom which they were to meet in a few hours. The Colonel climbed up the long stairs with me and accompanied me down the road. He spoke vaguely of the coming attack—it might be to-night. Anyhow, they were ready. The dusk seemed to accentuate the meaning of everything he said. As I was bidding him good night, he asked me, as though by an afterthought, to do something which I realised had been lingering in his mind. "You know that sketch you did of me just now in the dug-out? I wonder if you would send it to my sister?" He then flashed his torch on a piece of paper and wrote out an address. I left him to retrace his steps towards Vourcelette Farm, his lonely figure facing the enemy side, where more than 2,000 guns pointed towards him were ready to support forty-two divisions in the biggest attack ever known.

Immediately away from the line I felt the dearth of troops—once past the artillery I hardly saw a soul for miles, except men from labour battalions moving round their camps.

As I rode my motor-bike through the night I felt and saw a mist rising off the ground. I thought little of it, as this often occurred on the Somme. I did not suspect that this was to turn into a fog, which would deprive us the next morning of the most valued factors of our defence.

That evening I was in General Gough's room. Like a man fully alive to the facts that confronted him, he told me he expected the storm to break over the Fifth Army that night, and that he knew for certain that forty-two divisions were massed before his army. As he was giving me other details the telephone-bell rang, and I heard a one-sided conversation with G.H.Q. General Gough was laying stress on the advisability of having his two reserve divisions right up ready to intervene. I could gather that the man at the other end of the line held a different opinion. The conversation was brought to a close by General Gough saying energetically: "I shall fight the blighters in my battle zone as long as we can hold them there. Good night, good night." He then turned to me and told me to come and see him early in the morning.

I walked over to my billet to change my dirty clothes, very conscious of the approaching danger. The night was clear with stars, but the mist still hung on the ground. Hardly a sound came from the line. W— was in the mess alone as I went in for dinner. Feeling rather strung-up, I nearly exploded with laughter when I saw the mysterious expression on his face. With a Captain Kettle beard, W— came from a neutral country and had volunteered to serve in the British Army at the outbreak of the war. His job in the Intelligence Department was to trace spies and arrest them. Unfortunately, he was constantly being taken for one himself, and arrested on account of his very strong accent. He was a charming fellow, really very brave, but as his work didn't actually bring him into the firing line, he lived it all in his imagination. He carried a revolver in each of his hip pockets. Mysteriously he gazed around him as he moved, stroking his beard. If you asked him where he was at the beginning of the war, he would tell you, with a deep look, that he was "galloper to Allenby." One could see him galloping through bullets and cannon-balls. If the staff were preparing an attack he would at once assume an air of mystery and importance that gave the whole show away. He couldn't help it. At the first intimation of movement in the line his horse was saddled ready, for he always dreamed of the "gap," and I am sure he would have been the first through it, too, if he had been given a chance, but it never came.

His greatest ambition was to earn the M.C. and the Legion of Honour. He suffered agonies at every honours list that came out. He turned quickly to the end of the list to see if his name was there. He never gave up hope— with a smile he would say: "For next time"; he had the ribbons ready in his pocket-book. One day he pulled out the red ribbon of the Legion of Honour and said: "My dear Maze, on a blue suit at the French races, wouldn't it look awfully nice?" He said it in such a suave voice and with such benign innocence that I longed for him to win it.

He also wanted a wound stripe, and that he got within the next few days. During the retreat I ran into General Maxse's headquarters, hearing shouts of, "Carry on, I'm all right," and saw W—— bandaging a scratch on his hand. He hurried off to the casualty clearing-station to have it dressed so that his name should be quickly on the casualty list, and I am sure that on that very night the wound stripe figured on his arm. I saw him again after the war walking along Bond Street, carrying a dispatch-case and looking as mysterious as ever. . . .

As we walked through the streets of Nesle that night after dinner, the place seemed plunged in perfect peace. Not a sound came from the line.

THURSDAY, MARCH 21ST, 1918.—It must have been shortly after 6 o'clock the next morning when I responded drowsily to the calls of my landlady, who, having planted herself at the foot of my bed, said in a complaining manner: "It's been bombarding like this since early morning." Though she had no reason to be annoyed

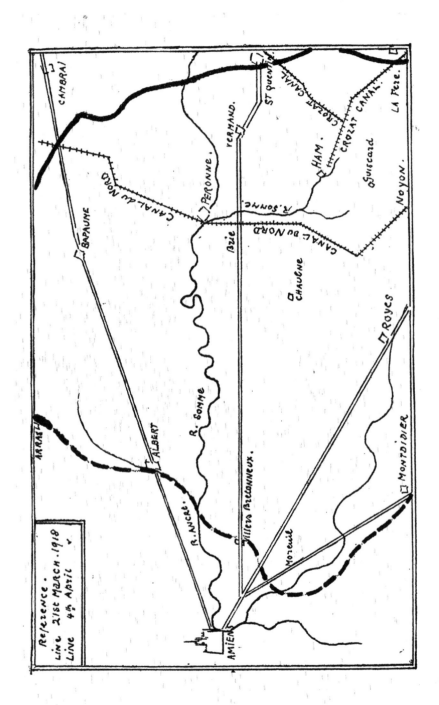

Reference.
Line 21st March. 1918
Line 4th April

CAMBRAI
ST QUENTIN
CROZAT CANAL
CROZAT CANAL.
LA Fere.
VERMAND.
HAM.
Suiscard
NOYON.
PERONNE.
CANAL DU NORD
R. SOMME.
CANAL du NORD
Brie
CHAUBNE
BAPAUME
R. SOMME
ROYES
ARRAS
ALBERT
R. ANCRE.
Villers Bretonneux.
MONTDIDIER
Moreuil
AMIENS

with me, she had plenty to be anxious about, for the roar coming from a very wide front had reached a most unusual intensity, rattling the window-panes as though heavy traffic had been continuously passing.

There was a thick fog outside. While I dressed hurriedly I could hear motor-bikes rushing off in every direction. Acting on an acquired principle, I had a good breakfast and went to the office, leaving my reproachful-looking landlady. Every corps had already reported a heavy bombardment on their front, also a very thick fog, but no infantry attack had so far developed. General Gough was at the telephone when I went in to see him, so I paced up and down in front of the headquarters, my mind riveted on the line. Staff officers were setting off in cars and immediately vanished into the fog. I was told to wait until further news had come in. I fidgeted outside, eager to feel a breeze that would lift the fog. Tired of waiting, I went and had a second breakfast, the tension prevailing everywhere, suggesting that the chance of another meal that day was remote. The fog isolated us mysteriously from the line. At 9.30 I started off for the left of the front, where we linked with the Third Army, the same place I had wandered over the day before. I first made for General Congreve's headquarters, the 7th Corps. Through the thick fog the noise of roaring cannon was like thunder.

The Corps Headquarters was in huts on a chalky knoll, perched up like a platform; bombs had shattered them a few days before, giving the place a desolate appearance. The air was vibrating continuously from distant explosions as I knocked at the doors of the offices, most of which were empty. The General and best part of the staff had gone off to the divisions, and there only remained an A.D.C. and a few clerks. A dog, its tail between its legs, was slinking round the huts, stopping to turn and snarl at the artillery roaring five miles away.

The enemy infantry attack had by then started; beyond that no other news so far had come in. So I left and went on. But for a battalion of the Italian Labour Corps that

I passed, gesticulating with their picks and shovels, I saw no one on the road until two ambulances rushed past. I was by then nearing the zone from which our heavy guns were firing somewhere in the fog, and I felt the first crash of an enemy shell pitching near the spot from which came the loud report of our guns. I accelerated nervously—conscious of my nearness to the line—and of the added horror and danger of the fog.

Soon the village of Sorel le Grand loomed before me. Reserves were solemnly marching through it. A lot of our guns were scattered about between that village and Heudecourt, for which I was making. On the way I heard the shouts of drivers slashing at their horses and the jerk of chains strained from a sudden pull as guns were leaving their position. The firing falling on our battery positions was steady and incessant, while the reports from our guns seemed more erratic and sounded muffled in the fog. I managed to get through the block barrage at the entrance of Heudecourt, about 3,000 yards away from the line, without mishap. Amongst the ruins of the village men could be seen hurrying here and there intent on their jobs. A few lorries were lying on their sides abandoned in the middle of the road. Artillery limbers rushed past, the drivers with a look of fear and haste in their eyes. Nobody could tell me what had really happened so far. The fog, still very thick, showed no signs of lifting; the village seemed endless. Shells flew overhead and crashed with a thud into the houses. I became more and more paralysed by terror and anxiety. I went on, not knowing quite where I was making for. Vaguely I registered the shapes of shattered trees and the stones of the crumbled houses, the shape of which seemed transformed and magnified by the fog. Carcases of horses lay on the road. Our guns thundered away further on, while the general tumult from the not so distant barrage left me utterly confused. Only the previous night I had cycled through those very streets, unperturbed, feeling the first touch of spring in the evening light. Every familiar landmark now seemed obliterated. Soon the splutter of musketry was audible—violent in parts, dying down in places to rise again with a sudden and terrific clatter, especially from the left of the 9th Division front.

I left my motor-bike and followed a party of signallers, who were uncoiling a wire from their headquarters to their batteries. All communication appeared to have been severed. Avoiding the road, I strode into vagueness to look for our "brown line" about 800 yards north of the village. The visibility was very bad. I stumbled forward, thinking of the seriousness of the situation, a feverish anxiety growing all the while in my mind. The smoke from the steady shower of German 5.9s mingled with the fog. The ground was marked everywhere with fresh shell-holes; the uproar rising from the line had become alarming. Shapeless figures were running through the fog past me. I saw a few men on the ground with their eyelids closed and then attached myself to a party of men making for the brown line which, happily, was easily found. It was only partly occupied by a few reserves with machine-guns trained and ready. I had strayed far more to the south than I thought; instead of facing Vourcelette Farm I was a good 1,000 yards to its right, facing the village of Epehy on the ridge skirted by our defences.

The men were under no illusion as to what they were in for. I struck across to get on to the Gouzeaucourt road in an endeavour to reach Revelon Farm. It was only about 600 yards away in front. The road was being very heavily shelled when I reached it. The place reeked of gas, and everybody was wearing gas-helmets; nervously I slipped mine on. A field artillery gun, burrowed inside a bank, pointed its muzzle straight over its protection of sandbags, with its ammunition piled in rows, showing the bright copper cases. I could not see the expression of the men with their goggled eyes and the snake-like rubber tubes hanging from their mouths. Seen through my goggles the men moving in the opaque atmosphere might have been divers, and the trees coral reefs under the sea, round which

the smoke from bursting shells was drifting like an under-
current.

I had to shout to make myself heard by the officer in
command of the gun. They were waiting for the Germans
to break through at any moment. They enfiladed the
valley, he said, and if they could see at all, they would
have a good target when the enemy appeared. I knew that
other guns were placed for the same purpose along this
stretch, and at any moment they might open fire. I was
not keen to get in their way. He thought that I had no
chance of getting anywhere near Vourcelette Farm, and
strongly advised me not to try, so I made for Revelon
Farm, keeping well off the road.

After going a few hundred yards I stopped to consider
what I should really do. I was now about 800 yards from
the ridge, and from the sound of rifle-firing I could un-
ravel approximately what was going on. Obviously the
enemy had penetrated into our forward battle zone; the
ridge was rattling from machine-guns as though it were
being drilled; they must have been near our "red line"
fringing it. I could not, therefore, think of reaching the
Northumberlands marooned in Vourcelette Farm; I could
not have found out any more by going there than I already
knew. I only risked getting into the confusion and probably not getting out again. At times I could detect
isolated firing from posts which must have been surrounded and were still resisting.

It was more difficult to make out what was happening
on the left, where the violence of the firing rose unevenly
from different areas and seemed to indicate imminent
further penetration by the enemy. A jagged piece of shell
that thumped into my shell-hole startled me to my feet,
and I realised that if I stayed there and the Germans broke
through, I stood the risk of being caught in the fire both
of our own defences and theirs.

I crossed the road to Revelon Farm without seeing a
soul. Bursting shells were tossing up earth all round. A
hundred yards beyond was the road to Chapel Hill, along

which an officer was hurrying back. In order not to waste
his time, I ran alongside him while he told me that he was
trying to get a message through to his guns to fire on
Gauche Wood, which, although they were otherwise holding the enemy, had now fallen into their hands. Stationed
between the "brown line" and Revelon Farm, muzzles of
machine-guns and isolated forward guns were sticking out
of the ground in a comforting way; so far they had not
fired a shot. The men, wearing gas-masks, were waiting
in tense readiness, expecting the enemy at any moment.
Only a very few wounded, so they said, had managed to
stray back from the line; everywhere I went I got only
meagre information. I wondered then if it was advisable
to get back to headquarters and tell the General the little
I knew of the situation. Certainly there was nothing he
could do; the battle was now well out of his hands, and
the fate of the army depended entirely on the courage
displayed by the battalions.

Anyhow, I decided it was best to get back to the corps.
It was past noon; the mist in parts was thinner, and as I
was looking for my motor-bike amidst the mass of ruins
where it had been left, the fog seemed suddenly to split,
letting through the blue sky. There immediately followed
an increased outburst of shelling and general musketry
firing. Our guns seemed also to have taken a new lease of
life, and the valley which I had just left burst into a clatter
of machine-gun and artillery fire—something obviously
had happened. Our forward guns were then firing at
point-blank range—suddenly the reports ceased and were
replaced by musketry clatter. I little knew then that the
gunners were surrounded and defending their guns with
their rifles. I was whirled away with the movement of
galloping horses and limbers, while a swarm of enemy
planes appeared, flying very low, showering the ground
with bullets and in places dropping bombs. Our own
planes had also come on the scene, and battles were raging
in the air. Now there were guns on the road moving back,
and further along in the open field large guns on cater-

pillar wheels were crawling along like prehistoric beasts, pointing their awkward elongated necks to the sky. Everything suggested anxious hurry. The shells pitching all round made the progress of the guns appear slower than it really was. Aeroplanes were harassing the batteries. Some reserves, made up of sappers, were marching up. German balloons had already climbed in the sky; ours, packed up on their lorries, were trailing back to safer positions.

As I arrived at Corps Headquarters, one of General Congreve's A.D.C.s was going off in a car to make a round of the divisions, so I went with him. The 21st Division on the right was anxious. Ronsoy had fallen and the enemy had penetrated into Cologne Valley encircling the ridge, where Pozières and Epehy, undaunted, were holding on.

The enemy had pushed up his guns and all divisional areas were now being thoroughly shelled. We had to work our way round to get to the 9th Division. I heard then how the Germans had broken through into the valley in front of Vourcelette Farm and had been caught as in a trap by our guns immediately the fog had lifted and revealed them. Obviously the fog had disorganised them, but they had penetrated into our "yellow" line system of trenches. We had lost Chapel Hill, which, however, we were ordered to re-take. So far on that front the battle line was still pretty well intact. I rode back to Corps Headquarters on my bike, where the calm of the road was a soothing change after the infernal roar from the line. I was struck by the absence of troops anywhere back of the line. Generally, at this juncture of a battle, reserve divisions are marching to the guns. Alas! none were to be seen, for the simple reason that there were none available beyond two divisions which the battle had already engulfed.

General Gough was away visiting his army corps. Messages had poured in from every part of the line, but so far one could not know how much ground the enemy had won. It looked as if the III Corps on the right had been more heavily pressed than the others, but on the whole line the fighting had developed into a huge battle, and the army was now facing a situation that none other had ever been called upon to face before. Aeroplanes were reporting that every German road was crammed for miles back with troops. Knowing that I would take soon to the roads again, I gulped down a good meal.

Later I was sent to the XVIII Corps. I found General Maxse absolutely calm, and apparently happy, as was his wont; he asked me for news of the other parts of the front. His had stood the strain. His look of satisfaction was no doubt due to that. He had held the line of his battle zone, having only lost a few of his outlying posts and some of his redoubts. Although he was satisfied, he didn't deceive himself as to what the following days had in store for him and the rest of us. He told me General Gough had been in and told him that he was not to count on receiving any help from army reserves for some time.

I rode back to Nesle, tired out, leaving behind me an uninterrupted wavering of gun-flashes. I had not been back five minutes when I was sent with a message to a French Army Headquarters in the south. I was so weary that I was only semi-conscious of the road sliding under me. After delivering my message I lay down for an hour's sleep, and returned to our headquarters in the early morning, riding through a mist which completely shrouded the country. I had little rest before I was sent early to the III Corps on the right.

I had gathered from General Gough that the French reserves were not coming up as he had hoped, and that beyond the two divisions of reserves, which he had at the start, no others were forthcoming—at least, for the time being. During the night, orders to retire had been issued to certain units whose positions were either precarious or threatened the safety of others. He could not hope to hold the Germans in his battle zone, as with insufficient reserves there was no way of preventing the enemy breaking through. He wanted the army to retire gradually, fighting a rear-guard action all the time and holding on to strategically valuable ground as long as possible. He appeared pleased with the fight his army had put up. What was vital, he said, was to see that units kept in touch with each other and didn't retire without giving warning to the units alongside them. He asked me to help in that way particularly.

MARCH 22ND.—I didn't feel too fresh when I set out from Nesle making for Buchoire, twenty miles south, where the III Corps had its headquarters, but my own fatigue was nothing in comparison with that of the infantry who, after fighting all the previous day, had spent the night in extricating themselves from their dangerous positions, which involved fighting and forced marches in the general confusion and darkness. However, the retirement had been successfully accomplished. Even some of the garrisons of the forward posts had made their way through the enemy and rejoined their brigade, which had shaken its feathers and stood grimly waiting for the next ordeal. The corps during the night had retired this side of the canal without being interfered with by the enemy. Bridges had been blown up, but in some cases the fuses laid by the French a long time before had failed to do their job. On the extreme right, south of the River Oise, two brigades which had not been attacked still held their original positions.

In spite of the previous day's hard fighting, the corps had plenty of artillery left, the infantry had reorganised and some of the most tired units had been replaced by reserves. They were therefore awaiting the day under rather favourable conditions.

It was still misty as I passed our gun positions, making for the little towns of Vouel and Tergnier, which together straggled as far as the canal. Some of our cavalry regiments were waiting in reserve and entrenching, battalions were hurriedly digging trenches. Except for a violent rumble from the north and the steady shelling of villages,

the line in front still seemed comparatively quiet, but
when I reached the outskirts of Vouel a heavy barrage
opened, spreading towards the north along the Crozat
Canal. As the mist cleared the town of Tergnier rose up
wreathed in smoke. At once the clatter from our machine-
guns started, and from its violence I realised what a target
the enemy on the other side of the canal must have been
offering our men at that moment. I saw detached companies from a battalion rush through Vouel in double-
quick time. Considering their previous day's experience,
the men looked well, but I noticed a scarcity of officers.

I had no difficulty in finding Brigade and Battalion
Headquarters; everything was still well organised and
under control, ready for the coming storm. They had still
their own reserves at hand and good cohesion existed between units. I heard from some men of their experiences
during the night, and how they had worked their way
through after being surrounded.

I climbed on the bank of a railway-line parallel with
the canal, where a few reserves were taking shelter. As a
wall of smoke screened the view, it was only from the noise
that I could gather what was going on. It was now about
11 o'clock. After the mist had completely lifted, the bombardment from both sides increased; enemy balloons had
taken up a line in the sky and their aeroplanes began to
circle everywhere like hungry gulls.

I then worked my way up north, not unlike a man who
visits a stormy shore and stops to watch the waves. The
enemy was hammering hard at all the bridge-heads.

Quessy, Liez and Menessis each in turn were being
rushed by the Germans and being re-taken by our counter-
attacks. The cavalry, which had so far been in reserve,
was now involved everywhere.

I ran into the headquarters of General Lee, who commanded the 18th Division. I knew him well, as he had
been the Fifth Army's chief engineer. He showed me on
his map the disposition of his troops, marked by multi-
coloured pins which he moved from place to place, look-

U

ing at them through an eyeglass. Although he preserved his usual calm, he was naturally anxious about the immediate future. He asked me if the army was expecting any reserves. I had to tell him there were none.

The line held remarkably well during the afternoon, although at times the violence of the repeated attacks augered ill. We were, however, counter-attacking when we could, and at one time I had the unexpected sight of a large group of German prisoners being marched down the road.

Late in the afternoon the volume of sound of our own bombardment was increased by a roll peculiar to the French seventy-fives. I learned afterwards that two French divisions were on their way, and that already their artillery was in position. On nearing the approaches of Chauny, I met the leading battalions, and for a long way south I could see the roads covered with this welcome relief force. The enemy captured Tergnier in the evening.

Further north there was no change all along the canal-bank. The enemy had been successfully held wherever he had forced the bridges. But as I rode back to the Army Headquarters, my mind was filled with misgivings about the situation of the army.

During the day the rest of the army had been heavily attacked. The XVIII Corps on the left had been obliged to retire on the Somme after very severe fighting.

I slept that night at Nesle—my last sleep in a good bed for many nights.

In the meanwhile the line was again being straightened, and by the mercy of God, all retirements were made without interference from the enemy. Darkness and fog gave the troops some respite and time to reorganise.

CHAPTER XXXII

THE RETREAT CONTINUES

MARCH 23RD, 1918.—From an early hour lorries were loading the archives of the Army Headquarters preparing their removal to Villers-Bretonneux. It was foggy, and the inhabitants were rushing about anxiously, not knowing whether they were to go or stay. They were calling on each other from doorsteps to windows. What could one do but tell them to leave their homes? They hoped that we could pack them all into lorries and save some of their furniture, but this was out of the question. The soldier's attitude towards civilians in a crisis is necessarily ruthless.

I caught up with General Uniacke, commanding the army artillery, who, spick and span, was on his way to his breakfast. We talked of the situation. He said he had lost many guns during the first two days, but he had helped himself out of G.H.Q. Siege Park, and many guns were now in trains on their way up to replace the losses. The value of this immediate supply of guns was to be a great asset during the next few days.

The XVIII Corps lorries were driving into the town as I left, for this corps was taking over our headquarters. The development of the previous day had started a general westward retirement which filled the roads. Camps and canteens had already cleared away; trains at railway-sidings were being loaded up. Chinese and every other available labour were working at the dumps—what could not be shifted was being blown up. Forward casualty clearing-stations had folded and packed up their tents; bonfires were clearing up the rubbish. As I passed one of the hospitals I saw the nurses in their long coats, holding their little bags, waiting by the side of the road to climb on to the lorries that were taking them away. They might

have been passengers standing by the lifeboats of a sinking ship after a collision in the fog. Thousands of
prisoners who had been encamped behind the lines were
being marched away from their camp to safer places,
guarded by a mounted escort. Had it been clear enough
for the enemy aeroplanes to have seen anything at all,
their long columns might have been taken for our reserves. The distant booming of guns filled the atmosphere
with foreboding.

I was on my way to the III Corps, to keep in touch
with the French, who had arrived with two divisions.
General Gough had hoped that these forces would relieve
some of his troops, which he would use as reserves, but
this was not to be. General Pelle, who commanded the
French Corps, had taken up his headquarters alongside
General Butler's III Corps H.Q.

I passed elements of French divisions working their way
up along the roads. They were a fine lot of men, particularly the dismounted cavalry. All these blue uniforms
gave us hope, as we understood more were coming.

A French division had already entered the fight by
making a counter-attack on Fargnier—the 75's were
thundering hard. I gathered at Vouel that the attack was
progressing successfully.

But the storm battering against the Crozat Canal had
risen to gale fury. It could only be a question of time
before the dam gave way. The bad visibility helped to
create a most uneasy atmosphere.

I wandered on to find touch with the left wing of the
French taking part in the counter-attack in progress.
Some English transport was leisurely retiring, the men on
their wagons cheerily eating their breakfast as though
nothing serious was pending. As soon as I came up to the
French Regimental Headquarters I heard grave news.
Their counter-attack was being held up, and they were
being heavily attacked on their left flank instead of being
in touch with British troops. This implied that the enemy
had forced his way over the canal and was filtering through

between the British and the French. Fierce fighting was
going on. I placed myself at the disposal of the Colonel
and rode off to get the situation clear in my own mind. As
the increase of machine-gun-fire on the left of the French
showed that unmistakably the enemy had crept up, to
allow myself a margin of safety I worked my way along
a loop-way back and round the French to come out by
our English troops. The roads were very much encumbered with a mixture of French and English transport,
as well as artillery, retiring. A staff officer held up in his
car made me realise what an asset a motor-bike was, for
I kept off the road where I could. It was useless to try to
find any headquarters at the moment, for they were on
the move with the rest.

On the edge of a wood men were digging a trench. I
talked to the officer in charge, and all he could tell me
was that a staff officer had ordered him to prepare a line.

I overtook some companies of French dismounted
cavalry who were labouring with their loads across the
open in order to keep off the road; they were the tail end
of a regiment hurried up to Bois Hallot. They said something about looking for their ammunition transport,
which had not followed up. The hurry of troops going
up and of those coming away from the approaching roar
of battle made a significant picture then in my mind.

I had climbed on to a wooden knoll, from where I had
a survey of about 300 yards of partial visibility, and could
watch the progress of limbers and carts on a road below.
The enemy guns began to extend their firing, and shells
were now leap-frogging over my head and bursting on the
roads behind me. The uproar made by the French
counter-attack on the right and the continuously increasing thundering on the whole line from north to south
sounded most ominous. Anything at that moment seemed
possible. The fog had thinned a little, which permitted
me to see vague groups of men ahead, and gradually a
further patch of country rose to view beyond. Immediately the tac-tac of machine-guns was heard on the right,

which brought to their feet a number of men I hadn't seen before, who started running, obviously for shelter. The fog then completely lifted, and the volume of machine-gun-fire increased. Aeroplanes swooped down on to our troops and dropped flares that brought an immediate response from their artillery. On leaving my position I certainly apprehended the worst, but unexpectedly to my forward left Bois Hallot sprang to life with the debouching lines of French infantry, who were advancing to counter-attack under cover of machine-gun barrage. This propitious intervention seemed to divert the enemy's fire from the British, who were now springing to their feet and quickly retiring.

In the meantime graver happenings were taking place further north, where the enemy had captured Ham in the morning and had driven the 30th Division from the Somme Canal. This thrust on the left flank was coming on the rear of the 36th Division, engaged with some cavalry in a grim counter-attack to check the progress of the enemy by Ollezy.

The French counter-attack south had in the meantime come to nothing, and on the right French and British divisions were falling back, fighting alongside each other. It was an anxious day. By the time a situation had been reported to Headquarters and they were taking measures to meet it, a more serious one had arisen, upsetting all their plans. This state of things was continually recurring.

As I rode that night on the long way back to Army Headquarters I felt that the reports of the right wing for the day would alone be enough to worry the Army Commander; but the gravity of the situation was still greater than I thought, for the centre and the left wing north of the Somme had been forced back and, furthermore, the retirement of the Third Army alongside the Fifth Army was increasing the danger to our left flank. General Gough asked me to remain with the XVIII Corps and keep in touch with the French troops that were coming to its help. "Wherever you can," he said, "impress on the troops with

whom you are in contact that on no account are they to
retire without warning units on either flank. The line
must bend and give, but the enemy must not be allowed
to break through."

As I rode on to the XVIII Corps, lorries with supplies
for the troops and ammunition for the guns were crawling past me; the organisation for the feeding of the army
never once broke down even in the face of our increasing
difficulties.

I unlaced my boots and rested for a few hours in a room
next door to where General Maxse sat enveloped in his
heavy coat, his cap pulled over his eyes, puffing at a cigar
and facing his map like a professor studying a problem.
Now and again a shout for "Tom" would bring forth his
Chief-of-Staff, General Holland, who was calmly dealing
with all the intricate problems of the anxious situation
in another room. The green bed valises rolled up in the
room indicated that sleep was out of the question for anyone that night.

MARCH 24TH.—The fog was again thick the following
morning. On the 36th Division front, to which I had
gone, everything seemed relatively quiet. From the report
of the field-guns firing it was evident that the line there
made a very dangerous semi-circle. Now and then rifle-
shots from outposts cracked out like a fire that has gone
down and only needs stirring to flare up again.

The enemy did not wait for the fog to lift to put down
his barrage, and their infantry attacks followed soon after.
The day cleared brilliantly; enemy balloons took their
places in the sky and their planes flew over us to seek the
weak spots in our line. The 36th and 20th Divisions so
far were holding their own, but wedged in that salient I
awaited developments with misgivings, in spite of the fact
that the French had come up in force on their right, and
from the sound of their guns were well supported by
artillery.

I wandered south to see how they were getting on as I

had been told to do. I went via Villeselve and then cut
through a wood where the many wagons of a French
division had halted; on proceeding I was dismayed to see
some of their artillery on the move, and when columns
of infantry appeared marching back, I realised that the
whole of the French 9th Division was giving way—what
seemed worse was that they were conforming with the retirement of one of their divisions on their right—the
whole of the right wing then was withdrawing. I realised
at once the consequences this retirement would have on
the British divisions fighting north of them.

It takes time to find a headquarters. One has to stop
and enquire here and there, and then go to some place
where one is told somebody will put one right. In a
short while one is sucked into the chaos of a retirement
as a cork drifting on a river gets held up by current pools.
When I did find a staff their minds were entirely preoccupied with the problem of getting their own troops
safely through the wooded country, which rendered the
retirement difficult. I knew there was no possibility of
stemming the tide, but I hoped to try and delay it by explaining the dangers to which the British on their left were
now exposed. But the Colonel replied, and perhaps wisely:
"But they must also withdraw."

The 36th Division, which in the meantime had been
pressed back, had thrown in their meagre reserves, and
General Harman had just rushed his cavalry into a breach.
Counter-attacks were in progress. To make the situation
still more perilous the enemy had advanced southwards
from Ham, threatening to cut off our ultimate line of
retreat by closing up the circle behind us.

I raced off to inform Headquarters, but soon became
caught in a web of columns that were being held up by
the baggage and artillery of other French units going
north and which cut across their path. The anxiety of
each column to proceed was only making matters worse.
I noticed a French officer's car jammed in the block
and ascertained that this officer was endeavouring to get

on to reconnoitre the route his division was expected to take when they came into the line during the night. The thought of available troops stirred me to give him a picture of the situation the XVIII Corps was now facing, and I impressed upon him the necessity of immediate help. He suggested that I should ride back with him to his Divisional Headquarters. We extricated ourselves from the traffic and I followed his car.

The General commanding the division was away, so I explained the situation to a chief-of-staff. He certainly saw its gravity, for he got on to his Corps Headquarters. I had to wait a long while, probably because the corps was consulting the Army, for no division moves a battalion on its own initiative so easily when it is not in the line. I then rode on to find the XVIII Corps Headquarters, which in the meantime had fallen back.

I found General Maxse in conversation with General Robillot, who commanded a French corps that was coming up. General Gough had arranged with him for a counter-attack to be made the next morning south of Nesle by his 22nd Division, and his troops were now on their way to take their position behind the XVIII Corps. The command of British troops then passed automatically under French orders the moment they came into the line. This arrangement was to cause at first great complications, for the French staff could not, on arriving, immediately realise the state of the British troops after four days' strenuous fighting, and their plans were often incompatible with the reality of the situation. No two men could have presented a bigger contrast than these two Generals; General Maxse, very quiet, sitting grimly at his table, and the rather exuberant French General dressed in the palest blue with two rows of medals tinkling on his broad chest.

It was no light task to ensure the necessary preparations for the relief of the British troops by the French and co-ordinate arrangements for a joint counter-attack. Most of the orders had to be hastily transmitted verbally. I was engaged that night in seeing that the French troops

reached their expected position and got into touch with
British troops on their left when they arrived. I had hours
of anxious wanderings on the dark roads, for everlastingly
unexpected new problems kept cropping up. Ammunition had not followed and had to be found; if there was
any delay one knew that the enemy would renew his attack
early and forestall all our plans. Having been shifted
about from place to place the British troops had had no
rest again that night.

One or two stars glittered in a paling sky. Another
night had gone. Every soldier was weary as the anxious
day dawned. How much longer would they stand the
strain? I myself felt sore with fatigue as I motor-cycled
to headquarters and got a whiff of eggs and bacon being
fried on a petrol lamp by the drivers of an ammunition column; I gratefully accepted a generous offer of
some breakfast. I always ate when and where I could, and
never failed to refill my bike with petrol whenever the
opportunity offered. Later on it became difficult to find
petrol, so I carried a spare tin behind me.

The French had now taken over most of the III Corps
front. Its line had been pressed back the previous day to
a depth of about ten miles, but what seemed a miracle was
that the British 36th Division, exposed to encirclement as
it had been throughout the day, had successfully extricated
itself from its dangerous position and was now prolonging
the French left.

The situation north of the Somme continued to give
alarm, for there had been a general withdrawal to the
Somme Canal. Péronne was lost. Although the French
were now arriving in strength, the Fifth Army was facing
a task beyond the power of its depleted forces, for the
enemy attacks, strengthened by daily reinforcements, were
showing no signs of relaxing.

The town of Nesle which, within the last six days, had
been Army, Corps and Divisional Headquarters in turn,
could now be seen from the line 2,000 yards inside the
enemy's territory, and it seemed strange to see it like a

familiar rock cut off by the rising tide.

On looking for the 18th Division mixed up with the French right wing, I saw early that morning indications of the renewal of the retirement. I came on the 17th Lancers trotting along in answer to an urgent call. On seeing me, Colonel Melville stopped his regiment and asked me for news. But for their own experiences, they were all ignorant as to what had happened in the north, except for unfounded rumours which always circulate at such times and sound more alarming than the truth. As I saw the men lean forward in their saddles to catch what I was saying, I spoke loudly so that they would hear that the French were arriving in force and that the situation, though serious, was being taken in hand. The men smiled with relief. "How is Goughy?" asked the Colonel as he gathered his reins and rode off, followed by his regiment. "All right," I called back, "he is very pleased with you all."

I went from place to place, gleaning here and there information, trying to keep in touch with brigade staffs which were constantly on the move. We had lost Abbécourt and Cailleul early in the morning, and there had begun a general withdrawal of the French towards the Oise Canal. The troops I saw everywhere were sweating as in summer; it was very hot.

By the middle of the afternoon I felt the complete exhaustion of one who for days has had insufficient sleep. I rode on to some high ground in the middle of thickly wooded country and came to a place where I could lie down and at the same time see the country below and beyond me. I flung myself on to the first patch of withered grass and felt sleep overpowering me like the action of a drug; in a few moments I was soundly asleep. Was it for seconds or minutes?—I don't know—but when I awoke I remained for a time in that delicious comatose state when only a vague contact exists between oneself and one's surroundings. Now and then I could hear the rattle made by horse-drawn carts passing on the roads below, and the scraping feet of retiring troops rose like the sound pro-

duced by the rubbing together of two sheets of sand-
paper. Where roads could be seen through gaps in the
woods the blue of French troops marching along gave a
semblance of flowing water. In the afternoon light the
trees shone a warm brown. All the same, I kept a vigilant
eye on the creeping barrage, for the splutter of rifle-fire
was re-echoing louder and louder across the wood. I felt
refreshed once more, and suddenly everything became
precise and clear.

My map spread out before me, I identified the various
roads on which I could see the retirement of infantry
and artillery. On a straight stretch of road more visible
to the right, pontoons raised on wagons above the blue
tunics might have been gliding on the shining waters
of a canal. A succession of explosions as bridges were
blown up added to the significance of the retreat. I could
tell by the sound, the direction of the enemy's advance,
accentuated on the left towards Noyon and on the right
towards the Oise Canal. Aeroplanes were following the
movement as gulls follow the wash of a ship. Immediately in front of me the heavy firing of rifles and machine-
guns seemed to hold back the advance. After a time the
main body of the divisional troops had passed, leaving
an empty gap on the road and then a battery went by.
Near a village I saw the flash of some guns that had unlimbered to shoot off a few rounds and then gone on again.
Then appeared, intermingled with the blue uniforms, the
khaki of our troops. They were threading their way
through the edge of a wood, making for an agglomeration
of buildings, and spreading out to cover the approach to
the village. Some armoured cars were moving up towards
Montescourt, over which enemy shrapnel was now bursting with vicious sharp cracks.

I was anxious to see what was happening more to the
right, so I walked through the wood which resounded
with the echo of guns. The trunks of the trees hemming
me in filled me with a sense of loneliness. I couldn't find
a better view than I had before, so I returned to my

former position. From there I saw spinning rockets rise through the writhing smoke below me on my right, and heard sharp firing much nearer than I had expected, which soon developed into a violent action. I rushed for my motor-bike. On my way through Bois d'Autrecourt, where I expected to find the 18th Division retiring, I was told that they were more to the right. Events had followed each other in quick succession. I learnt from a group of cavalrymen that the village of Babœuf had not only been lost, but had been retaken by the 18th Division.

I set off in that direction, and on my way saw a bunch of German prisoners coming towards me; one of the exhausted-looking escort told me that a good many more were round the next corner; there were about 200 of them. I then found General Sadleir-Jackson, whose brigade had made the counter-attack. With his moustache curled up as usual, he looked very smart and bright. "We've given the blighters hell," he said, "and have stopped them for a while. I am going to hold on here as long as I can; I wish you would go and tell the French corps." So to Noyon I went, where I found General Pelle's headquarters in an old building of the town. He was a very distinguished-looking man, with a charming manner. He said he did not intend to defend Noyon, and that he had ordered his troops to fall back on the canal. Orderlies and officers had packed their papers and were obviously waiting for the word to jump into the waiting car outside. But General Pelle, calmly immersed in his thoughts, sat looking at his map, giving instructions to his impatient entourage while the building shook from the wheels of heavy artillery rattling by with an agonising sound. He didn't seem ready to leave until he had settled everything to his perfect satisfaction.

Noyon fell in the evening. The French on the right had retired on the canal line, but the 18th Division still held Babœuf. I rode on to Army Headquarters at Villers-Bretonneux.

It was now dark on that straight main road towards

Amiens. I was tired and dazed. My legs felt stiff inside
my long boots. All I could see was a circle of silver spray
made by my lamp lighting the pouring rain, and I could
hear the water sizzling on my hot engine. The events of
the preceding days were passing through my mind in a
succession of constantly changing pictures, and the darkness was stirring my imagination, for I could see village
after village falling like ninepins into the enemy's hands.
I could hear above the roar of my engine the everlasting
sound of retiring troops like a haunting theme. At times
the possibility of German cavalry breaking through in
force obsessed me. I was, however, cheered to a certain
extent when the rays of my head-lamp, flashing on to the
husks of buildings in the ruined villages, showed me the
desolation of the land which the enemy had wilfully
wrought the previous spring and of which his troops would
soon taste the discomforts. Sometimes a brilliant light
would approach and flash past—a staff officer in a car on
an urgent mission.

All these days on my way to back areas I rode without
once seeing approaching columns of fresh British divisions
marching up as I had so often seen in other battles. But
the French were arriving in force now and fine troops
they were, too. At Roye buses crammed with their infantry splashed their way along, and their 75's were
following in lorries.

When I came on to the devastated places the civilians
who had been allowed to return and restart their lives
were on the roads again in flight. They walked along in
the dark in the heavy rain alongside heavy artillery slowly
trailed by caterpillar tractors. The impression I had of
this drab mob, which included excited Chinamen of the
Labour Battalions, was of a crowd pressing against the
shaky chariots of a carnival cavalcade, the camouflaged
barrels of the guns wobbling like the long necks of diabolical dragons. As my lamp in passing lit up the edge of
the sprouting fields on which these poor devils had so
vainly laboured, I felt the horror of war.

General Maxse was in a bad mood when I found him, for Nesle had been lost early that morning and the counter-attack had failed. First of all the French had been obliged to postpone the hour as they were not ready, and then at the appointed time something had gone wrong; either they were themselves attacked by the enemy, or their orders cancelling the movement never reached the British troops. At all events our khaki lines strode forward unsupported on their right, their flank exposed. This was the result of the French staff taking over the command of our troops immediately theirs were pitched forward into the battle. General Maxse said that he was not going to allow his divisions to take orders from anybody but himself in future and that he would keep firm control over his troops. Two of his divisions, the 20th and 36th, had at last been relieved by the French and were now in reserve in the neighbourhood of Roye about six miles behind the line, having left their artillery to cover the French division whose guns had not yet arrived. I passed by these two divisions the next morning on my way up. Most of the men were lying like dead men, tired out. Little did I think then that they would be called upon that very day to intervene and save one of the most critical situations in the whole phase of the retreat. Some of them were shaving off a five-days' growth of beard. There could not have been more than 1,500 able-bodied men left out of each division of about 6,000 strong.

The battle had been raging hard on the XVIII Corps front for some hours when I proceeded towards it. At the time, although the firing seemed patchy and irregular, my fears that there would be a further withdrawal were confirmed by a motor-cyclist I came across who was vainly searching for some Brigade Headquarters.

Not having passed any gun positions nor seen any reserves, for all troops by then were in the line, I found myself approaching a group of tired men who directed me to some farm buildings 200 yards off, towards which I

crept, not knowing how safe it was of approach. In the
first building I found a young officer pale with fatigue.
He had the remnants of a battalion with him, some of
which were scattered in the broken ground beyond.
"What the hell is happening?" he asked. "We withdrew
here to conform with the left, but I can't make out whether
they are French or English in those sheds," pointing to
them standing prominently in the plain 500 yards away.
A heavy rifle fire was concentrated on them as on a firing
range. One of his officers had gone to find out who was on
his immediate right, where the ground rose thickly covered
with brushwood, from which intermittent firing of rifle
shots gave the assurance that somebody was there. As the
French should have been somewhere near I started working my way round towards where their guns could be
heard firing, to tell them to fire across our front, which was
completely unsupported by artillery. I saw half a dozen
men resting in a ditch, who having seen neither their
troops nor the enemy, had strayed like sheep and were
just vaguely waiting. They were done up and had lost
all sense of initiative; they were grateful to be directed
anywhere, so I sent them on to the farm buildings I had
come from.

My next recollection is an empty road closed in on my
left and a certain apprehension creeping up as I swung
round a curve and suddenly came on to a hushed plain.
In a flash I caught a glimpse of a bunch of German steel
helmets moving up through the rough ground in line with
my road about 200 yards to my left. Unconsciously I
pressed on the accelerator, making one with my machine,
expecting to hear the whistle of bullets. I covered an
exposed stretch of about 500 yards and during that
anxious spell all I passed on the road was a broken-down
lorry with its driver hanging limply from the seat and a
soldier on the ground some distance away who had feebly
waved to me. The road thereafter sank and I flew down,
jamming on my brakes suddenly as I came on to a French
armoured car. Another one was beyond in the main street

of the village with an officer in charge, to whom I quickly explained what I had just seen. The first armoured car at once moved carefully forward. This officer was under the firm impression that British troops were in front of him on the right and his mission was to keep in touch with them, and he was trying to find them.

My next move was to find the nearest French artillery to get them to fire across the space of ground where I had seen the German advance party. When I did so I realised the risk of firing on our own people as well, so it was decided that they should drop their shells on roads well ahead of where I presumed the British front line was at the time and down which the Germans must have been advancing. The French gunners were at once willing, knowing that the British artillery was supporting their front further south.

As the morning wore on the pressure of the German attack forced the French back southwards towards the River Avre; this was an entirely different direction from the one which both armies had been ordered to keep. The XVIII Corps, for their part, were withdrawing as arranged in a westerly direction. This meant that the two armies were separating, leaving an ever widening and unprotected gap for the enemy to come through.

General Maxse was already acquainted with this danger when I reached him. Already his resting divisions had been ordered to come up and take up a defensive line. He was worried as they had not a gun behind them with which to face the battle. He had sent orders to the French staff to have his guns sent back, but nothing had been done. He therefore ordered me to go immediately to the French Fourth Army and put the situation to General Humbert personally.

At the end of a ride of about 25 miles with many anxieties on my mind, the sudden entry into a luxurious panelled room where sat a hyper-military French Army Commander, acted like a cold douche. Standing in front of a table on which maps were displayed, officers were receiv-

W

ing their orders and with a smart click of spurs and clang
of sword saluted and went out. The dignified atmosphere
and luxury of the room contrasted greatly with the anxious
but human world I had just left in the line. My turn
came. Two sharp black eyes behind a pair of spectacles
were turned on me and I was curtly asked what I wanted.
I felt even more shabby than I must have looked when,
to justify my presence, I answered that I had come from
General Maxse himself to ask for the immediate release
of our artillery. I explained that the XVIII Corps troops
were fighting without a gun. He turned to one of his
officers and asked him if he knew anything about it. He
didn't. "Well, I will go into the matter at once," he said.
As I had been told not to leave without a written order
which I was myself to place in the hands of those responsible for our artillery I had to importune him still further.
"Very well," he answered, and gave orders for the written
document. While I waited for it I attempted to impress
upon him the gravity of the consequences which the retirement of his troops southwards was likely to cause, but I
don't think he liked it, for he dismissed me with my paper
saying, "We are looking after that." With a smart salute
I shook the dust off my boots and rushed into the night
to look for our artillery; it started that same night on
its long detour round Montdidier to rejoin the XVIII
Corps.

That day north of the Somme the Fifth and Third
Armies had fallen back across the old Somme battlefield
and the enemy was in front of Albert. On the front of the
XVIII Corps the night passed with a succession of alarms,
for at one time there was a gap of several miles between
two brigades of the corps, but in spite of this opportunity
the enemy did not break through. He advanced feebly
and even the counter-attack of our weakened troops
checked him.

In the morning, parties that had been surrounded since
the previous evening managed to fight their way back to
their line and the links of the chain were joined again

even with the French on the right who had put in new troops. The lack of initiative on the part of the enemy showed that he was as sorely tried by his advance as we were by our retirement. By then his Storm Troops, on which he had relied during the first days, had also suffered considerably, for our men had taken every opportunity at targets with machine-guns and artillery.

The enemy was now about 25 miles from Amiens, gradually gaining ground along those three straight roads from Bapaume, St. Quentin and Noyon, all converging towards that town, the taking of which would crown his offensive with success. What was there to stop him? The French Army was certainly arriving in force now that another new army (the Second) was being formed. I couldn't help feeling that they were giving way all the time on a set plan and that when they chose to turn they would. On the other hand, all that remained of the Fifth Army were men whose bodies were tired out but whose spirits were unbroken. Not one of them looked upon himself as a beaten man.

An incident characteristic of the British soldier was when on an occasion I commandeered a British lorry to take from a railway station some ammunition which had arrived for the French and which they urgently needed. There was no officer there to give the necessary authority and no time to go looking for one, so I took the responsibility, and the driver, though willing to help, was rather perturbed as it was "against orders." However, the ammunition was loaded on the lorry and a French N.C.O. climbed up beside the driver and off it went towards the attacked village. I followed some distance behind. Soon I saw the driver running back towards me; his lorry was ditched. The French N.C.O. had been shot; but what the driver demanded, first of all, was a receipt for his lost lorry.

To defend Villers-Bretonneux, the Army Staff had gathered a composite force of various elements, including American Engineers, which were the only fresh troops on

which the Army could turn for support, and when the
hour came they behaved as splendidly as the others had
done. General P. G. Grant, Chief Engineer of the Army,
took over the command.

I rode to Dury that morning with a message for the
Army Commander. I spent the day out of touch with the
line, for I had to go to St. Just to General Debeney's
headquarters, a long ride which took me most of the day.
His headquarters were much less formal than those of
General Humbert. A sympathetic atmosphere permeated
it, inspired by the charming personality of the Army
Commander. While I stood before his table messages
were coming in, and I followed his marking with a charcoal the progress the enemy was making on his front. As
I was leaving, he said: "I would advise you not to go too
far north of Montdidier, for we are falling back." Although
I followed his advice I was astounded when I reached the
heights just above that town to see infantry deployed along
the ditch of the road ready to let the retreating troops
come through them and receive the enemy. There was
then no sound of artillery. The enemy had advanced at
least nine miles that afternoon and quickly. I had to
make a large detour to reach Moreuil in safety, where
General Maxse had retired his headquarters. His corps
had held its own throughout the day and had hardly given
any ground.

.   .   .   .   .   .

MARCH 28TH, 1918.—We were facing the eighth day of the
battle. It was very misty and the pulse of the line beat
very low that morning. From both infantry and artillery
hardly a shot was heard. I enquired of a sergeant, who
was lying on the ground with a group of men, the whereabouts of the line; he pointed out a vague line of men
strung up in the grey of the morning and said: "There it
is." I had seen no troops behind them and knew there
were none except for the force in front of Villers-Bretonneux. I showed some surprise at the quietness of the line

and the sergeant replied, "Blimey, they are as done as we are." Had we had any fresh troops there that morning we could have walked through the Germans. I wonder now what our poor Tommies would have thought had they known of the hundreds of thousands of trained troops being treasured for some unknown reason in England at that very moment. . . . !

I asked where their Brigade Headquarters were and was told that some General was 300 yards down the road, so I set off in that direction and finally found General Malcolm, who commanded the 66th Division, together with General Jackson of the 5th and General Heneker of the 8th. The frontage held now by three divisions was so small and the troops so few that they had amalgamated as at other times brigades had amalgamated to form a battalion.

General Malcolm looked grey and tired. He asked me what reserves there were behind and if I knew of any coming. All I could tell him was about General Grant's force. "What a pity!" he said. "Had we fresh troops we could walk back to where we were a few days ago."

An odd shell or two was pitching in the sodden fields as we talked sitting in the ditch. A Brigade Major was writing orders and two dispatch-riders had just come in with messages showing that the organisation still existed. I left General Malcolm and promised to send a wire to his wife to tell her that I had seen him and he was all right, but my wire reached her after she had been informed that he was in hospital with a shrapnel wound.

I was now on my way back to Dury to the Army on the Villers-Bretonneux road leading to Amiens. I rode towards some cars against which I could see the blue uniforms of French officers who, to judge from the fanions on the cars, were Generals. Thinking of coming reserves, I ventured to give them some information of the line. I was asked sharply who I was, to what unit I belonged and when I replied that I was attached to General Gough I was told "he is not in command any more." I was speaking

to Marshal Foch. Dumbfounded, I saluted and dashed
off to Dury.

The streets were crowded with lorries of the Fourth
Army marked with a Boar which were unloading, while
lorries of the Fifth Army marked with a Fox were loading
up. I needed no further evidence. In a small garden in
front of the office I saw General Gough immersed in his
thoughts. He at once informed me that he had ceased to
be in command of the Fifth Army, "but before I tell you
what has happened," he said, "if you have any urgent news
you must give it to General Rawlinson, who is now in
command. I have arranged with him for you to remain
with his Army and for you to continue doing the work
for him that you have been doing for me. He is a fine
soldier; you will like him." I followed him into the office
where I was presented to General Rawlinson, who impressed me with his astounding health and confidence.
He took me into his Chief-of-Staff, General Archibald
Montgomery, and introduced me, adding that I was hence-
forth to report the result of my activities to him. I recognised one of his A.D.C.s as Lord Dalkeith, whom I had
last seen at Festubert in '15 with the Guards just prior
to an attack.

I then went back into the garden with General Gough
and quite simply he told me of Marshal Foch's visit, how
abrupt and short he had been to him and the depreciatory
terms in which he had referred to the conduct of the Fifth
Army. During the moments we were together in the
garden he neither made a complaint nor passed an
opinion. His thoughts dwelt on the problem the Fifth
Army was still facing.

As we parted he said, "We must win the war; we must
not let our personal feelings distract us for a moment from
our purpose." He drove off with his A.D.C. to G.H.Q.

Within a few days of leaving his army he was pacing up
and down the deserted promenade of a seaside resort in
England, his energies condemned to inaction. As it had
often seemed politic to the authorities to describe some

of our disastrous offensives as victories, so it was now the
the policy of the moment to refer to the Fifth Army
retreat as a calamity. Everywhere it was being discussed
by people whose opinions were based on ignorance.
General Gough was being reproached particularly for
doing what the enemy least of all wished him to do. After
the first day of the battle the enemy tried to pin him down
to a stand. It would then have been easy for them with
their overwhelming forces to annihilate us and walk
through, but General Gough was not to be lured into this
heroic gesture. It would have been the destruction of his
army. He felt the danger. He gave rope all the time,
ordering his army when it could to turn and strike back.
Meanwhile he preserved his front until the French came
up to our rescue and indeed saved us in the end. Small
recognition was shown to the many thousands who died
and the few hundreds that survived who, from the first day
of the retreat, were hopelessly outnumbered.

CHAPTER XXXIII

THE END OF THE RETREAT

MARCH 29TH, 1918.—We were now entering upon the last phase of the retreat. Although the enemy went on attacking, during the next days the flow of his advance was gradually becoming more uneven. Our resistance everywhere was stiffening. The French were now well organised and were settling down; and numbers of their reserves were coming up to strengthen the wall which was gradually being built up to stem the danger threatening Amiens. It was a joy to see their smart battalions of Chasseurs à pied marching up towards the line in artillery formation behind their deployed companies' fanions. The French were daily taking over more and more of the front and shortening the line held by the exhausted British troops. The greater part of what was left of the front of the Fifth Army was now held by Carey's Force, originally commanded by General Grant in front of Villers-Bretonneux, and some of the cavalry. A brigade of Australians had also arrived. I had known lots of their officers on the Somme in 1916 whom I found now risen to higher commands.

Only a few hundred weary men of the divisions which had fought since the first day were still in the line. These were again to give a good account of themselves before they could be relieved. We had left behind the grim and exposed spaces of the flat devastated areas and were now fighting in broken and hilly country more suitable for making a stand, but the danger was not yet over. The enemy pressed on, renewing his efforts to break through somewhere, and all our energies and resources were called upon to hold an unbroken front. The line again gave way on March 29th, but we lost relatively little ground and the continual din of our counter-attacks marked our intentions. The following messages reflect the prevailing tension:—

Toutes troupes que vous recevez, doivent être employées sur votre gauche en face Mézières et Demuin. Il faut maintenir à tout prix le moindre pouce de terrain et continuer cette nuit à renforcer la ligne occupée avec tout ce qui arrivera. Ne craignez rien pour votre droite ni pour votre gauche, je compte dans la nuit pouvoir envoyer un bataillon d'une autre division vers Hangard.

We want the French to take over this place and a little more if possible. If Boche attacks now he will get through as we are very thin.

The enemy was now facing Villers-Bretonneux, shooting up its streets and the little house in which I had slept so many nights had already begun to crumple. We had lost Demuin; the enemy had crept up the heights overlooking Moreuil and had entered the wood which General Seeley's Canadian Brigade was to retake the next day. Grim fighting went on round Moreuil during the next 48 hours. The 8th Division, still in the line, held part of the wood alongside the French and showed that they still had a kick left in them by also counter-attacking to improve the work done by the Canadian Cavalry, but the line was very much strained; the attacks had spread south and there the French had given way.

On a road running out of Moreuil Wood I felt the swish of bullets about me and heard the noise from an enemy plane as it swooped past and rose in front of me, then turned to come down the road and enfilade it again. I realised in a flash that he meant to get me and flung myself into the ditch to avoid another spray of bullets which made the road curl up in dust. I saw the fuselage of his plane stained with the drips from the engine and smelt the reeking oil; he flew so low. Slinging out my carbine I took a careful aim; but he rose over the wood and disappeared. He must have reported some French infantry coming up,

for the smoke of German 5.9s was soon spreading amongst
them.

The battle on the heights of Moreuil had reached a
climax. I was approaching the town, walking alongside
French reserves, when I heard in front of the bridge over
the River Avre a hubbub of voices and saw some French
troops gesticulating in a most disorderly way as they came
from the town. On the bridge I found General Mesple,
who commanded a group, holding a revolver in one hand
and his map and spectacles in the other, exhorting these
unruly territorials to discipline. It appeared that on
being relieved they had broken into the wine cellars
in the town and had drunk themselves into this excited
state. Although the moment was tragic, for at the time the
enemy fusillade was steadily creeping up to the hill and
lines of Frenchmen could be seen falling back, I could
not suppress a nervous laugh at some of the remarks made
by these excited men. While the kind old General was
clutching hold of two of them, the others were slipping
past brandishing bottles and hurling invectives at him.
When, however, he saw machine-guns in the hands of
these drunken men it was more than he could bear. "Take
out your revolver," he said to me, and he fired a shot that
immediately made an impression on the mob. It was really
a most unpleasant situation, for the men were not young
and were not really running away. They had just been
relieved. As we were marshalling them into some semblance of order General Heneker, who had just taken his
8th Division out of the line, came up and asked me what
was happening. "Do you think I had better bring up my
few hundred men?" he said, and I answered, "No."
Certainly at that moment it looked as if the French Army
had got out of hand, for this small group of drunken men
managed to create an appearance of far greater disorder
than actually existed.

While General Mesple was writing out a message which
he wanted me to take to the French Headquarters I kept
an eye on the ridge where the enemy lines were now

appearing. So distinct were they that I could see in-
dividuals falling as they were met by the volleys of the
French retiring troops.

On my way to the Army Headquarters I had to cut
across the transport lines of English and French units
falling back from the Avre. The traffic was very congested
and an English Major was sitting on a bank shouting the
directions which the passing units were to take. The
exodus of French inhabitants was increasing the com-
plexity of this mêlée, which at one time became a tight
jam. I rode along the edge of a field and at last came to
the cause of the hold-up. In front of an agglomeration of
peasant carts was one drawn by a donkey which simply
could not be induced to budge. An old man and woman
dressed in black sat in the cart, the old boy hanging on
to the reins while the woman hit the beast with a stick.
I tapped him gently on the shoulder and told him that
he must draw to the side of the road as he was holding
up two kilometres of traffic. He looked up in despair and
burst into sobs. The whole bag of tricks had to be lifted
bodily off the road while for some unknown reason the
old woman heartily cursed her weeping husband.

The roads all the way down to Breteuil were in a
constant whirl of dust made by the buses streaming past,
crammed with troops and batteries on lorries hurrying up
to the line. It was evident that the French now meant
business.

I came to General Debeney's headquarters very late
and found him with some of his staff just finishing dinner.
After reading my report he begged me to sit down by him
and have some food. I must have been very tired, for I
slept almost immediately; when I woke up the room was
empty except for a fat cook sitting next to me smoking a
cigarette. It was nearly midnight. He said that the
General had instructed him not to waken me before 12
o'clock. "Laissez-le dormir," he had said. I was touched
by this small friendliness, and felt immediately at home in
that headquarters.

As I left that night I was confident that the situation would soon change.

By April 1st, 1918, the French had extended their line to Hangard and had relieved most of the Fifth Army troops who had fought since the beginning of the battle. The following message which I received from some units reveals their exhaustion and anxiety as they eagerly waited to be relieved:—

See if the French troops coming to relieve us are on their way up. If so, tell them to get a move on.

Meanwhile the enemy had brought up his big guns. He concentrated his fire on all the roads leading to Amiens. At Boves I saw a stampede such as I had never seen before. Salvoes of 5.9s were falling on French artillery columns as they were approaching the viaduct. Limbers at full gallop struck the brick walls of the bridge and were hurled over, wounded horses and men lying all over the place, at the same time as the French Foreign Legion was marching up, apparently unaware of what was going on. At Longueau, an important railway junction just outside Amiens, a hush had fallen. Trains were running no more. This vital bifurcation which always hummed with the busy sounds of passing engines and rushing trains was now dead. The tracks were empty.

Just on the outskirts of Amiens in a network of waterways made by the Somme, where a section of the population cultivated their vegetables, shells were falling, shooting up high spouts of water and smashing the many globes that were forcing melons and other vegetables for the spring market in Paris. I punted across to one of these small islets to get at some lettuces and fresh radishes which were delicious after all these days without fresh food.

The bombardment of Amiens had begun. The station roof was already holed and the town was empty. Some of the shops had been ransacked. The front of a "Pâtisserie" had been torn open by a shell and sweets were strewn all over the pavement and across the street. Military police were grimly patrolling the town, which was now out of bounds. The Cathedral was being hurriedly protected by a wall of sandbags. Otherwise everybody had gone except Josephine, whom I found packing her cooking utensils into a cart. She had kept her head, for she was going to open a place further off. As I left she called out: "Tiens, grand," and threw me one of her last cooked chickens which I held like a Rugby pass.

My activities during the next few days were concentrated at the junction of the French and British troops at Hangard. I was attached to General Butler's III Corps. The demarcation line of the two armies was the Amiens —Roye road that cut through Demuin and rose across the front dividing Rifle Wood and Cavalry Wood spread astride the ridge. The road had been daily shortened for us in the last twenty-one days. It had been a stretch of more than 90 kilometres to our front line on March 21st, and now we only had the run of about 16 kilometres of it, but these 16 kilometres were to make all the difference between victory and defeat. Although during the next few days the enemy did not attack again, they had not yet accepted defeat, for they were to make several more vain attempts on Amiens.

Hangard had become a very nasty spot. The shelling on and about the road had become intense. Already it was strewn with shattered trees as after a violent storm. It seemed strange, after being on the move as we had been for so long, to remain in one place. I was glad of the rest, for I was feeling the reaction of all these busy days creeping over me. The hot spring mornings made me feel weak and sad, and overpowered with emotion. Now it seemed to hurt to see this country, budding with new life, being shelled to blazes. Lying relaxed in the sunshine I saw the whole valley below me cut by a line of freshly upturned earth, showing the extreme limit of the enemy advance. Fields ribbed with furrows were interlaced with sprouting velvety crops shining in the sun. What I had taken for

scattered manure heaps across the field were corpses of
the enemy who had been caught in the open. The crucifix
surrounded by four trees on a road over which I had cycled
many times during the past days was now reduced to
splinters.

When one feels weak one envies the energy of others. I
watched two French soldiers singing as they walked up the
slope towards me carrying pails of soup and I envied their
gaiety, when some 5.9s burst near them and they took to
their heels. I heard their laughter between the shell-bursts
until a smart crack slew them both and sent their pails and
tin helmets flying. They were now lying quiet near me,
mere patches of blue, the colour of the sky, stretched out
on that green spring field beside the gaping hole made by
the shell that had killed them. The larks continued to sing
above them. I wondered vaguely whether to envy them
even more now.

On April 4th we learnt from a prisoner that the
enemy was going to renew his attack that night. I spent
the night in the cellars of a farm at Hourges, 600 yards
from the front line and realised then that my nerve had
really gone. Two reserve companies crammed the cellars
which at the same time acted as a headquarters of a regiment. I lay down on the straw surrounded by fully
equipped men packed together. A Major commanding
the battalion sat at a dimly lit table. When a man was
ordered to go out the steely clash of his bayonet and
helmet resounded through the place as he fixed his gas-
mask on and prepared to face the din outside. The line
was being heavily shelled and the building shivered from
the uninterrupted shocks. Some wounded men were being
brought in; the atmosphere was stifling.

As the night wore on I got tired of being cooped up. I
felt like a rat in a trap, so I stumbled out into the night
and crossed the road to our English lines. Gas shells made
a screen of foggy fumes. Ghostly figures gasping for breath
were swaying along holding on to the trees. The following morning I remembered Josephine's chicken in my

haversack and shared it with some men squatting between tombstones in the cemetery. Never had chicken bones tasted more delicious.

However, the enemy gained no further advantage. Australian brigades had arrived in front of Villers-Bretonneux and the line now remained stationary, until the enemy made his final attempt on April 24th, when he attacked Villers-Bretonneux and held it for a few hours.

In the meantime his great attack on Lys had started a new phase of strenuous fighting with our Second Army. Like an agonised monster he was striking wildly everywhere, and our poor divisions that had been taken out of the line after having lived through all those gruelling days of the retreat, reinforced with new troops from England, were being packed into buses and sent up to meet the new danger.

I went in to see General Higginson near Boves. I knew he had been given command of a division. I found him just as his brigade, which he was to lead for the last time, stood ready to go off to an attack. He was genuinely sorry to leave three battalions with which he had been so long connected.

I was by this time worn out; I was thankful when General Buller suggested to General Rawlinson that I should be granted a short leave. I returned on April 24th, the night that the enemy attacked Villers-Bretonneux and were driven out by two Australian brigades.

The next morning I was roaming about on the spur on which stood Villers-Bretonneux. The red château was now in ruins, and its famous aviary was a thing of the past. Some wounded flamingoes were hopping about on one leg crossing the main road, gazing mysteriously at the dead lying all around. . . .

Had the enemy machine-gunners who were now lying dead in their shell-holes survived the night, they might have seen rising out of the distant mist the spire of the Amiens Cathedral dominating the valley of the Somme, the pinnacle of their coveted goal.

CHAPTER XXXIV

DURING the months of May and June the Fourth Army fronts remained quiet, but behind the line extensive defence work was in progress to safeguard Amiens from further danger. Digging, wiring and the building of concrete machine-gun emplacements were going on. The possibilities of a break-through by the enemy had been so remote in the minds of the General Staff that extensive lines of trenches which had been made early in '15 had been filled in to allow the peasants to plough their fields. It showed what confidence we had then in ourselves, for our thoughts dwelt only on offensive. The March attack had been a great awakening. The Australian Corps had come into the Fourth Army and the III Corps with its division reconstituted also held the line which ran from the north of Albert to the south of Villers-Bretonneux. Battalions, which had been so heavily depleted during the retreat, had received their reinforcements and were settling down to steady training. The weather was hot and the Somme battlefield had become very dried up. There were certain areas where at times the smell of thousands of bodies shallowly buried in the course of three years of battle permeated the atmosphere.

We were beginning the fourth summer of war, and one hoped it might be the last. During that period I was engaged in making panorama drawings. I found it restful, for my work brought me mostly into the valley of the River Somme, which had retained a picturesque aspect, in spite of the heavy shelling to which it had been exposed. The river bent in graceful loops along the foot of thickly covered slopes, where the mellow ruins of villages stood outlined against the green. I worked from a ridge and looked right down into this sunny valley, having observation on the enemy line running along the next spur. The report of their guns coming from the distant high ground or ours fired behind me could not disturb my contact with the radiant landscape. I would forget that I was drawing for military purposes, and become engrossed in form and colour, letting myself go completely. The spurts of water from shells falling into the river didn't disturb me either. Sometimes a man diving into the river made the same splash as the shells. A whole battalion would be bathing, and their gleaming bodies gave an illusion of life and gaiety pleasantly remote from the actual dreadful reality.

Civilians had gone back to Amiens with a feeling of safety, and life there had resumed its normal aspect. I remember seeing a wedding procession with several British soldiers in the cortège proudly escorting French girls, and it struck me at the time how most of our soldiers had won many French homes. I had often heard it remarked that these two nations were too different from each other to get on together, and can only conclude that the people of either race who make such assertions have never come into contact with the other. Probably the same applies to all nations.

The enemy's artillery activities went on as usual, but their infantry had become very passive. It was obvious that after the strain of their various unsuccessful offensives all they wanted was to be allowed to recuperate, but the Australians gave them little peace. Whenever a newly constructed trench line showed itself it was promptly captured. Thus they were not given a chance to improve the defences of their front.

Reconciled to another summer of war, I wandered about the line and really enjoyed it, although often I wondered how much longer this struggle would drag on. As Albert was now within the enemy line, a barricade had been erected on the main road from Amiens to Albert, and there one entered a trench. It seemed strange to me after

x

three years, during which I had always whizzed straight
down that road on a motor-bike or in a car. From the line
one looked right on to the roofs of Albert. Most of them
were holed like a tapestry canvas. One afternoon I was
going round with the G.S.O.2 of the Army, and we had,
for a few seconds, the nasty shock of finding ourselves in
No Man's Land by mistake. The trench we had been
following ended abruptly at the main Amiens–Albert
road, therefore we presumed that it continued immediately on the other side. We had climbed up the bank,
sidled along the brushwood fence and dropped down on
the other side, where we at once discovered that our own
trench was sixty yards behind us. We bolted like rabbits
and got back on to the road. The men in our front line
were running to their stations like sailors on the bridge of
a sailing-ship, their rifles pointed at us. As we scrambled
breathlessly into the front line, we were given a cold
welcome. It was a hot day. Evidently the enemy was
enjoying his siesta, for not a shot was fired at us. Another
incident I remember of those peaceful summer days was
crawling along a spur where one of our forward observa-
tion-posts had a plunging view on a German trench the
other side. I had started sketching when I saw the bald
head of a German framed against a shirt laid out to dry
on the parapet of his trench. In a hushed voice I called
the sentry and pointed towards the man. "I know," he
said, "he's been there all the morning doing nothing but
picking fleas off his body. Lousy, that's what he is." It
hadn't occurred to him to shoot him. Evidently in his
opinion being lousy was trouble enough for one man.

The Army Headquarters were far back behind Amiens
in a factory village called Flixecourt. On my way home
in the evenings, I branched off just before Amiens on to
a neglected towpath along the canal-bank, which the run
of my tyres rendered daily more smooth and even. Thus
for some miles, within hearing distance of the rising
murmurs of a busy town, I felt some peace. The coolness
of the shady banks and the calm reflections in the water

were refreshing after the heat of the sun. Although I always rode as slowly as I could, I invariably felt a pang when I came on to the noisy thoroughfare again. Only once did I feel that I had lost the proprietorship of my peaceful track, and that was when I met a pretty girl and stopped to talk to her. She gave me her address: Charlotte, chez Boulotte, rue d'Amour at Pegnigny. Although I never saw her again, the name of the street where she lived gave my evening rides an everlasting enchantment. I was far too busy to look for Rue d'Amour—perhaps it was just as well.

Sometimes I used to escape to Montreuil-sur-mer for the day. It was a long ride there and back, but it was worth it, for the view of the sea from the top of the cliffs was always refreshing. I had made friends with some lady ambulance-drivers, who were all very charming, so perhaps that was another inducement for my occasional jaunts. We would picnic on the beach, but nearly every time a message would come in the middle of it that a train-load of wounded was due in, and they all had to rush back to their ambulances to transport the men from the station to the hospitals. These girls were very hard-worked. Many of them never recovered from the strain of it.

Towards the end of June I accompanied the Chief-of-Staff of the Army, who was inspecting the defence lines in course of construction. During our walk he surprised me by some of his remarks, which indicated that his mind dwelt on the possibilities of resuming the offensive. By then the failure of the enemy's offensives in Champagne and at Compiègne had greatly diminished his reserves. His line on the front of the Fourth Army was held with comparatively few troops. Their power of resistance was tested in a small attack against Vaire and Hamel Wood. Taken completely by surprise, the enemy retaliated feebly to our assault, in which we had sixty tanks supporting the infantry. I remember the early morning light revealing to me the first American dead as I walked over the newly

won ground. Alas, I was by then indifferent to the sight
of our own dead, but those, somehow, moved me; they
looked so new and smart with their long leggings, they
symbolised also the hope on which the Allies were relying
for the future.

This attack was really the prelude to a wider offensive
which the Fourth Army had prepared in the hope of dis-
engaging Amiens. Its success was ultimately to propel the
allied armies forward to the general offensive, which
eventually gave us the final victory.

On July 15th, 1918, as the Germans were marching
against Rheims and crossing the Marne again, we followed
on the map the gradual formation of a salient which, like
an over-inflated balloon, was to burst with the first prick
of the French and American armies massed against its
flanks.

The time was coming for the Fourth Army to strike
opportunely. Although the attack was fixed for August 8th,
during the period of preparation, which started at the end
of July, no one not immediately concerned with it had an
inkling of what was intended. The chance of success of
this offensive depended on absolute secrecy. Only at night
did trains move the troops and materials necessary for the
attack, while the cavalry and tanks moved at the same time
by road. Guns came into their positions at night and were
at once camouflaged, as were ammunition-dumps. The
registration of targets was done according to a programme
so as not to increase the normal firing. On the afternoon
of August 7th the troops were waiting for darkness to fall
to move to their final assembly positions. Throughout the
day our aeroplanes had unceasingly patrolled the air to
prevent any observation, and, but for a raid by the enemy
the previous day, in which they had taken some prisoners,
there was every reason to believe that our intended attack
was unsuspected. The front of the attack extended from
Albert south to the River Somme, then in front of Villers-
Bretonneux astride the fork made by the River Luce and
the Oise, where the First French Army linked with us.

The III Corps was on the left, the Australian Corps in the centre and the Canadian Corps on the right. We were really attacking on the ground over which the Fifth Army had retreated in March. General Rawlinson and his staff may well have been satisfied with all their arrangements on the 7th, for up to then everything had worked out perfectly.

I had arranged to dine with the 17th Lancers in bivouac outside Amiens. As I motor-cycled through Amiens nothing indicated the pending event, except perhaps a long line of tanks sheltered from observation under the trees of the outer boulevards. The whole of the Cavalry Corps of three divisions was to move after dark along the only available road through Longueau and on to the Gentelles Plateau. Infantry and tanks also had to move up, and every unit was to start off precisely at its allotted time. At dinner I observed how all the officers were inwardly keyed up with excitement, for wasn't the cavalry to have its chance of a gallop at last? Yet, confident as we all felt, the next few hours was a gulf of uncertainty and inevitable apprehension. At 10 o'clock the orderlies cleared the tables, officers went off to get ready, and gradually our gay party disbanded and I parted from Colonel Melville. I was to see most of them again the next day in the full elation of a pursuit after the demoralised Germans.

It was pitch dark outside. Troops and cavalry were passing through a cloud of coal-dust rising off the road. My destination was a hole near Cachy, where I was to meet Major Priestman, the G.S.O.2 of the Army. Zero hour was fixed for 4.20 a.m. There was heaps of time. For a while I stood watching the progress of the troops on the Longueau—Villers-Bretonneux road, the prolonged clatter of cavalry horses reminding me of earlier days. They were marching slowly to keep within their time. I overtook infantry and tanks moving along in weird masses in the dark, following troops all the way to the Gentelles Plateau. There the ground was taped and pegged; boards indicated

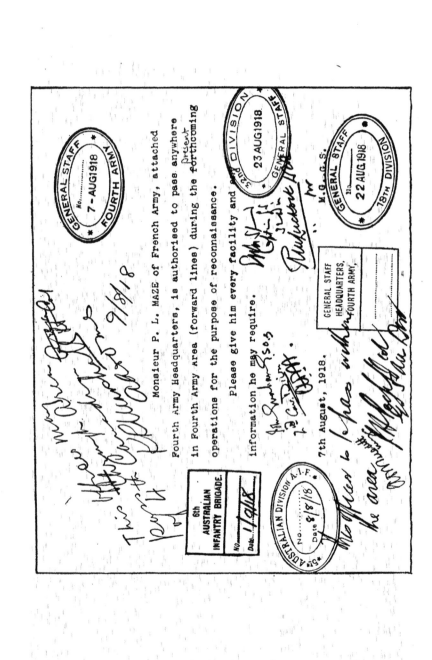

Monsieur P. L. MAZE of French Army, attached
Fourth Army Headquarters, is authorised to pass anywhere
in Fourth Army area (forward lines) during the forthcoming present
operations for the purpose of reconnaissance.

Please give him every facility and
information he may require.

7th August, 1918.

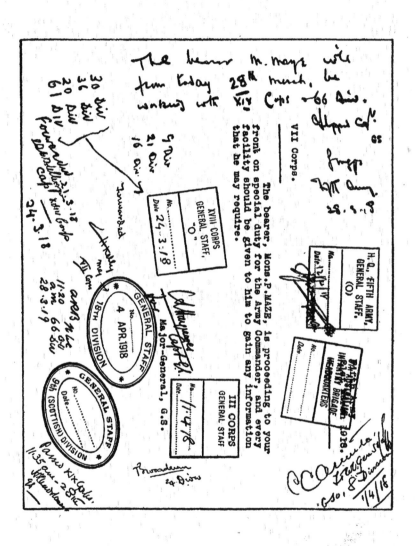

The bearer M. Maze will from today 28th march, be working with XIX Corps & 66 Div.

29.3.18

VII Corps.

    The bearer, Mons.P.MAZE, is proceeding to your front on special duty for the Army Commander, and every facility should be given to him to gain any information that he may require.

H.Q. FIFTH ARMY,
GENERAL STAFF,
(O)

No. .... Date 12/4/18

INFANTRY BRIGADE
HEADQUARTERS

No. .... Date ....

XVIII CORPS
GENERAL STAFF,
"O"

No. .... Date 24-3-18

GENERAL STAFF
18TH DIVISION

No. 4 APR.1918

III CORPS
GENERAL STAFF

No. .... Date ....

GENERAL STAFF
9th (SCOTTISH) DIVISION

No. .... Date ....

Major-General, G.S.

14/4/18

Broadsea
24 Divn

9 Div
21 Div
16 Div

30 Div
3c Div
20 Div
61 Div

XVIII Corp
24.3.18

VII Corps
11.20 a.m. 66 Div
28.3.18

Passed XIX Corps.
11.35 a.m - 2 Bde

the way each unit was to take as far as the approach to the line, to avoid any mix-up or delay. The whole area might have been the scene of a gymkhana. Aeroplanes were droning loudly overhead so as to drown the noise of the approaching tanks. Every object looming in the darkness hid something—the woods sheltered hundreds of silent guns awaiting their signal. I looked for a place to park my motor-bike and then found the G.S.O.2, who had wisely brought some food along. Our hole had been dug on the slope of the spur about 1,000 yards from the line.

At 2 a.m. we were squatting between four narrow earth walls with a mackintosh sheet for roof. We had a direct wire laid on to the Army Commander. Priestman tried the buzzer, it was working—all was well. The light of our torches by which we read turned the earth red. We tried in vain to sleep. Without admitting it to each other, we felt an increasing tension. Now and then the purring of the engines of the tanks or the report of a gun broke the silence which was now falling. I got up and looked out into the night. The atmosphere had grown hazy, the ground felt clammy. I had a hint of troops through the mist moving down the slope to their assembly position like long shadows, darker than the night. All I could see of them were their fumbling feet. Every hour had increased the conglomeration of troops on the plateau. It seemed too marvellous that so far the enemy had not fired a shot. Could he know anything? He had blown up a petrol supply tank that afternoon in Bois l'Abbaye, which in turn had destroyed many other tanks surrounding it, but he could not have known of their presence. Anyhow, all was quiet now. The plateau had gradually stilled and every unit now lay concealed in their proper places waiting for the moment to move.

Our buzzer squeaked like a tiny kitten. Priestman took up the receiver, and his voice may well have sounded as though it came from the grave with his non-committal answers to the Army Commander of "Yes," "No," "Right."

Now and again a heavy gun fired a low thudding shot
that deepened the night, and our field-guns would fire as
they usually did at night. We talked and waited. At about
3.30 a.m. the whistle of a German 5.9 pierced the air and a
shell crashed not far away. Then came another whistle,
and a crash followed by a quick succession of distant reports. But it was only one or two batteries firing, not
more. We listened to every crash until the last made us
think that the next must either bury us or pass over.
There was no next, and the night relapsed into complete
silence. I looked at the drawings which in my nervous-
ness I had carved on the walls, shivering with excitement
and cold, for the air had grown chilly with the early
morning.

As time crept on our watches became our sole interest.
It was now 4 a.m. Twenty minutes more! There was a
murmur of engines as the tanks moved up to their starting-off places. There were now only a few seconds left to
go, and then the sudden report of 2,000 guns fired together
rocked the earth. Our creeping barrage was falling in
front of the infantry and the men had gone forward. I
sprang outside. Thousands of guns were firing through
the mist. I could hardly hear the near-by bursts of a few
German shells falling like drops of rain in a passing storm.
We waited. The barrage was lifting according to the pre-
arranged time-tables, and in my imagination I followed
the progress the troops must be making if, as we hoped,
the enemy had been taken by surprise. So far there was
hardly any enemy artillery retaliation.

It was dawn, without any sign of daylight, just fog, mist
and fire. The visibility was not more than 100 yards. I
didn't know quite what to do at first, then I clambered
down towards Domars, where I hoped to get some news
from the Third Canadian Division who had a report centre
there. All around the khaki-clad reserves were merging
with the fog. No definite news had been heard so far, but
hopes ran high. Rumours and bad news, which always
travelled fast and had so often shattered our expectations,

had not come through. At about 5.30 a.m. a message was
received that hundreds of German prisoners were marching in and the advance was progressing favourably. Forward casualty stations were also reporting few casualties.
The atmosphere in that headquarters was tense. I left
them to their work.

I was anxious to get back to my motor-bike, for I knew
that the time was coming for the cavalry to move, and I
didn't want to miss them when they started. Our guns
were still blazing away, and not a German shell was falling
anywhere near our reserve troops, who were now moving
off towards their starting lines to get through and exploit
our first success. Their spirit had passed from one of suppressed anxiety to one of excitement—the report that Fritz
was "on the run" seemed to hasten their steps. It was then
that I saw a sight which remained engraved on my mind.
General Harman, who commanded the Third Cavalry
Division, was riding quietly down the slope followed by
his trumpeter. I hurried forward to give him the news.
He greeted me cheerfully, gave a sign of satisfaction, then
put his horse into a trot to meet the return of the patrols
that had gone forward with the infantry to report whether
the cavalry could cross the river. As he moved off the
leading squadrons of his divisions appeared surging forward out of the mist from the brow of the hill as in a
shifting mirage. In a moment the slopes were moving with
cavalry and tanks rolling down like a cascade. The tanks
were zigzagging along, back-firing as they went like jumping crackers. A yellow balloon was ascending in the sky,
and now, visible above the dispersing mist, aeroplanes were
buzzing above us. Something kept saying to me: "Look,
for you will never see such a sight again." If those who
had synchronised the advance could only have shared the
enthusiasm that surged through every man who stood
watching the cavalry pass! I was swept off my feet. I
waved to passing friends in the cavalcade and longed to
be with them. I ran to where I had left my motor-bike,
and saw near-by General Kavanagh standing beneath his

corps pennant surrounded by his staff, taking the salute of
his passing regiments. The din made by our firing guns,
the vibration of the air, the rattle of machine-gun-cases
on the pack-horses trotting down, the roar of the tanks and
the crash of our distant barrage were deafening.

The infantry was reported to have reached the green
line, their first objective, at 6.20. The 3rd Cavalry
Division was eventually to pass through the infantry who,
after a pause of two hours on their first objective, were renewing their advance and were progressing towards their
second goal. I had to follow the horses. I left Priestman
at the telephone. By then the Army Commander's
anxieties were allayed. He must have known that the
attack was a success.

I took the Marcelcave road for a while, leaving on the
right the squadrons of the 3rd Cavalry Division cutting
their way across country towards Hangard Wood, with the
2nd Cavalry Division advancing on my left making for
Marcelcave. The Scots Greys were visible in the distance,
their grey horses pressing on as I had seen them doing
early in the war. I soon saw ahead of me a grey mass filling
the road, obviously prisoners. I stopped to watch them as
they passed. They still looked dazed with surprise. I
couldn't wait until they all passed, there were so many of
them. I went on and came to our reserve trenches, showing everywhere traces of the passage of our troops. The
pegs and tape lines were now entangled after having
served their purpose. I saw very few of our casualties at
our starting-off lines and on the road which cut across No
Man's Land, but noticed arms and top-booted legs of dead
Germans protruding all along their front line so effectively
cratered by our bombardment. Plenty of machine-guns
lay about, and here and there derelict tanks sent up a black
smoke. Some were still burning.

In my haste to get on I rode into a deep hole, and as I
strove to pull my machine out of it, my anxiety was as
desperate as in a nightmare when, in spite of frantic
efforts to move, one remains rooted to the spot or forced

back by some invisible power. At last I succeeded in getting my machine out and went on, catching up with the cavalry as it was trekking through Morgemont Wood. Here groups of Germans were being gathered together, and men were chalking up some of the machine-guns with the names of the units that had captured them. I could see by the tracks of the tanks how they had been rounded up one by one. Some dead Germans, run over by the tanks, were lying flattened out like pancakes.

Near Aubercourt the Canadians had suffered severely. They had been shot in the open ground from a trench which defended the approach to the village. I did not remain in the river valley very long, for the enemy were dropping some 5.9s, and I also wanted to be with the cavalry before they went through Ignaucourt. Our barrage could now be heard preceding the infantry as they continued to advance. The spirit of the men had suddenly passed from one of resignation to one of enthusiasm. Hopes were raised—it looked as though this battle was to be the beginning of the end.

It was now past 9 o'clock. The light was still slightly diffused. The moment had come—the cavalry was going to realise its dream. Regiments were waiting echeloned down the slopes as far as the village of Ignaucourt, large groups of horses gathered here and there. I thanked God the enemy was not shelling. Flushed with excitement the men held their horses. When the whippet tanks were reported safely across the river, the Canadian Cavalry Brigade set the pace through the village and over the bridge, followed by the rest. There were jambs in places, just as when a hunting field is pressing to get through a gate. On and on they went, striking across the open to catch up our advancing infantry 1,000 yards ahead, and then go through them. All these passing horses bewildered me. I found it difficult to get on, so I turned down the first ridable path, which brought me on to a road, but I didn't have it to myself for very long. I heard the clop-clop of hoofs behind me and was overtaken by a regiment,

which irresistibly I followed down a winding road through
a thickly wooded gully. It thrilled me to see the leading
horses taking the turns below me at a gallop, some of the
horses rearing wildly. The distant outbreak of machine-
gun-fire sounded as exciting as a hunting-cry.

We swept through what had been a German headquarters, which had the picturesque aspect of a beer
garden with ingeniously constructed huts and tables made
of branches, on which we caught a glimpse of plates with
untasted food still in them. We passed some infantry
waving excitedly, and then, as the squadrons were rounding the elbow of a hill-side, I saw them disperse after
victory.

As no more infantry was to be seen ahead and knowing
the danger of this folding country so suitable for snipers,
I stopped to consider what I had better do. If I followed
on the heels of the cavalry my observation would inevitably be limited to the happenings in my immediate
vicinity. I also had to keep to the roads or paths on my
bike, and I wasn't anxious to run straight into the barrel
of a gun. So I turned back making for a near-by spur, from
which four months ago I had watched the enemy advance
and from which I now hoped to contemplate his flight.
The dead horses of his artillery teams were lying about,
killed, probably, as they were galloping towards their guns
in an effort to save them, for a little way on was a battery
of artillery with its dead gunners around it. One man
must have been killed as he was inserting a shell into the
breech of his gun, for he had collapsed with it on his lap
and looked as though he were nursing it. Further on I fell
in with some of the Canadian infantry, who had been
passed through by a forward lot, and I gathered some details of the attack. Naturally their experiences varied.
Some had had a walk-over and were thrilled with their
easy victory; others had had a harder time, it all depended
on where they happened to be.

Everywhere our barrage had thoroughly ploughed up
the ground. Some crosses, marking the spots where our

men had fallen and been buried by the Germans during
the March retreat, were still standing. Could they only
have seen how the tide had now turned they would have
felt that their sacrifice had not been altogether in vain!
Here and there prisoners were being rounded-up and
marched off to the rear by beaming escorts.

I was now riding up the Ignaucourt—Mézières road and
approaching the crest of the high ground. I realised then
how the day had cleared, giving an impression of sudden
expansion to the whole country-side. Between where I
was and the river valley 2,000 yards beyond, the ground
from which the enemy had been driven was now alive
with the movement of our men. The guns were now firing
this side of the river, marking the success of our attack.
Even the balloons which had come up quite close seemed
to me at that moment to be actually smiling in the sky,
but what was even more exhilarating was to see the Fourth
Canadian Division coming up to go through the Third
Canadian Division on the other side of the spur. Their
lines were curving across the broad flat accompanied by
tanks, shooting jerkily forward as though they were being
squeezed out of the earth. I could just see burning dumps,
a compact mass of grey uniforms being marched towards
the already packed prisoners' cage in the rear, as I turned
and rode on across some dead ground to where I hoped to
catch a glimpse of the progress of the cavalry in the
next valley. They must have been encountering some
resistance, however, for I could hear the sound of heavy
firing.

Gently the road began to descend. Three of our aeroplanes came from behind me then, swooping over the brow
of the spur, and dived into the valley below where a battle
was going on. I had scarcely time to take my bearings
when some spent bullets flicked past me and I just saw a
village lying below, with a wooded spur standing beyond
it like a wall. I heard the report of guns coming from a
distant ridge, and my eyes travelled from horses working
their way round the village of Beaucourt towards the

wooded high ground on the right, to some whippet tanks advancing towards the left of the wood in the thick of bursting shells. A terrific clatter of machine-gun-fire came from this wood, directed at the mounted men who, after a vain attempt to enter the wood, were now swerving round at a gallop, unable to face the deadly fire. Some of their horses with empty saddles were cantering madly in all directions. The whippets were also withdrawing.

While this was happening Beaucourt village was taken at a gallop. I moved to the right to watch the progress of mounted men who were now striding along towards the Amiens—Roye road. Hammon Wood prevented my seeing where the French were coming from on the other side.

There was no sense in the cavalry trying to force the capture of Beaucourt Wood, as the 4th Canadian Division were by now near at hand on their way to the "blue line," their third objective. So the task of clearing this high ground above the village was wisely left to them, and they took the wood in their stride.

It was afternoon. Hours had passed in a flash. From the various Cavalry Brigade Headquarters scattered about I got news of what had happened elsewhere.

The infantry fought its way forward, and by 5 o'clock had reached the "blue line," which was the limit of their advance prescribed for the day. I followed behind the cavalry, who had again gone through the Canadians and beyond, and who were finally held up in front of Le Quesnel, where it was obvious that the enemy had rallied and would attempt to hold the high ground which commanded the area over which the next advance would be made. The villages of Beaufort, Vrely and Rosières en Santerre were also firmly held, and it appeared that the 1st Cavalry Division further north faced a similar situation after their day's gallop.

Although it seemed imperative to go on striking before the enemy reserves had time to arrive, it was thought wiser to wait until the next day, when the attack would be adequately supported by our heavy artillery coming up behind.

It was evening. The sunset coloured the white surplice of a padre who stood by a grave in a circle of bowed heads of Englishmen and Germans, forming an oasis of common fellowship in a setting of war. Near-by brigades of cavalry which had been withdrawn made a large square in the middle of the plain. All the horses had their heads down and looked tired out.

The corps staff seemed very happy. I was glad to accept their invitation to a meal, for General Seligman, who was now in command of the corps artillery, maintained a high standard in his mess.

It had been a good day for the Fourth Army. The Australian Corps forming the centre of the attack had advanced beyond expectations, taking a great many prisoners, guns and machine-guns. The left wing, comprising the III Corps, had had a more difficult task, but had progressed well along the Somme. The French were beyond Frenoye en Chaussé, which the Canadians had taken at a gallop. They were the same men I had seen cross over the main Amiens road. In one day we had won back what it had taken the enemy four days to gain during the retreat.

I was tired out. The Cavalry Corps headquarters were billeted in the houses in the villages that were so wrecked that I preferred sleeping with some of the cavalry brigades which had been taken out of the line and were bivouacking in the shelter of a wood. The cavalry had paid for its success. I heard at once which of my friends had been killed. It was a dark night. I could just see the forms of the tired horses with their drooping heads. Some of the men were anxious about the hostile aeroplanes murmuring overhead, but most of us were too tired to care and wouldn't have moved a yard to get out of the way of a bomb.

I woke up as a heavy bombardment on Le Quesnel serenaded the dawn. There was a stir among the men,

followed by the jingling of chains and the clang of stirrups
as the saddles were lifted on to the horses. Kettles were
boiling for tea, and even bully-beef at that hour was welcome. The regiments were soon under way to rejoin the
infantry attacking about Le Quesnel, as there was hope of a
gallop through again. I had run short of petrol, and also
discovered that both my tyres were very much cut about,
so I had to ride first of all to the nearest supply depot. It
was really wonderful how quickly things could get done.
I applied for two inner tubes and two outer covers, and
that very evening they turned up.

I thought I had missed my chance of seeing the cavalry
go forward, but they had been held up after the taking of
Le Quesnel by heavy machine-gun-fire coming from a wood
near the village of Beaufort. I had taken the road over the
high ground, and presently saw some dismounted men
lying facing the road. They motioned to me to get down,
and I jumped off my bike and crawled up to them. They
had been held up in their advance by rifle-fire coming
from a knoll south of the village and had drawn back into
cover while the rest of their squadron was working round
the enemy, who appeared to be much more on the alert
that morning. There we lay for hours in the full glare of
the sun, trying to follow what was going on in the valley
below, where the infantry had come up to attack the wood
and the village. There was a lot of firing, but we could see
very little. We passed the time throwing stones at the
apples on the trees, but as soon as anyone tried to cross
the road to gather the fallen fruit, bullets began to flicker
past. In spite of this we managed to get some. Hours
passed while we waited for the taking of the village, and
it was not until the afternoon that the cavalry eventually
went on.

I followed in the rear, but very soon when I saw that
they were striking north, avoiding places from which
firing was still coming, I let them all go on and found myself alone on the road, for the infantry coming up behind
were still some way back. My motor-bike instead of being

a help was then rather a source of danger. I was just considering whether I should wait for the infantry to come up or follow in the tracks of the cavalry when, round the base of a rise about 400 yards away, I noticed a wash made by a file of grey-clad men crawling back through the standing crops. I promptly plunged into a hole off the road and fired several shots at them with my carbine. As quickly they disappeared. I thought it wise not to expose myself in the open again, and remained where I was firing shots at intervals as much to reassure myself as anything else. I had a sudden shock when I heard the approach of men behind me, but they turned out to be an advance-party of the Canadian infantry. As I wore a French helmet with a khaki cover and was alone, they couldn't make out what I was at first, so to put any suspicions at rest I produced my pass.

As all the attacks that morning had started with some delay and at different times, it was rather difficult for me to follow the course of events. I knew the French had been advancing on our right and went to look for them. I found Canadian armoured cars and motor machine-guns working their way up the Roye road, from which I saw the French infantry in the open on the other side. The village of Follies had been taken by the Canadians and the French were preparing to push on and attack Buchoir. French and English were now advancing together over the identical ground which they had defended elbow to elbow in the March retreat. At the time they had not started their advance, and the men of their forward lines were resting in the little holes each had dug for himself. They were all high-spirited and I thought they looked fine.

Meanwhile I had entirely lost touch with the cavalry. They had had an 8-kilometre gallop. I only reached them in the evening at Maucourt, where they were held up. They had again done well, but the First Cavalry Division on the left north of us had been checked from the start and had suffered many casualties.

It was obvious that the enemy had pulled himself

Y

together and his resistance was stiffening, although so far
he had made no counter-attack. The fight continued until
sundown. I learnt from a prisoner that a quantity of
machine-guns had been hurried up and troops were on
their way. Taken as a whole, this second day of fighting
had again brought us great gains. In spite of considerable
opposition, the Australians and the II Corps had advanced,
and an American division which had participated had
greatly distinguished itself.

The next morning, August 10th, I was in touch with the
Third Canadian Division, which, with the help of tanks,
was advancing towards Le Quenoy en Santerre. Although
they were meeting stiff resistance, the advance was progressing and the 32nd Division, which had arrived in the
night and which had followed close behind the Canadians,
passed through them in the course of the day and went on.
The cavalry then tried to get through on their right, but
soon came under heavy machine-gun-fire from the old
trench system which the enemy now held and of which
he was taking the fullest advantage. The nature of the
ground we were now on made it very hazardous for the
cavalry to advance. The horses had to hop over trenches
and pick their way through belts of wire which in many
places was hidden by the long grass. Many of the horses
fell into holes. After several unsuccessful attempts to go
forward the whole of the cavalry had to be withdrawn.
Throughout the day the fighting was most severe. German
reserves had obviously arrived and were putting up a
determined defence. Our tanks, now very much reduced
in number, were facing the fire of enemy guns waiting for
them with open sight. Our attacking divisions were beginning to pay heavily for the little progress they could
make. It was plain that the fighting was reverting again
into trench warfare.

During the two days in which we persevered in our
efforts to get on, the enemy launched strong counter-
attacks well supported by artillery. In spite of this, however, the Canadian Corps steadily managed to win some

ground. The Australian Corps further north with the
III Corps also improved their line. The notes I took
down during these two days show the atmosphere of the
line:

3 o'clock. Boche is running away to Warvillers. Our
guns firing into them. A dismounted Uhlan has been
captured.

I think 32nd Division must be in the Chavatte. 4th
Canadian Division were not in touch. Heavy machine-
gun opposition. There is thick wire in front of Fouquescourt. 2 tanks are going forward to clear the place.

Hallu is strongly held. Strong machine-gun enfilade
is coming from there.

Attack by 4th Canadian Division impossible until late
to-night as our line must be further advanced at
Fouquescourt. German prisoner reports that they have
not got many troops in rear, but a great quantity of
machine-guns have been put in line last night.

Enemy counter-attacking by Hallu—heavy bombardment.

Men are fatigued, but far from finished.

Afternoon. Boche again counter-attacking our most
advanced post of Hallu after a concentrated bombardment directed from both sides on the salient we make.
Our heavy guns firing into German infantry after our
men had withdrawn a few hundred yards—shelling hell
out of the Boche.
Will try to take Hallu back and straighten out line
provided flanks are protected. Meharicourt and Chilly
are being heavily shelled.

Y*

Canadian Division is going to attack with 12 tanks.

Attack postponed 24 hours. Boche shelling with gas-shells.

South. 32nd Division has had a bad time and back on their original line. In touch with French at Cambuse—French attacked 3 times Bois Z without result. Situation obscure. The Division has no fresh men, has used all reserves bar a couple of companies.

3rd Canadian Division relieving 32nd Infantry Division. 3rd Canadians in fine trim. Not more than 1,800 casualties since attack started.

We are now in trench warfare and must have another jump off.

When I left in the evening the line was in a hectic state. Preparations for renewed attacks were being hurriedly made while the enemy was counter-attacking. On my way to headquarters I met the quartermaster of the 17th Lancers, a lonely figure striding along the dusty road in search of his regiment. He bulged out of his tight tunic and, mopping his wet brow, expostulated vehemently at having been on leave during the offensive. He felt that he had been badly treated as he was not warned—nobody had been, for that matter, as the attack was to be kept secret until the last minute. I felt rather contrite returning to the army after four days' absence without having given them an inkling of my whereabouts. But what was there to tell them that they didn't already know when things had been going so well? The first thing I heard was how Priestman, the day after we had parted, had rushed in pursuit of the Germans in a brand-new Army car, only to have it destroyed.

I was not surprised to hear that further offensive operations were cancelled for the time being and that the

Army was to restrict itself to consolidating the ground and harassing the enemy in order to make him believe that the renewal of the attack was pending. It was a wise decision, for the Fourth Army had achieved a great success, so far with very few losses, and now that the enemy was strongly entrenched we couldn't possibly hope to gain any more ground except at very heavy cost. In four days the enemy defences had been penetrated in places to a depth of twelve miles, and we had forced him back into the old waste land of the Somme battle-fields where no accommodation existed for his reserves and lines of communication were very bad. Twenty-three thousand prisoners had been taken and over 400 guns and hundreds of machine-guns.

But while the Fourth Army marked time during the ensuing days, it was preparing a new offensive further north, where the enemy least expected it to come from. The idea was to drive him off the high ground stretching from Albert to Bray-sur-Somme and oblige him to withdraw from the River Somme, which formed a strong obstacle in the way of our eventual objective, Péronne.

This attack, launched on August 22nd by the III Corps and the Australians, was a complete success. It gave a new *élan* to the offensive which had started on August 8th and which continued relentlessly until the day of the Armistice.

CHAPTER XXXV

ENVOI

OF the events of the succeeding days a few pictures remain among kaleidoscopic impressions registered during a period of ceaseless activity.- I remember vividly the sight of the advancing waves clearing the enemy out of Albert in a cloud of smoke and dust on that hot August morning; "Happy Valley" will always recall hell, enfiladed as it was from the dominant surroundings by constant machine-gun-fire and shelled by every variety of gas-shell; and lastly there remains the picture of the Australian advance over the high ground beyond Bray-sur-Somme, made on a moonlight night, that gave to the old Somme battle-field an unreal aspect, the men moving furtively forward with fixed bayonets as though pursuing their own fugitive shadows.

For days the Fourth Army fought forward, breaking through the most stubborn resistance. The impetus was now general—it had spread from Soissons to the Scarpe, where all the allied armies were attacking in turn. The enemy was not given a moment's respite; he was to be continually harassed until victory was within our grasp. Often we had him down, but, like a plucky boxer, he was still game for a good many rounds, as he proved in the fight he put up at Mont St. Quentin, by Péronne and in other places vital for him to hold.

The rush of the last few days had brought the Army within reach of Péronne. Although we had stuck close to the enemy's heels, we had been unable to prevent him from blowing up the bridges on the River Somme, and the time it took us to repair them gave him the few hours' respite which he needed to reconstitute his forces amidst the strong system of defences east and north of the river bend. This strong position had to be taken before a general offensive could be pursued. The Australians undertook the task.

The afternoon of August 29th found them streaming along the river-banks as they concentrated near Cléry-sur-Somme for the attack at dawn. The movement of all these troops—enemy shells splashing into the river—bullets flopping and ricochetting off the water like flying fish—the steep sunny river-banks gleaming through the grass, all combined to make a memorable scene.

After day broke the enemy gun retaliation and the confusing reports of the situation made my wandering in search of news painful and exasperating. I remember seeing flares spin skywards from the high ground of Mont St. Quentin, as with difficulty I crept into Save trench and found its occupants having the most nerve-racking time. They were being shot at from Bois Halle behind by some Germans who had been left there, and also from Anvil Wood in front by a gun with open sight at a distance of not more than 300 yards. The gun report, the displacement of air, the shock as the shell crashed, were all registered in one reflex of terror. We waited breathlessly, knowing exactly how long it would be after a shell had passed over the parapet of the trench till the next one would be fired. There was, too, in that area a newly captured system of enemy trenches named after God and Love which in parts now resembled a shambles, mostly the result of the work of the bayonets. Some German parties were still here in between our troops, which made any movement in the open a constant source of danger.

On hands and knees I crawled in the tracks of the 20th Battalion, which had successfully reached Feuillecourt. But the sustained enfilading fire from the high ground made my progress towards that village most unsafe and very slow. At times I would look back towards the river valley, which was being heavily shelled, and see Divisional Headquarters on a distant high spur where, with their field-glasses, they were getting a more placid view of things than I had on the spot. The explanation of the precarious position of our left flank turned out to be that the division operating next to it had failed to come up, thus leaving this flank exposed.

By the afternoon I was in touch with the battalion that had fallen back from Feuillecourt, and knew that we had only a footing on Mont St. Quentin. I thought then that I had some idea of the situation, but, by the time I left for home, the Germans were counter-attacking violently, and when I reached the division the whole of our position was again transformed. On the way back I found the river-bank swarming with reserves, which were awaiting their turn to cross the river. They were sheltered against the bank and looked like a huge crowd at a football match. Some had climbed to the very top of the steep bank that was fairly safe from the unending stream of shells which were falling into the river in a continuous play of spray. The troops crossing the river in Indian file wearing tin helmets reminded me of Japanese prints showing little figures in round hats walking over planks no higher than the weeds rising from the water. From where I stood I watched the men ducking, trying to avoid the spray, and I saw one man hold back the whole line to point at something in the water; he was probably an enthusiastic fisherman pointing out a floating dead fish.

While I was interested in all this activity I heard my name called, and saw an old Liverpool friend jump out of a lorry whom I had not seen for over ten years. He was arriving with the Life Guards, who were now machine-gunners and were coming up to give a hand in the battle.

The attack was continued that night, and, after fierce fighting, the Australians entered Péronne and the heights of Mont St. Quentin were finally stormed. Meanwhile the III Corps had driven the enemy from his strong position on the heights between Bouchavesnes and Morval, and their losses had been very heavy. Quickly the artillery was pushed forward over the river to take every possible advantage of our advance. The gunners had to work like Trojans. But news of the continual advance of the French further south and our armies in the north acted like a tonic to all. The Army was going to maintain its pressure on the Germans and drive them further and further back. In places the morale of their troops was found to be on the wane. Every success was increasing the ambition of the staff. The plans of the Hindenburg line were now unfolded and the storming thereof was the Army's next aim.

By September 18th we had reached its outer defences, and the Army was now in front of Epehy, Ronsoy, Pézières, le Verguier and Agincourt, all names which evoked memories of the gallant resistance of the Fifth Army when the Germans had broken through on March 21st.

The enemy, however, was reinforcing his front. He meant to hold these outer defences of his main line of resistance, knowing only too well that their loss would give us observation on a great part of his defences and would naturally aid our assault in every possible way.

On the morning of the attack I was walking up to get news; the atmosphere was heavy after rain. I had been passed by tanks, which I could see now swerving to the right and left down the slopes, trying to avoid the shells searching for them as they made for the valley which, with the silhouetted top of a village rising from it, the smoke-screen and accompanying roar of machine-guns, made up the classic setting of a battle-front of those days. I had stopped to study my map by an abandoned trench where a man was sitting, his elbow on his knee, his chin in his hands, staring straight before him towards the village which was being heavily shelled. He might have been the "Penseur" of Rodin. He was a runner, loaded like a Christmas-tree. I thought he was just tired, and it occurred to me, as it had often done before, how absurd it was to send dispatches by men so heavily accoutred instead of by lightly clad runners, who would be specially picked for a job which demanded agility, fitness and resourcefulness. Often I had seen men with dispatches in a state of collapse, due to nothing more than excessive smoking. This man was so deep in thought when I approached that he didn't even turn round. When at last he answered me, he said that he had been to Brigade Headquarters with a message and was now returning to his battalion. "It's hell out there," he said, pointing to the village. . . .

As I was going on my way I saw him pick up his rifle and make towards the shelled slopes I was purposely skirting, not that there was much to choose between the two routes, but I remember thinking at the time that I should have induced him to come my way, seeing that we were both going to the same place. However, I hadn't done so, and my day passed in the usual atmosphere of noise, rush and confusion. I didn't think anything more about this man until the evening when, after having walked back over the newly conquered ground, I came to the spot over which I had last seen him walking. It came back to me then how pensive he had been, and I wondered if, like so many of us, he had been feeling that the end of the war was at hand, and speculating on the chances of getting through the last spell. But, anyhow, he had lost—a few yards beyond I found him lying with his mouth open, gazing with unseeing eyes at the coloured sky, a streak of blood across his face. . . .

Although the day's fighting had gained for the Army a great portion of the outer defences of the Hindenburg line, hard fighting continued for several days thereafter for the capture of the remaining positions which were still a great obstacle to us, and some of which remained to be captured in the main attack which was planned for September 29th. Before troops could be ready to storm the Hindenburg line they had to be rested and artillery preparations had to be made. The undertaking of such a task as storming this very formidable line of defence required the most detailed preparations. The Army was greatly helped by a plan of the system of the Hindenburg fortifications found on August 18th in a German headquarters which had been hastily abandoned.

An American corps with two American divisions had now come into the Fourth Army. I was to spend the last days of the war with one of these divisions. New as they were to our kind of warfare, they had settled down to their job with great spirit. I remember coming on a battalion for the first time at night, at a time when a barrage was making a fearful din, and I thought they were all talking at once, but on closer inspection it turned out that they were only chewing gum.

During this spell I was still riding back every day to the Army, but my journey was not so long now, for the Army Headquarters had come up and were established in a sort of semi-underground camp, in which huts were linked up to each other by duckboard corridors covered over with camouflaged wire-netting, so that we moved about rather in the fashion of animals in a zoo.

During these days of intensive successful activities General Rawlinson remained the same. In the mornings he always looked as though he had just enjoyed a hearty breakfast. He was never exuberant, although always genial. One morning after I had received my instructions from him, he told me to go into the next room, where I should see something that would appeal to me, and there I found William Orpen squeezing paint on to his palette preparing to paint the portrait of the Army Commander. The smell of the oil-paint went straight to my head and revived a longing which had been sternly suppressed for over four years.

My ride backwards and forwards to the line each day carried me over the ground won by our troops in their colossal effort. Derelict tanks were still lying where they had been hit, like milestones marking the advance. Everywhere fresh troops were coming up to continue the fight, with their untiring tenacity. I often tried to guess their civilian occupations and by what magic they had been turned into such splendid soldiers.

During three consecutive days and nights prior to the main assault of the Hindenburg line, every available gun bombarded the enemy front. The expense, work and organisation needed to supply the guns in order to keep up this sustained bombardment were terrific. Train-loads of ammunition came up every day; they had to be unloaded and every shell reloaded on to lorries which in long columns made their way through the inevitable congestion of moving troops and transports, the forerunners of an attack.

Came September 29th, the day of the attack on the Hindenburg line. After three days of incessant shelling which, starting with gas-shells, ended up with every imaginable variety of explosive, at 5.55 a.m., zero hour, the noise of the bombardment suggested a *coup de grâce* as the troops went forward to storm over twelve miles of strongly fortified defences reputed to be able to repel any attack.

Whatever the scale of an attack, beyond hearing the general barrage, one's observation is restricted to a small area, especially when the atmosphere is foggy, as it was on that morning, and when one has not followed the troops immediately from the start.

The 27th American Division, with whom I was, had been given one of the most vital positions to capture—namely, Gillemont Farm, Quennemont Farm, and a place called the Knoll, which the enemy was bent on keeping at all costs. Several attempts to take these places the previous days had failed. My first intimation that they were again encountering a stiff resistance was the sight of a number of tanks already out of action, due to direct gun-fire. The most confusing situation existed throughout the day in that area, although on the rest of the fronts, unknown to us, everything had gone well.

I remember entering a dug-out of one of the attacking

American regiments. The muggy atmosphere outside
made the deep dug-out absolutely stifling. At a table sat
a Colonel and two staff officers, in stiff jackets with high
collars facing a map at which the Colonel kept glancing
through tortoise-shell glasses attached to a silk cord, which
he kept putting on and taking off his big nose. They had
had no news of their attacking regiments. "Waal," he
drawled, adjusting his glasses, "I have no news yet of how
the boys have gotten on, but they went over at skeduled
time, and I am confident that they have done their
dooty." I expressed surprise as a considerable time had
elapsed since the beginning of the attack, and suggested
that perhaps someone should go and find out how things
were. The Colonel talked in technical terms as if he had
come straight from a military school, and rather in the
manner of a doctor facing his first patient. We climbed
up the steps of the dug-out and, while the Colonel was
deciding which of his available "lootenants" should go, I
suddenly saw a movement of men some distance away
coming down the sloping ground. "What's this?" I asked.
"Waal, I guess it's some of the boys coming back," replied
the Colonel. "Lootenant —— had better go and see what
it is all about." Not waiting for the lieutenant to put on
his kit, I had jumped on to my motor-bike and rode as far
as I could, running the rest of the way up to the crest.
The men were indeed retiring, but simply because they
were not in touch with anybody; they had no news,
and most of their officers had been killed in the
advance. I made some of them stay where they were
and place their machine-guns facing the battle, then
ordered the rest to go forward and rejoin their comrades,
which they immediately did. They were not in any
sort of panic, but had merely sauntered back for want
of instructions.

When I got back to Battalion Headquarters to tell them
about these men, to my amazement I found the place
shattered as if by an earthquake. Three corpses lay there
partly covered by a sack. They were the sentry, who had

been standing at the door of the dug-out, and two of the officers with whom I had spoken before I left. Down below the Colonel sat alone, mopping his brow. "Say, Captain, this certainly is war," he commented as I entered. The casualties of the American Division that day were very heavy.

The 27th American Division resumed their attack the next day, helped by the Australians on their right. After wandering about trying to elucidate a most obscure situation, towards the afternoon I happened to reach a battalion of Australians, and after a conversation with the Colonel, he wrote down in my note-book the situation on his front, and asked me to take it to Brigade Headquarters. His message, reproduced from the original, read as follows:

MACQUINCOURT VALLEY
Elements of 108th Am Regt,
are reported on the GREEN
LINE but left of
~~the~~ 97th American Div
are mostly in a very
disorganized state
to the SOUTH and WEST
of the KNOLL. Officers
are out in the attempt
to reorganize both
3·3 + 5·4 Bde. Our troops
are certainly in BONY
but so are the Boche
~~............................~~
Mr Maze will supply
all further details /

ff   A. Crowther
          H Col

With this message I started to walk towards Brigade
Headquarters, meaning to ascertain at the same time what
the position was exactly at Bony, a little village standing
on the rising ground, which the Americans had captured
earlier in the day. I had left the Australian troops and
was now crossing the ground over which the Americans
had advanced. I was over the main road leading to
Bony and had settled down to ascertain who were the
figures popping in and out of the houses in the village,

when I was immediately shot at from the intermediate
ground, still held by the enemy. I dropped into a shell-
hole trying to see where the shots were coming from. I
then saw not more than 200 yards away to my left the tops
of German steel-helmets above the earth. I raised my field-
glasses to have a look at them, and as I did so my left arm
dropped in excruciating pain with a bullet in the wrist.
My next step was to crawl out of my shell-hole, without
giving the enemy another chance. At last I reached the
bank of a road which brought me safely to some
Australians waiting in reserve, from whom I got a field-
dressing for my wound.

I remember, as I walked from the Brigade to the nearest
place from which I could get a lift back to Headquarters,
that I registered sharply everything I saw, for, half unconsciously I was taking leave of the war.

I bid good-bye to the Fourth Army staff to which I had
become devoted as I had been to the Fifth Army. Of my
friends on that staff, I remember with particular gratitude
General Sir Archibald Montgomery. I left him at his desk
where for months, during the day and most of the night,
he sat dealing with his work with cheerful capacity and
untiring command. When in the evening, day-weary, I
reported to him, as I entered his office his genial welcoming smile was refreshing. Such men drew the best of one
and certainly kept up in us the spirit which won in the end.

That evening I was in an ambulance train riding slowly
away from the atmosphere of battle. I could still hear the
guns making a thundering row, and as I looked out at the
desolation gliding past the windows and saw all the reinforcements coming up to finish the assault on the Hindenburg line and sweep all before them in the next fifty days,
I thought of the comment of the mother of a French
friend of mine who had succeeded in reaching her soldier
son in a village immediately behind the line during a
battle. She had sent word and was waiting for him, a tall
black figure in the middle of the road; as she spied him
coming towards her down the shattered street she called

out: "My dear child, why all this noise? What is it all about?" . . .

We were landed at Havre the next morning. We had to alight quickly, for the train was wanted immediately to fetch another lot of wounded. Railway stations at 6 o'clock in the morning are never pleasant; the smell of smoke and coal-dust has something particularly depressing about it at that hour. We had to wait, as the ambulances that were to take us to hospital had not turned up, and there we lay like emigrants do when they wait to go aboard an ocean steamer after their journey across Europe.

At last I was between cool white sheets. It was a lovely September day, and the band of an American regiment was playing as the men landed from transports on the quay beyond. I could also hear the blasts from other transports coming in with the tide, and it took my mind back to that day in August, four years before, when I had stood and watched the transports of the British Expeditionary Force arrive and land their troops within 200 yards of where I now lay.

I was finishing exactly where I had started. I turned over wearily on my pillow and dreamt that the war was over and all nations were united in a common Peace . . . !

FINIS

Printed in Great Britain
by Amazon

86799905R00222